RICHARD HUGHES

A WEIGHT OFF MY MIND
MY AUTOBIOGRAPHY

RACING POST

This edition first published in Great Britain in 2012 by
Racing Post Books
Raceform, Compton, Newbury, Berkshire, RG20 6NL

10 9 8 7 6 5 4 3 2 1

A catalogue record for this book is available from the British Library.

ISBN 978-1-908216-06-9

Cover designed by Jay Vincent
Interiors designed by Soapbox
www.soapbox.co.uk

Printed and bound by the CPI Group (UK) Ltd, Croydon, CR0 4YY

www.racingpost.com/shop

CONTENTS

For helping me to turn my life into a book, I want to thank
Lee Mottershead, my ghostwriter and friend.

For their constant love and support, I wish to thank my family.

For believing in me from the start, I owe a debt of gratitude
to Richard Hannon and Mick Channon.

And I say a special thank you to those people who helped me
through my darkest days. They know who they are.

FOREWORD

I have long thought of Richard Hughes as one of the most stylish and effective jockeys of the current generation, but it was not until I was invited to write the Foreword to this book that I thought about just how much we had in common.

Like me, Richard is tall in comparison with most of the other Flat jockeys, which means that in a race it's not easy to hide yourself away. So it says a great deal for his skill and nerve that he is a past master at putting a horse's head in front right on the line. To see him produce Canford Cliffs or Paco Boy at precisely the right moment has been a joy to watch.

Richard's riding career also echoes my own in his battle with the scales. I know from long experience that getting your weight down to a level well below your natural mark is one thing, but stabilising it at that level is another challenge altogether. Richard has done a marvellous job to keep his weight stable over the years, but – as this book graphically illustrates – the process can be a nightmare, and it is a mark of Richard's character that he has managed it so well.

And like me, Richard has ridden plenty of times over hurdles – partly as part of his effort to help keep his weight stable, but more because he loves the hurly-burly of a hurdle race, as did I when I rode over hurdles in the 1950s.

This autobiography is a wonderfully readable and remarkably frank account of a great riding career, and I wish Richard all the very best with it.

Lester Piggott

PROLOGUE

Never in my whole life had I been so desperate to pee. It felt as though I was fighting a battle I could only lose. Ascot racecourse, my final destination, was still a whole mile away. The road taking me to it was full of racing traffic, the pavements either side dotted with racegoing pedestrians, some with binoculars draped over their shoulders, others carrying *The Sporting Life* or *Racing Post*. It was the day of the 1996 King George, the Flat season's summer jewel, and I was far from alone in wanting to get to Ascot. My need, however, was greater than theirs. I was in grave danger of wetting myself.

The irony is that I had wanted to pee all day. By 'wanted to pee', I mean I had been trying to make it happen without success. No man had ever worked harder to stimulate a bit of bladder action, but all my efforts had come to nothing. Until now. All the way from Newmarket to the M25 there had been not the merest discomfort. Even after I left the motorway and headed into Berkshire my desire to urinate seemed certain to be unfulfilled. Then, suddenly, everything changed.

I had brought it all on myself. I had ridden at Ascot the day before and driven from there to Newmarket, Flat racing's headquarters. My one ride at Ascot had finished nowhere and my single mount at Newmarket's evening fixture fared no better, but at least I was riding at Ascot and Newmarket, Britain's two premier Flat tracks. It was only two years since I had quit Ireland, frustrated at the lack of opportunities

1

my homeland was affording me. For a while it had looked likely that I'd be the next big thing, but Irish Flat racing has room for only a certain number of big things and it turned out that I was not going to be one of them. I accepted it and moved on, to Britain to be precise, and the relocation had reaped dividends. I had ridden three Royal Ascot winners, landed two of the country's biggest handicaps (the Cambridgeshire and Stewards' Cup) and enjoyed two European Group 1 wins for British trainers. I had also become popular with leading trainers Mick Channon, David Loder and Richard Hannon, whose daughter, Lizzie, was my girlfriend.

Life was good, but not entirely straightforward. I had started drinking too much while in Ireland. Since quitting County Kildare for Wiltshire, I was drinking even more. The previous night was a case in point. After racing I had headed to Newmarket's high street, intent on getting pissed. I found a shitty little pub, partly because there are lots of them in Newmarket, partly because that was the sort of pub I preferred. I hated people coming up to me, fawning over me, asking questions, probing. At the grubbier end of the pub market, that was less likely to happen.

I got through a bottle and a half of champagne. I was becoming increasingly fond of champagne. You have to be quite fond of it to survive a bottle and a half. Truth be told, vodka and tonic was probably my drink of choice at the time, but I was drinking for a reason that night. Two reasons, in fact. One was to get pissed. That was often the sole reason, but so was the second factor: I was drinking to stimulate weight loss. I was drinking in the name of my job, in the name of sport. Some athletes use protein shakes. I used champagne.

People often call me a natural, but in terms of stature I am anything but. Men who stand 5ft 9in tall are not supposed to be Flat jockeys. Men who are 5ft 9in tall are not supposed to tip the scales at 8st 8lb, the weight I needed to make if, with my lightest saddle, I was to ride at 8st 10lb, the burden allotted to one of my Saturday mounts at Ascot. And for me it was a burden. An enormous burden. At the time, I was waking up most mornings between 9st and 9st 2lb. You do the maths.

The answer came in the form of a tablet – to the medically minded a diuretic, to jockeys a piss pill. They dehydrated the body and slowed up the process of rehydration. So much of the body is made up of water. Piss pills got rid of it. They were the perfect quick-fix solution, far simpler than spending hours in the sauna or driving to the races in five layers of clothing with the heaters on full blast. Some jockeys even went for long runs. Perish the thought.

I did what jockeys had done for years: I took piss pills. The problem for me was that I had taken them for so long and in such quantities that my body was becoming immune to their effects. Most jockeys found that taking one was enough. That morning I had started the day by popping four. By nine o'clock, nothing had happened. I had six pounds to lose in the space of a few hours. I began to worry. So I took four more. Still nothing. I remained as dry as a bone. Not good.

I took the pills with me to Ascot. By the time I had got to within sight of the racecourse I had taken 14. It had now suddenly transpired that though my bladder laughed at a single diuretic, it found 14 hard to deny.

The urgent, bursting need to pee was coming close to inducing tears. I wriggled around in the driver's seat, doing whatever I could to ease the unrelenting pressure. Finally, I was there. I sped into the jockeys' car park and pulled up as close as I could to the old brick toilet building within it. As I got out of the car a friend approached and tried to start up a conversation. Politely but clearly, I told him that I needed the loo and couldn't stop. This was no time for chit-chat.

I ran into the building and made for the nearest cubicle. I did not have the strength to stand up so I shut the door, pulled down my trousers and sat on the seat. The discomfort I was experiencing was overwhelming. So too, after I had been peeing for at least 30 seconds, was the relief. The agony was over.

And then I passed out.

I woke up ten minutes later on the floor of the cubicle. I know it was ten minutes because I had checked the time on my watch while I was peeing – I had plenty of time to kill – and I checked it again when I regained consciousness. That was an instinct thing. I was booked to ride Oscar Schindler in the King George VI and Queen Elizabeth Diamond Stakes, one of the world's most prestigious races. It would have been unfortunate in the extreme to have missed it due to collapsing in a lavatory.

My situation at that moment was somewhat worse than unfortunate. I was lying on my back, dirty, smelly, my shirt sodden and black with sweat. I looked like a well-dressed tramp. But I had a job to do, and while doing that job I would be watched by 30,000 racegoers and not far off a million people on television. If only they knew.

I got to my feet and brushed myself down. I waited for a few seconds to make sure the toilet was empty. When I was certain it was, I opened the cubicle door and walked towards a mirror. I tried to make myself look presentable, doing up my suit jacket as tightly as possible to hide as many of the sweat stains as that allowed. I returned to the car, got in and put on my tie. I attempted to compose myself. I wanted to put out of my mind what had happened, but that was impossible. The side effects of the piss pills, all 14 of them, were kicking in. I was cramping up. My fingers and hands were completely stiff. I was totally dehydrated. It felt as though every last drop of liquid had been drained from me. Exactly as I had wanted.

Funny the things you willingly do to yourself.

I walked slowly, very slowly, to the weighing room. I was living a life of excess. A bottle and a half of champagne, 14 diuretics, and now ten whole oranges. I knew I needed calcium and the oranges were going to give it to me, so I ate one after another. Soon enough, I felt better.

Had it been a Hollywood film I would have won the King George, but it wasn't, and I didn't. Oscar Schindler finished fourth – perfectly respectable and pretty much where we had expected him to finish. Two of my other rides that afternoon trailed in last, not because of their jockey but because they were not good enough on the day. My final mount of the afternoon, Nasrudin, was the one I had been worrying about. Despite all my efforts, I still put up a pound overweight. To rub salt in the wound, he only finished ninth.

That night I made the mistake of mentioning what had happened to Lizzie. She only ever wanted what was best for me, but at the time I did not always see that. Passing out in the toilet had scared the hell out of me. Lizzie felt the same. She did what she always did in similar circumstances. She phoned my dad.

Dessie Hughes, once an Irish hero at the Cheltenham Festival, was not just my father but my mentor. After Lizzie told him what I had done, he got on a flight from Dublin to London the following morning. He rang me and told me to meet him at Heathrow.

I did as I was told.

He got off the plane, met with me in the terminal, lectured me for an hour and then got the next flight back to Dublin. He told me how upset Lizzie had been when she spoke to him. He said he understood why. He tried to convince me that piss pills were not an easy way out of a weight problem. He mentioned the names of former jockeys whose bodies and lives they had ruined. He made me promise that I would not take them again. I promised, and I kept my word.

Back home, Lizzie and I argued. We were arguing a lot. The way I saw it, she was constantly nagging me, generally about my drinking. She said I drank too much. I knew I did, but I drank for a good reason. I drank to control my weight. Partly, that was true. It was also true that I drank because I was an alcoholic – not that I recognised it at the time. I thought alcoholics drank from bottles concealed inside brown paper bags. It turned out they came in all shapes and sizes. One of them was a 5ft 9in Irishman.

I had a weight problem and a drink problem but I was, by common consent, a brilliant jockey. I no longer wanted to be a jockey who passed out on the floors of racecourse toilets. I never did again. My life, however, remained complicated. The best and worst was still to come.

1

WELCOME TO MY WORLD

Even now, nearly four decades on, I can still remember the smell. Just the thought of it and there it is, back in my nose, as powerful, satisfying and addictive as ever. It would almost certainly do nothing for you, but I loved it. Always did, always will.

That smell is the first thing I can remember. I can only have been two years old, three at the most, when I first experienced it. I was on the back of a horse at Mick O'Toole's yard just on the outskirts of the Curragh. I couldn't tell you what the horse looked like, or how it felt to be on top of a thoroughbred for the first time, but I can tell you that I was wonderfully overwhelmed by the smell of everything to do with the horse. There was the animal itself, but there was more than that. Like a fine wine, there were undertones: oil, saddle soap, leather, and a deliciously pungent paste called Cribox that stops horses from crib biting or gnawing at their boxes and rugs.

It can't be a coincidence that my first memory is linked to horses. At no point in my life have I not been around them. Since the age of seven I have used them to earn a living. Almost everything I have done, everything I have achieved, has been completed with their help.

My first horse, however, was bought purely for pleasure. It was made of wood, a rocking horse that I must have sat on more than any chair in the house. I rode my first finishes on that horse. It would be an exaggeration to say I used it to begin perfecting the art of riding a finish, but it played its part and is still with us, safe and sound back home with Mam and Dad. Mam often says that she would never part with it. I wouldn't be overly sentimental but I'm glad she feels that way.

When it became obvious that a wooden horse would not take me very far, I switched to more active animals, primarily under the tutelage of a father who had been equally obsessed with horses as a child.

Dessie Hughes was an Irish racing legend but he was certainly not born into the sport. Neither of his parents had any involvement in racing, but one of their six children quickly gained an appetite to spend as much time with horses as possible. There wasn't a whole lot of money in the family so Dessie used to help out on a horse-drawn milk cart. Like me, he remembers the early smell of horses as much as anything else, and, like me, he loved it. There was an aunt in Wexford that the family used to visit for holidays, and on every train trip down the only thing that Dessie would think about were the ponies his aunt kept on her farm. He would ride the ponies from one end of the day to the other and vowed to himself that he would become a jockey.

He not only became a jockey, he became one of the best and most successful in Irish racing history. Initially educated in Flat racing by Dan Kirwan in Kilkenny, he rode in his first races in 1959 as a 15-year-old, but it was after Kirwan died and Dessie's apprenticeship was switched to Willie O'Grady, on 11 June 1962, that he first experienced the feeling of going past the winning post in front. Unfortunately for Dad, he also first experienced the feeling of having victory snatched from you by the stewards just a few minutes later.

His mount, Sailaway Sailor, one of six runners in a mile-and-a-half race, narrowly beat the 2-1 favourite, Duffcarrig, who represented the Arkle team of Pat Taaffe and Tom Dreaper. They won the Cheltenham

Gold Cup three times with Arkle and they won that considerably less prestigious Tramore Flat race with Duffcarrig when the stewards disqualified Sailaway Sailor after Dad was found guilty of squeezing up his somewhat more experienced rival. Taaffe lodged an objection, but he must have felt bad for doing so because he later apologised to Dad and slipped him £2!

Luckily Dessie did not have to wait long to make amends. Sailaway Sailor was turned out again just three days later at Ballinrobe and came home two lengths clear. Dessie, who had become used to travelling home from the races in O'Grady's horsebox, was this time allowed to make the return journey alongside the trainer in his car.

In what might be seen as an omen for what would happen to his son, Dad became troubled by his weight. In the space of two years he got taller, bigger and heavier, expanding from an eight-stone lightweight to a ten-stone heavyweight. Mother Nature had robbed him of a career in Flat racing. The only alternative was to switch to the jumps.

It turned out that Mother Nature had actually done Dessie a favour, although there were still plenty of dark days to come. He took up a new riding job in Scotland before heading south to join Reg Akehurst in Basingstoke. It was while riding for Reg in 1966 that he was brought down at the second flight in a Wolverhampton maiden hurdle contested by 29 extremely ordinary horses. Dessie was a sitting duck for a lot of galloping jumpers, and although, as is the way with horses, the majority did their best to avoid him, one pounded a leg into his chest. The next three months were spent in hospital, where none of the doctors seemed able to diagnose what, apart from a lot of painful bruises, was ailing him. In the end, a specialist at Churchill Hospital in Oxford worked out that a rib would have to be taken out so that blood clots caused by a punctured lung could be removed. Just in case he ever came close to forgetting what had happened, Dad was left with a huge horseshoe-shaped scar on his chest.

When he came back from injury, Dessie was still a long way from being a household name. However, in the years that followed he was helped by two people in particular.

One was Mick O'Toole, a former butcher turned greyhound and racehorse trainer, to whom Dad became stable jockey. Together they enjoyed some great days, not least with Davy Lad, who gave Dessie his first Cheltenham Festival winner in the 1975 Sun Alliance Novices' Hurdle and then, two years later, won them the most prestigious jumps race of all, the Cheltenham Gold Cup, in which they pulled clear of Tied Cottage to give Ireland a famous one-two. Mick was an enormous punter, who famously took bookmakers to the cleaners more than once. Teamed up with Dessie Hughes, he became an even more potent force.

The other new and major influence on Dad's life was my future mother, Eileen Lyons. Eileen, like Dessie, was from anything but a horsey family. Brought up in the south side of Dublin, she was only nine when she lost her father, a lorry driver for a dairy company. Although she was not introduced to horses until she met Dessie, she did know something about racing because her mother, who came from a farming background, had been a fan of the sport, and particularly of Pat Taaffe, whose mounts she used to back every Saturday.

Eileen and Dessie married in 1968, two years after which they celebrated the birth of their first child, Sandra. They had been living in a mobile home in Mick's yard, but with a baby on the way Dessie bought a small house near his employer's Curragh stables. Dessie became invaluable to Mick, and at one point was working not only as stable jockey but also head lad, travelling head lad, and sometimes even as box driver. On one occasion he collapsed through exhaustion while in the passenger seat of the horsebox. I have no doubt that Mick missed him when he left.

I came along in January 1973, three years after Sandra and six years before what was by some way Dad's most famous achievement as a jockey. He had stepped in as and when required to ride Monksfield, an ugly duckling but an extremely talented ugly duckling, most famously in April 1977. On what turned out to be one of racing's most iconic days, they dead-heated with the great Night Nurse following a thrilling home-straight battle at Aintree that was fought out just 45 minutes before Red Rum won his record-breaking third Grand National. Monksfield was widely regarded as the rightful mount of Tommy Kinane, who steered him to victory in the 1978 Champion Hurdle. Monksfield's owner Michael Mangan and trainer Des McDonogh thought differently, and exactly one week before the 1979 Champion Hurdle, Kinane – whose son Mick scaled even greater heights on the Flat – was told he was being jocked off in favour of Dessie Hughes. To say he was not happy would be something of an understatement.

It was a difficult situation for Dad, but one that so many top riders have experienced, on both sides of the equation. Dad and Kinane regularly sat next to each other in racecourse weighing rooms, but for some time after being parted from Monksfield, Kinane refused to speak to Dad, at least not in public, as he sought to reinforce the image of a wronged man.

He felt even more wronged on 14 March 1979, when Monksfield fought off another iconic jumper, Sea Pigeon, to retain his Champion Hurdle crown. The two horses were locked together through the closing stages of the race, but it was Monksfield who found the most under pressure and eventually edged three-quarters of a length clear. Dad had never been associated with a more famous victory; he never was again, and I doubt I ever will be either. With a few rare exceptions, jumpers capture people's hearts far more than their Flat counterparts, and Monksfield, both at home in Ireland and across the water in Britain, was about as popular as they come.

I was six years old when Dad won on Monksfield at Cheltenham but I would be lying if I said I could remember much about the day. I've watched the tape, plus the one that shows Davy Lad winning the Gold Cup, hundreds of times since, but, by and large, Dad always tried to keep work and home separate. Sandra and I were seldom taken with him to the races, and certainly never to Cheltenham. Back in the late 1970s racecourses were not the family-friendly places they are today. You would not have found crèches, face painters, bouncy castles or fairgrounds. If Sandra and I were taken racing it was only really during school holidays and only then to coastal tracks like Laytown, situated about 30 minutes out of Dublin, or the seaside racecourse Tramore.

As we got older and Dad switched from riding horses to training them, we did go racing much more often. One such trip was supposed to be to an evening meeting at Leopardstown. After I got back from school I pleaded with Mam to let me go and she relented, but only if I promised to have a rest first. The good boy that I was, I went to my room and began reading a book, almost certainly one in which my hero, Lester Piggott, figured prominently. Prince, our Lassie look-a-like dog, came in with me and fell asleep on the carpet. Mam must have known I was tired because I quickly nodded off while reading. It proved the wrong thing to do. As I slept, I turned over and fell off the side of the bed and on to Prince. Normally a quiet, affectionate dog, Prince was startled by the accident. It was as though a switch flicked inside his head and he turned into an animal nothing like the one we knew and loved. He started to attack me and began biting me repeatedly. I screamed like a baby, hopelessly helpless as he dug his teeth into the crown of my head. Dad rushed into the room and tried to pull Prince off me but he couldn't. He ran out and returned with a brush which he had to beat Prince with before the dog would scarper. Dad was forced to hit Prince so hard that the handle of the brush broke.

I had been mauled and was covered in blood. Mam remembers that it was on the day that Dad trained Chow Mein to win the Galway Plate that she took me to the doctor to have the stitches removed. Prince seemed to return to normal but I was left terrified when anywhere near him. The local vet told us that once a dog does that he can always do it again. Prince was put to sleep.

I had more luck with ponies than dogs, even make-believe ponies. As a young boy I would often substitute a human for a horse. My late Uncle Hubert had many a finish ridden from his back; even Sandra failed to escape, as a picture Mam treasures shows all too clearly. Fortunately for Uncle Hubert and Sandra, there was also Dino. A Shetland pony, Dino was the first pony I ever owned. The craic I used to have on him was immense. Perhaps because I felt Mam was always a bit too concerned for my safety, I enjoyed it much more when Dad supervised my lessons on Dino. He would sit on the little lad first, the result being that Dino had his back down and was ready for action by the time that I got on him. He was a fresh little devil and would take me as fast as his legs would carry him round and round the garden. God, it was fun.

Even then, I think I knew that Dino was a means to an end, a stepping stone to what I hankered for most. I wanted to be Lester Piggott. The walls of my room were full of pictures of Lester, cut out from the racing pages of the newspapers. I idolised him and loved the way he rode, ultra confident, stylish, strong, and with his backside so high in the air that it almost pierced the clouds. I kept scrapbooks detailing his seasons and big-race wins, some of which I watched again and again on a video of Lester's greatest rides that Dad had bought me as a present. To read about him and see him on television was thrilling enough; the prospect of getting to within touching distance of him excited me like you wouldn't believe. You can see that from a photograph Mam and Dad have in their dining room. It was taken in the paddock of the now defunct Phoenix Park racecourse on Irish Champion Stakes day. In the foreground is Lester, waiting to be legged up. In the background, looking sheepish and awestruck, is a young Richard Hughes, just delighted to be in the same parade ring as the great man.

Looking back, I suppose I did have some right to be seen in a racecourse paddock. I might only have been 11 or 12 when the picture was taken, but at that point I was already a successful jockey. Dessie's boy was making a big splash in the world of pony racing.

2

A CHAMPION ON A CHESTNUT

I became a jockey at the age of seven. I would have started even earlier if it had been possible. I'm sure that's how most young sportsmen feel. You often hear of footballers, still of primary school age, who get watched by scouts from the major clubs and then, before the boots are off their feet, are signed into academies on long contracts. That's their way into football. The way I got into horseracing, and the way so many Irish jockeys got into horseracing, was through pony racing.

When I go to work these days I'm often a spectator for the first couple of contests. That's because pony racing is beginning to take off in Britain. Lads like Sam Twiston-Davies and Harry Derham are among an increasing number who have established themselves as professional riders off the back of racing on ponies. From early summer into deep autumn you often find that meetings at tracks as prestigious as Ascot, Goodwood and Newmarket are preceded by two pony races, contested generally by the same riders, week in, week out. A real circuit has developed, one that also takes in point-to-point fixtures. In Britain it's a heavily regulated sport but it is not an entity in itself. It has no life of its own. In Ireland, it's a very different story.

Back home, pony racing does not have to share a stage with horseracing. It lives and breathes alone. Most parts of the country will stage at least one fixture a year to a minimum of six races at each one. Invariably held on Sundays through the warmer months, the meetings bear close similarities to point-to-points. They have a relaxed, amateur feel to them and are held on makeshift racecourses, made up for the day by rails being laid out around the perimeter of a farmer's field. Chip vans do a brisk business, burger sellers stick cheap patties of meat between untoasted buns, and racegoers try to keep warm with the aid of steaming tea drunk from paper cups. And, as at a point-to-point, there are bookmakers, for therein lies a crucial difference between pony racing in Britain and Ireland.

In Britain the racecourse bookmakers will lay a few small bets on the pony races but there are usually only one or two runners in each event with a serious chance of winning, which means that odds become prohibitive and the betting is uncompetitive. In Ireland it could not be more different. The men and women training the ponies take it extremely seriously and teach the jockeys to do the same. Prize money exists but, as at a point-to-point, it seldom exceeds £100 per race. To those people who view pony racing as something more than a chance for their son or daughter to have fun and learn the art of race riding, the only way to make real money is through gambling.

For me, though, it was all about the craic. I wanted to be a jockey, sooner rather than later, and pony racing presented an opportunity to make an early start. Dad did nothing to discourage me.

He had taken out a training licence in 1979, not long after his great day at Cheltenham with Monksfield. He needed somewhere to train from and we didn't have to go far to find the place. Osborne Lodge, a racing yard situated a stone's throw from the four-furlong pole on the Curragh's sprint track, became the family home, and remains so to this day. Training had been on Dad's mind for years before he actually took the plunge, and having spent so much time with Mick O'Toole, he had learnt his trade alongside a master. He knew the difference between a good horse and a bad horse and he knew how to get the best out of horses, good or bad. Mam happily settled into the role of trainer's wife and Sandra and I enjoyed being surrounded by thoroughbreds and the people who worked with them. Straight away it felt right.

It did not take Dad long to make an impact. Every aspiring jumps trainer yearns of saddling that breakthrough winner at the Cheltenham Festival. For some, even the finest, it can take years. Paul Nicholls spent eight years searching for his debut Festival success, David Nicholson considerably longer. Dad's wait was much shorter. His first runner anywhere was sent out in 1980, and just two years later he added to his Cheltenham Festival wins as a jockey with an opening Festival winner as a trainer. Miller Hill, ridden by a former pony racing graduate, Tom Morgan, gave Dad a notable first when landing the traditional curtain-raiser, the Supreme Novices' Hurdle, in 1982. It was a significant year for Dad, and also a significant year for me, as it marked a notable first for me as well: it was the year I rode my first ever winner.

I shall always be grateful to The Bear Smith. I can't tell you what his real name was because I don't know. We knew him as The Bear Smith, The Bear or even just Bear. Never Mr Smith, though. That wouldn't have seemed right.

The Bear Smith was a walking caricature of how some English people perceived old Ireland. A bit of a tinker, he was rough to look at but not as rough as the place he lived in. Home to The Bear was four miles from Osborne Lodge, on the other side of Kildare, where he lived with his much younger wife and very many children in a property that was every bit as messy as its owner. Neither The Bear Smith nor Mrs Bear Smith did much in the way of dusting, and neither seemed to have what you might call a real job, but they got by. The Bear, although dishevelled to look at, was far from stupid. He was the sort of man a character actor would love to play, a larger-than-life Irishman who would get into scrapes but invariably get out of them in one piece, and also a bit richer. In his dealings with the Hughes family, he most definitely ended up richer.

The Bear's children went to the same school as me, the De La Salle

Brothers establishment in Kildare town. It was well known at school that Dad was a famous name in racing – although to me he was just Dad – and it was equally well known that his son was pretty smart on the back of a pony. The Bear's children had a pony at home but, much to their old man's frustration, they couldn't manage her. They did, however, tell their dad that they knew a boy who could.

They were right. The pony in question was a small chestnut thoroughbred, two years old, 12.2 hands high, and a smashing little animal to look at. For all that she ticked the right boxes, she was little use to The Bear's children. Every time one tried to sit on her back she would whip round, making it impossible for them to maintain any contact. All efforts had come to nothing. The children were bored and The Bear saw no sense in paying for the keep of a pony who was not giving anything back in return. I was seen as a way out.

The pony really only needed taming. The Bear loaned her to us and allowed us to take her home. In no time at all we had her behaving beautifully. We also quickly realised that she could run. Through 1981 we began training her, the goal already firmly in the minds of both Dad and myself. This would be my vehicle into the upper echelons of pony racing, but she would have to race under a name, so we gave her one, Chestnut Lady. She would become the most prolific winner of my riding career. When I got her I was only seven, but for the next few years she became one of my closest friends. My life soon revolved around her. In the mornings I would muck her out and feed her before going to school. After getting home I would head almost immediately to her box, in which there was a bench that I would do my homework on. We bonded brilliantly. There was nothing I loved more than riding her, which I did on a daily basis after homework was finished. I would saddle her up, get on her back and take her on to the vast acres of the Curragh, where thousands of Ireland's best and most expensive thoroughbreds were exercised on its plush gallops. So was Chestnut Lady.

In 1982, a nine-year-old boy and a three-year-old pony teamed up together on a racecourse for the first time. I already had a little experience having ridden in a couple of races in each of the previous two years, but they were just sighters. None of the ponies I had ridden had a realistic chance of success but they afforded me the chance to gain some extremely early practical education. That said, with Dessie Hughes as my father, it would have been criminal if I hadn't possessed some idea of what to do. I did. Dad had spent hour after hour instructing me in the art of jockeyship. He has always been a quiet man, so much so that it was a characteristic that defined him in the eyes of some. But while he seldom said much, what he said was always worth listening to. He explained to me that in pony races there was invariably a mad rush as soon as the flag went up. It was like the start of the Grand National, in which all the riders always seem desperate to get to the first fence. None of the budding jockeys ever really rode a race. Dad instilled in me that riding a race was exactly what I had to do. A pony race was, in that sense, no different to a horserace. You had to maximise the pony's energy and utilise its ability to the best possible effect, especially if all the other jockeys were just blindly trying to go as fast as they could for as long as they could.

Sporting a set of Monksfield's colours, I took to it like a duck to water. Our first race came over six furlongs in Wexford. We made a winning debut. Then we won our next race, the one after, and the one after that as well. From the very first race I attempted to emulate my idol. I had in my head the image of Lester Piggott on horseback. I tried to make the same shape that he made and I tried to ride the races in the way that he would have ridden them. I visualised his triumphs around Epsom and sought to copy the manner in which he'd brought Nijinsky from the back of the field to its front, cheekily, stylishly and with ease. I wanted to look like Lester, and for a nine-year-old I wasn't making a bad fist of it. And while Chestnut Lady was hardly Nijinsky, she was a useful tool, fast, enthusiastic and responsive to the way I wanted to ride her. We were a dream team.

This was not lost on The Bear Smith. He spied a chance to make a quick buck, and at the end of my triumphant first season on Chestnut Lady he decided that the time was come for the loaned item to be returned.

The Bear saw Dad out on the Curragh one day and said that, now that the pony had become something of a racing machine, it was the right time for her to come home. One of his children, he said, could have a lot of fun riding her and he said he was being pestered by his kids to take her back. I'm not sure that any of that was true. He had probably just sensed the chance to earn a few quid from nowhere. Dessie, knowing what The Bear was like, decided that the best thing to do was a deal, so he asked how much The Bear wanted. With hindsight that probably wasn't the wisest course of action. A pony like Chestnut Lady would have fetched somewhere in the region of £300 to £400 at auction and both Dad and The Bear knew that. 'I couldn't sell her for less than eight hundred,' said The Bear. Dad told him that he was trying to get the price of two ponies and walked off, hoping that The Bear, on realising that his attempt at daylight robbery had failed, would give up.

The Bear, however, had pound signs in his eyes. One Sunday we were having lunch together as a family when the dogs outside began barking. The Bear had turned up and brought a trailer with him. He had decided the time had come to take back his pony. I ran outside and was told, without any sugar coating, what he had come for. I ran back inside even quicker. I was in a flood of tears and pleaded with Dad not to let The Bear have Chestnut Lady. Dad put down his knife and fork, went outside and attempted to reason with a greedy man on a mission.

'Listen, Bear,' he said, 'you can't take the pony off the little lad. Look at the state you've left him in. What do you really want for her?'

Dad's expectation was that The Bear would this time settle for what Chestnut Lady was actually worth. He couldn't have been more wrong.

'I want a thousand for her,' he said.

Dad couldn't believe it. At that stage of his training career, even after a first Cheltenham Festival victory, £1,000 was hardly loose change, especially if it was being spent on a pony who was not worth half as much.

'What do you think, Eileen?' he asked Mam as I stood in the corner of the kitchen, watching their every move and crying my eyes out.

Chestnut Lady stayed with the Hughes family. In the end Dad wrote a cheque for £500. Fortunately for The Bear Smith, so did Mam. The tinker had got what he wanted, but I was keeping something I wanted even more.

Chestnut Lady became a diminutive winning machine. She was a miniature racehorse and far superior to the rivals she was taking on. Throughout my pony racing career we won a heap of races together each season, but the more races she won, the more other people noticed the boy who was riding her. Very quickly, I was in demand.

After a successful first season on my own pony, trainers of other ponies began wanting to use me. Because my tactics were so different to those employed by almost all the other kids, I stood out as much as my backside in a race. It was far from uncommon for jockeys to have more than one ride at a meeting and as I got older the number of rides I was taking began to increase rapidly. At each meeting you would have races limited to ponies no higher than 12 hands, 12.2 hands, 13 hands, 13.2 hands and 14 hands, after which there would be at least one race in which the jockeys rode not ponies but horses. Given that there sometimes might be more than one race in a category, I could leave a meeting having taken part in five, six or even seven races.

Thursdays and Fridays were the days when it would often become clear how busy I was going to be on a Sunday. The phone would start ringing with trainers offering me mounts at wherever the next fixture was taking place. I would keep a list of the ponies I had committed myself to and the races for which I was still available. I was my own agent, turning down rides if I thought a better one might come along.

This was not, however, a one-boy operation. Dad remained in charge of what I was allowed to do and where I was allowed to go, in no small part because I couldn't get anywhere on my own. Sunday racing had not yet started. These days there is barely a Sunday in the calendar without a quality fixture being staged at the Curragh, Leopardstown, Punchestown or Fairyhouse, but in the early 1980s it was a day of rest for racing folk – unless, that is, those racing folk had a young son who was plying his trade in pony racing.

And I was not just plying my trade. I was earning my living as well.

Pony racing was not like pony club games. You didn't get a rosette for winning, you got money. From the age of ten onwards I never had to ask for pocket money from my parents. I was self-sufficient. More often than not I would be given £5 by the trainer of every pony I rode. If we won, that would rise to around £20. For a boy of my age I was a rich man. I was also generous. Given that Dad would drive me to wherever in the country the Sunday races were taking place, I always gave him a tenner to pay for the petrol.

As The Turf Club, which runs Irish racing but has no control over pony racing, did not like the idea of a licensed racehorse trainer becoming too involved in an unlicensed sport, Dad was quickly told he could not be actively involved on race days. That meant he could only really watch from the sidelines. Sandra stepped in and helped out by tightening the girths of my mounts and making sure I weighed in and out before and after every race. She has always been a superb sister and she was incredibly protective of me. She would have done what she did for nothing, but I made sure she got a few quid to spend on whatever teenage girls want to spend their money on. As I wanted to feel I was giving something to every member of the family, I also gave Mam a little something each week too.

The way I did it was quite funny. When a trainer paid me at the races, I would slip the notes down the side of my riding boots. Then, when we were all back in the car and heading home, I used to take off the boot and shake out the money. I was Alan Sugar's ideal child.

I always knew that pony racing was just a stage in a journey. I wanted to become a professional jockey, earning not just £5 for a ride and £20 for a win but enough to make a decent living. Even so, it was never about the money. It was about the unparalleled thrill you get from riding a racehorse at speed. It was about knowing the difference in power between yourself and the animal beneath you but at the same time knowing that with just your hands on the reins and your toes in the irons you can control the beast. There is no sensation in the world that compares to it. Former jockeys like Richard Dunwoody have spent years searching in vain for something that will give them an adrenalin rush to match the one experienced on the back of a thoroughbred travelling at 40 miles per hour. But there is nothing like it.

Ponies can only take you so far. I was hungry to ride racehorses that were being trained to race on real racetracks. Dad had a lot of them and, from the age of ten, he put his trust in me to do it. He knew I was good. Why else would a father let his ten-year-old boy risk life and limb on a creature who was always going to win any sort of physical battle between them?

My pre-school routine was now more time-consuming: not only was I mucking out Chestnut Lady, I was riding out first lot for Dad on the Curragh. It was bliss. The thought of first lot finishing and the start of school drawing closer horrified me. It was not that I loathed school. I didn't. It's simply that I hated to be away from the horses.

That said, those mornings were not entirely uneventful. I remember one day being legged up on a horse called Fallahassa. We were on the Curragh's round gallop and Dad had instructed me to complete two laps. As I came by at the end of the first circuit he noticed that my foot was not in the iron. The stirrup leather had broken after half a circuit but I continued and finished the two laps as requested. Dad says it's something he has never forgotten.

Something I never forgot was the best present I ever received as a child (with the obvious exception of Chestnut Lady). Liam O'Donnell was a jockey who rode quite a bit for Dad and so also spent plenty of time at the yard getting to know the horses. He took a shine to me and one Christmas bought me a red whip. Dear God, I loved that whip. I never gave a toss about bikes or the presents that young boys normally crave for. No Christmas gift could ever have meant more to me than that whip. It was as if Liam was saying to me that not only would I become a professional jockey but that I was already a long way down the road towards being one. Sadly, Liam's own riding career came to an end when he suffered a brain haemorrhage during a race at Limerick. He survived and went on to run a farm.

While I loved my shiny red whip, Dad instilled in me that it was only ever to be used sparingly. I don't think there was ever a piece of advice he drummed into me more regularly than that it's the jockey who goes for his whip last who usually wins. He believed that a jockey should get a horse's revs up by pushing, squeezing and shoving. This was a time when jockeys, and in particular Irish jump jockeys, were beginning to get a reputation for being excessive when it came to their use of the stick. The animal rights lobby was beginning to gain momentum and racing's authorities, particularly in Britain, were just starting to sense that the public was becoming uneasy with the sight of tired horses being repeatedly thrashed at the end of long and gruelling races. Dad's opinion was that too many jockeys went for their stick too soon. He told me that if the whip was used too much it lost its effect. He was, and has remained, adamant that if the whip is employed as a last resort it has a greater impact on the performance of the horse.

Dad also knew what racing people were like. It was almost impossible to pull the wool over his eyes, which was of great benefit to me – although it would have been of even greater benefit if I had followed him exactly to his word.

Prior to a race I was riding in at Galway, Dad was absolutely insistent that I should follow one particular boy during the race preliminaries. 'Wherever he goes, you go,' he said, stressing to me, 'Don't for a second let him out of your sight.' Down at the start, the starter told us all to walk away from the flag and to take a turn. I noticed that the boy Dad had told me to follow had ignored the starter and stayed where he was. It immediately dawned on me what was going to happen. The starter let the field go, even though only one of the runners was facing in the right direction. I got a proper bollocking off Dad. He had learnt before the race that the boy I should have been following was the son of the starter and that the pair had executed the same trick at a previous meeting. From then on I was aware of being aware at all times.

I couldn't tell you the name of the starter's son but I could tell you the names of many of the other children I rode against in pony racing. Alan Roche was a brilliant jockey but he became too heavy as he got older and is now a key member of staff with Jonjo O'Neill at Jackdaws Castle. There was Adrian Maguire, who went on to become Richard Dunwoody's arch rival and in 1992 won the Cheltenham Gold Cup on Cool Ground. Adrian's brother, Vinny, was also a huge talent, but one that was tragically stubbed out when he was killed in a hit-and-run road accident. Adrian now trains, as does another of my pony racing contemporaries, Muredach Kelly. Muredach had three letters printed on his racing silks: R.V.D. They stood for 'Rides Very Dirty'. To be fair to Muredach, he didn't ride very dirty, but his dad wanted all the other riders to be afraid of him.

Even though Muredach largely played by the rules, not everyone was the same. As I began to do well, I increasingly crossed swords with another lad who was plainly jealous of how well I was faring. We were both down the back straight in one particular race, neither of us holding any chance of winning, when he urged his horse alongside me and steered me off the track while pretending that his horse was uncontrollable and hanging badly. I remember my horse colliding with the bonnet of a car. As the horse, who was thankfully unscathed, chested the car I was fired into its windscreen. Incredibly luckily for me, it did not smash; instead I bounced off it and landed on the grass. Bizarrely, the young girl sat in the front passenger seat got out of the car and shouted abuse at me as I lay winded on the floor!

The lack of sympathy was striking, as it once was from Dad, who watched me suffer a horrible fall during a race at Maynooth. I was making the running when my pony fell. I was a sitting duck for the rest of the runners, a good number of which proceeded to gallop over me. I got up with no broken bones but in considerable pain and with a dead leg. Even so, Dad told me I had to ride in the final race. I couldn't believe what he was saying and tried to explain that I could barely bend my knee. Like my knee, he wouldn't budge. My mother and sister watched the next race with their hearts in their mouths. So too did Dad, but he didn't want me to leave that racecourse with the freshest memory in my head being a chilling fall. He was being cruel – very cruel, my mother and sister thought – to be kind. He did the right thing, and I'm grateful to him now, even if I wasn't quite so grateful at the time.

Sometimes it wasn't the other jockeys who posed the biggest threats to my safety, it was the trainers. One, Liam McIntyre, grabbed me by the chest and pinned me against a wall after I gave one of his ponies, Denver Jessie, too much to do at Dingle. Given that I had messed up the tactics I had some sympathy for his actions, but neither Dad nor I had any sympathy for a different trainer who recklessly risked my life and that of everyone else riding in a race a month or so later.

It did not take long for me to realise that the pony had been doped to its eyeballs. Black as coal, the pony had been trained to within an inch of her life and, just in case that wasn't enough, the trainer had clearly given the poor animal a little extra something to ensure she was primed to perform. Down at the start I could barely control her. I have always prided myself on the fact that I have very seldom been run away with, but when this pony decided she was through with waiting there was nothing I could do. She was like a wild animal. The circuit was three-quarters of a mile long and she completed three of them before I was able to pull her up. Dad, who was watching, said that the pony's eyes were jumping out of her head as she carted me round and round the course. The effort I was putting into trying to pull the pony up was leaving me close to exhaustion. Each time I passed Dad he told me not to fight her as at some point she would tire herself out. After what seemed like an eternity she did but, astonishingly, the trainer and the pony's owners still wanted her to run. They were trying to pull off a betting coup, but Dad was adamant that I was not going to help them. 'You run her if you want to run her,' he said. 'Richard is not riding her.'

That was a bad day, but during my pony racing career there were many more good ones. I proudly wore the Monksfield colours to around 150 wins and in 1987 was crowned Ireland's champion rider. The support I got from my parents and sister was immense, as it was from the wonderful Chestnut Lady, who, when I retired from pony racing, was given to a nearby family so that other children could experience the sort of fun that she gave me. She continued to live a happy life well into her thirties, but long before that I had outgrown her.

The time had come for me to step into the real world.

3

TODAY ROSCOMMON, TOMORROW THE WORLD

For both Scath Na Greine and myself, 19 March 1988 was a day of great significance. It was the day both of us made our professional debuts. Being transported to Naas racecourse no doubt came as something of a surprise to the horse. I know how he felt.

At the start of the week, the Fishery Maiden was not figuring greatly in my mind, let alone that of the wider racing world. This was Cheltenham Festival week, the most important week in the sport of jump racing and, to the vast majority of racing fans, the most enjoyable week of the whole year.

On the Tuesday, Celtic Shot won the Champion Hurdle for the great trainer Fred Winter and his stable jockey Peter Scudamore. On the Wednesday, Pearlyman completed back-to-back wins in the Queen Mother Champion Chase, and on the Thursday, the biggest day of all, Charter Party won the Cheltenham Gold Cup for another legendary trainer, David Nicholson, and his soon-to-be legendary jockey Richard Dunwoody.

Then on the Saturday, while most other people were still reliving the memories of Cheltenham, I became a fully fledged jockey.

Bizarrely, given how long I had been counting down the days to it happening, news of my impending entry into the real racing world was completely unexpected. I knew that Dad had been planning to give Scath Na Greine his first racecourse start in the six-furlong maiden at Naas but at no point had he suggested that I would be the one riding him. For a start, I was still at school, including on the day before the race. In fact, it was only when I got back from a long, drawn-out Friday at De La Salle that he stunned me with the announcement.

'Richard, you'll be riding Scath Na Greine at Naas tomorrow,' he said, not long after I stepped foot in the house.

I might have thought he was winding me up, but that wouldn't have been Dad. He was telling the truth. He meant it. On Friday afternoon I had been in lessons. On Saturday afternoon, while some of my classmates were playing football or rugby for the school, I would be riding a racehorse against some of Ireland's best jockeys in a proper race. Admittedly, it was a terrible race for extremely ordinary horses, but that wasn't the point. In the life of Richard Hughes, this was to be the first day of the rest of my life.

I'm not sure Scath Na Greine was quite as excited. I had ridden him at home and knew that he was never going to be a champion. Some horses are brilliant on the gallops but only moderate on the racecourse. Some horses show very little in the morning but in the afternoons, revved up by the racecourse, are a completely different proposition. Many horses, however, are slow on the gallops and slow on the racecourse. Scath Na Greine was one of those horses.

That didn't matter. He could have been the slowest horse in the world – and that day at Naas we learnt that there were at least four who were slower – but he would still have meant a lot to me because of what he did for me that day. He was the reason why on that Saturday afternoon I was able to walk unchallenged into the weighing room at Naas. Not that this was a new experience for me. I had been going into weighing rooms – the places where jockeys base themselves before and in between races – since I was a young boy. Once a meeting had finished, the clerk of the scales would often let me have a look around the jockeys' sanctuary. It was heaven. I would gaze longingly at the saddles, pick up the whips and sit on the benches, imagining how it would feel to be a bona fide member of this most special place. On that Saturday afternoon at Naas, I learnt how it felt. It felt wonderful.

I had been 15 for only two months and there still wasn't much of me. Towards the end of my pony racing career, however, weight had started to become an issue. In some of the races, the horses were allowed to race off a minimum of five stone. I was ever so slightly heavier than that and on occasions would need to lose a pound or two to make the correct weight. I began to keep a ledger and every night wrote into it my exact weight that day. I was always the smallest boy in class but that didn't mean I wouldn't be too big to ride at the correct weight in some pony races without taking action. I wouldn't have to sweat – and I'm sure Mam and Dad wouldn't have let me anyway – but I did deny myself sweets and chocolate if I knew I had to make five stone. In truth, it didn't matter in pony racing if a boy carried overweight, but it mattered to me. I wanted to be a professional jockey, and a professional jockey would not last long if he could not ride at the weight his horse was supposed to carry.

For a while at least, things changed when I switched to horseracing. On the morning of Scath Na Greine's race I stood on the bathroom scales and saw them telling me I was 5st 4lb. Scath Na Greine's allocated weight in the Fishery Maiden Stakes was 8st 7lb. As he was allowed to have seven pounds taken away due to the apprentice status of his newcomer jockey, Scath Na Greine would have to race with eight stone on his back. That translated as all of me and an awful lot of lead. Funnily enough I don't recall a huge amount about the race, but I do remember that the lead bag was incredibly heavy. Its contents weighed almost half as much as I did. I was not only the youngest and most inexperienced jockey in the weighing room, I was also by some way the lightest.

There were some big names riding alongside me. Declan Gillespie, who would finish second on Silver Patrol for one of my future allies,

Michael Grassick, was a successful and senior rider who later that year went on to land two of Ireland's five Classics, the Irish 2,000 Guineas on Prince Of Birds and the Irish St Leger on Dark Lomond, both of them trained by the greatest of all trainers, Vincent O'Brien. Pat Shanahan, a weighing-room fixture and fitting, was taking part in the race, as was Stephen Craine, two of whose best moments would also come in the Irish St Leger, which he won in consecutive years on a horse I would also get to ride, Oscar Schindler. Much younger than Stephen but set to be more successful than anyone riding that day was Johnny Murtagh. Johnny had entered racing the previous year and made an instant impression. He would go on to become one of the most successful riders in the world. He also became one of my closest and most trusted friends, and someone whose life experiences would, in certain ways, mirror my own.

Back then, Johnny was already many rungs higher up the racing ladder than me. I was more than satisfied just to be grasping the first rung and riding in my first race. The form book shows that the race was won by the 4-5 favourite Sound Of Victory. Back in tenth, ridden by Richard Hughes, claiming seven pounds, was the Dessie Hughes-trained Scath Na Greine, a 20-1 shot who ran like one. Dad gave me little in the way of instant feedback but he did not say I had done a great deal wrong. That was enough for me.

Scath Na Greine and I teamed up once more, three weeks later at our local course, the Curragh. The race this time was the Straw Hall Maiden and it confirmed, were any confirmation needed, that Dad was not training a future champion sprinter. The horse was dismissed as a 33-1 rag by the bookies, whose judgement at no point looked like being challenged. In a field of 20, we finished 20th. Johnny finished first on a 12-1 shot called Dance Alone. Johnny and I would go on to have long and fruitful careers. Scath Na Greine would not. His time as a racehorse was over.

Over the next few weeks I continued to ride in races, primarily at the weekends but also, once the evening racing season began, at night.

The prospect of a mount at the Curragh, Naas or Leopardstown kept me going through my final months at school. So did my parents. Mam and Dad had insisted that I would not be allowed to become a full-time jockey if I did not pass what in Ireland was then known as the Intermediate Certificate, or, more commonly, the Inter Cert. That was certainly not beyond me. I would never have called myself intelligent but I would never have called myself stupid, either. Had I approached my studies with more application, I've no doubt that I could have bettered the grades I finally got. My problem was that I was like a lairy horse. I struggled to concentrate on anything the least bit academic. If I got to the third page of a book I couldn't remember what I had read on pages one and two. I'm still the same.

De La Salle was not a bad place and I didn't have a bad time there. I was the smallest boy in class so I was always chaperoned around by the bigger lads. I was cute in that sense and recognised that my diminished stature could be used to my advantage. It also helped that I wasn't bad at sport. I played scrum half at rugby and was invariably a mid-order selection for games of football. I was never the first lad picked, but I wasn't the last.

All the time I was thinking about racing. The prospect of a life in anything other than racing was too terrible to contemplate. I very much made that point clear when a science teacher detained me after school one day. He had not been impressed by my less than focused attitude to his lessons. He told me that I needed to show more dedication. 'You need a good education behind you,' he said, adding, 'What if you don't make it as a jockey?' To me that was a verbal red rag. It felt like he was threatening me, and I reacted accordingly. I kicked him on the shin and ran home, crying my eyes out. Relations between myself and the teacher were frosty thereafter.

With some other teachers I got along great, not least Pat McNamara. Mr McNamara loved his racing every bit as much as I did. We got on like a house on fire and I always felt he wanted me to do well. During one of my Inter Cert exams in June 1988, he was the invigilator, charged with staying in the exam room and maintaining quiet during the three-hour paper. In this role, Mr McNamara was clearly not supposed to offer pearls of wisdom, nor indeed to strike up conversations of any sort, but he did. 'I see your dad has been doing well recently,' he said. I agreed, and we exchanged a few words about the Dessie Hughes string. Then, before he walked away, I pointed to a question and quietly asked him which one of the three possible answers was correct. Good old Mr McNamara told me, and good old Mr McNamara has since become a friend of the family, regularly visiting Mam and Dad and sending them a Christmas card each year.

Thanks in part to Mr McNamara, I fulfilled my part of the deal with my parents. After the final exam that June, I left school for the last time, confident that I had done enough. In September, when the results were sent out, I was proved right. I had my parents' permission to devote all my energies to being a jockey. And by that time I had already ridden my first winner.

It had been a while in coming. From that first ride on Scath Na Greine well over four months had passed during which I must have taken part in about 50 races. Not once had I come close to a win, but, of much more importance, I was learning all the time. Christy Roche, in particular, became a mentor. Christy had famously lifted home Secreto in the 1984 Derby, the race that El Gran Señor was expected to win, looked like winning and would have won but for the strength of Christy. Towards the end of his riding career he was appointed stable jockey to Aidan O'Brien but back then he was number one rider to Jim Bolger and doing extremely well in the job. He generously took me under his wing and topped up all the excellent advice that Dad had passed on.

In my early rides I was impetuous and far too eager. I was fierce keen to go for any gap, however small it seemed. My instinct told me that I had to make the most of whatever opportunity came along in a race, but Christy taught me that you had to balance instinct with analysis. The first thought was not always the wisest thought. Sometimes it was better to wait. He also underlined what Dad had drummed into me about race tactics. When pony racing, I had loved practising the art of race-riding. Bringing a pony from far back in the field and stealing a race close home gave me a massive buzz. Christy told me that I should not be afraid of riding the same way now. He said that by sitting a little way off the pace you gave yourself more options. If you sat right on the heels of the leaders you were inviting others to come alongside you and trap you in. If you sat off the heels of the leaders, you were much more in control and could deliver a challenge to the inside or outside of the horses in front. They were wise words, and they have influenced my riding ever since.

But the biggest influence has been Dad, and in my apprentice years he did everything he possibly could to help. Then, as now, he was predominantly a jumps trainer, which meant there were only ever a certain number of rides he could give me. Given how competitive Irish Flat racing was even then, it was inevitable that only a handful of those rides would have a genuine chance of winning. Viking Melody was one such ride.

It is a measure of how bad the opposition was that she was returned no bigger than 4-1. The first division of the Roscommon Maiden Stakes, staged unsurprisingly at Roscommon, was weak in the extreme. A number of the bigger stables were represented but even the biggest stables have bad horses.

Viking Melody had raced five times before she went to Roscommon on 2 August. Owned by John Newe, an American who lived in New York, she had hitherto failed to trouble the judge. In four of those five races I had been the rider, and I had been unable to get her any closer than sixth. Even Mick Kinane was unable to offer much help and finished eighth of ten on her on the one time he was aboard. Even so, Dad fancied her that August night. She raced like a filly who would stay, so the mile-and-a-half trip was in her favour, as was the fact that my presence on her back meant that seven pounds of her allocated weight was not. Most importantly, though, she had worked well at home in blinkers and they were being worn in a race for the first time. Dad thought she might win, which probably explains why Mam and Sandra came along as well.

It was good that they did. Viking Melody proved Dad right and got home half a length in front after a final-furlong battle with Star Worshipper. The two of us came pretty close in the heat of battle, which prompted the stewards to hold an inquiry, but I was never fearful of my first winner, like Dad's, ending up being disqualified. We kept the race. Strangely, I don't remember being elated. I had won lots of times in pony racing so winning was nothing new. The feeling was more one of relief. I think Dad felt the same. He also still had a job to do because I wasn't strong enough to carry the lead bag back to the weighing room. This was a victory for all the family. The fact that Dad had to help out even after the race was won only goes to prove that.

It would be wrong to say that a torrent of winners followed in the wake of Viking Melody, but the tide definitely began to turn.

Only seven days after my first win came my second, again for Dad, on a filly called Glen Of Ealy in a long-distance maiden at Wexford. The following week it was off to Ballinrobe, where Dad legged me up on another filly, Daybreak Lady, who duly won a mile-and-a-quarter handicap.

My fourth winner, in October, was my first for an outside stable. Persian Valley, trained by Michael Grassick, won for me at Dundalk seven days before I steered Tawkin to victory for Arthur Moore at Punchestown. Then, to round things off for the season, there was another win for Michael, this time at Down Royal on the seven-year-old gelding Dochas, who took the grandly titled Her Majesty's Plate by a head.

There was absolutely no reason to complain. At the start of 1988 I had been a schoolboy with exams to pass. At the end of the year I was an apprentice jockey for whom school was a thing of the past.

Over the winter there was no school but also no racing with the Flat season finished. That didn't mean I was idle. Dad was employing me, and he was making me work. Like all the other lads who worked in the yard, I rode out and mucked out. I might have been the guv'nor's son but I was not shown any obvious favours. We also had the following season's two-year-olds to prepare so there was plenty for me to do. And when I wasn't doing plenty, I was looking forward to what I would be doing when Flat racing resumed.

When it did I was ready and raring to go. My efforts were rewarded in what was a fruitful year. Michael Grassick was once again a major supporter and supplied me with five winners, while there was also a Sligo success for the man who had once regularly selected Dad to ride Monksfield, Des McDonogh. However, for me, 1989 revolved around two horses who between them gave me nine wins as a 16-year-old. Thanks to Dotrecuig and Smoggy Spray, people began to notice me.

Dotrecuig, roughly translated (with a minor spelling mistake) as 'two, three, five' in Gaelic, was a horse I knew well. I had ridden him six times in 1988 and had finished second on him twice and third once. He had won towards the back end of the campaign under Christy Roche at Phoenix Park and he approached the new season with Dad considering him to be an improving and well-handicapped horse.

It was largely thanks to Dotrecuig himself that he remained well handicapped throughout 1989. He was a sprinter who had to be delivered late in a race and as a result never won by far, which meant the handicapper could only ever raise his rating by a certain amount. The tactics you had to employ on Dotrecuig were due to his own burning urge to race. Built like a sprinter, big and muscular with a powerful backside, he wanted to do everything in a hurry. He was by far the strongest horse in the yard and would run away with you given half a chance. Going down to the start of a race you would never dare let him break into anything faster than a trot. In part that was because you were trying to conserve his energy for when it mattered. It was also a matter of self-preservation.

Knowing how strong and enthusiastic he was, it was always essential to bury him in a race. Big-field sprints were perfect for that. In an ideal world you would put him to sleep in the stalls and then try to miss the break so that everything else got out running before he did. Then you would position him behind a wall of horses and wait, wait and wait some more before the time came to release the handbrake. When you did, Dotrecuig had the ability to unleash an excellent turn of foot.

His winning spree started at Phoenix Park in April. We got up by a head to win an 18-runner handicap and then followed up a month later in a 16-runner event at the Curragh. We justified favouritism back at Phoenix Park in July and then rounded off a lucrative season with a fourth victory, again as favourite, at Leopardstown in October. On top of those wins, we also finished second twice, third once and fourth once. He was a superstar for me, and it was particularly sweet that he was trained by Dad. Even so, my biggest money-spinner as a 16-year-old was a horse trained not by Dad but by the man who had taught Dad so much about the art of training.

I had never ridden a winner for Mick O'Toole before Smoggy Spray came into my life. On the afternoon I rode him for the first time at Leopardstown in May he had gone 11 races without a win. Moreover, he had gone 11 races without looking like winning. The form figures were not inspiring, but the fact that Mick was persevering made you sit up and take notice.

It's hard to imagine that there was ever a shrewder trainer in Ireland than Mick O'Toole. He knew everything you could possibly need to know about his horses, the form book and the betting ring. Mick did not see much benefit to be had from finishing second, third or fourth. When that happened, you merely alerted the handicapper to a horse's ability while gaining only minimal consolation from place prize money and each-way bets. When you went out to ride a horse for Mick the instructions were always 'If you can't win, finish last!' In the five times I rode Smoggy Spray I never once managed to finish last. Luckily, in all five races I managed to finish first.

The races we won were also more valuable and prestigious than the ones I had bagged on Dotrecuig. In some of Ireland's better handicaps over a mile and nine furlongs, Smoggy Spray and I mopped up. The first strike was added to next time out at the Curragh on Irish 2,000 Guineas day. Coming on such a high-quality card, a card that was broadcast on television, this was by far the most important win of my career to date. It was doubly satisfying because of the way in which it was gained. Smoggy Spray was involved in a scrap to the line with Popular Glen, who was ridden by the mighty Mick Kinane, then retained by Dermot Weld. The jockey can only ever do so much, but it was still an amazing feeling to walk away from a tussle with the great Mick Kinane knowing that I had come out on top. Having said that, it was a while before I could afford myself a smile. The two horses crossed the winning line inseparable from each other. Neither Mick nor I knew who had won and we were both left to wait for the judge to announce his verdict. These days photo-finish deliberations seem to be over almost as soon as they've begun, but back then you often had to wait for what seemed like an eternity before you knew if you had won or lost.

As we came into the paddock and headed towards the spots reserved for the winner and second, I didn't know what to do. Jockeys tend to be cautious and need to be very confident that they've won before dismounting in the first-place section of the parade ring. Mick, however, was insistent. 'Go into the first spot,' he said, adding mischievously and as a joke, 'I'm a good friend of the judge. If the camera hasn't worked properly he'll have to come to a decision on his own.'

The judge declared us the winner. Whether or not the camera functioned properly, I don't know.

I also don't know why Mick seemingly jocked me off Smoggy Spray in his next two races. When the horse reappeared two weeks later at Leopardstown and then again shortly after in the valuable McDonogh Handicap at the Galway Festival, I was forced to find other mounts when Mick decided he wanted to use somebody else. Fortunately for me, Smoggy Spray was a long way below his best in both those races. For his final three races that year I was once again in the saddle. We won all three, including the Irish Cambridgeshire at the Curragh in September.

Thanks largely to Dotrecuig and Smoggy Spray, my 16th year was very sweet indeed. To have won nine of your 16 races in one season on just two horses was no mean feat. It brought me to the attention of trainers, owners, racing journalists and punters. It was the slice of good fortune that every young rider needs. Knowing how important it had been, my parents put together a montage of pictures of all nine wins that hangs on a wall in their dining room to this day.

I was, as I always had been, their little boy, but I was also a little boy who was turning into a young man. I was getting taller, bigger and heavier. Few and far between are the easy, uncomplicated or untroubled teenagers, and I was starting to change from the person I had been up to that point.

I had a lot in my life, but I wanted more. I had always longed to be a jockey and the dream had quickly been realised. But I was still not satisfied. I wanted to be like my mates and to behave like my mates. I wanted to be one of the lads. My friends were allowed to party late at night. They were given free rein by their parents to go out on the piss. Not me. Dad was moulding me into the person he wanted me to be. I wanted to enjoy the craic with my mates but Dad, rightly and understandably, kept drumming into me that I could not and should not. He kept telling me that I was a jockey, an athlete, a professional sportsman, and that for me things had to be different.

There were times when I felt that I could not please him. If people praised me after a race he would point out to them the things that I had done wrong. It's not that he was not proud of me – he was – but he found it hard to accept praise, whether it was given to himself or his son.

Perhaps most of all I was uneasy being the son of the boss. I worked with the other lads in the yard, did the same jobs as them and worked the same hours, but I could not be like them. I was the one riding winners, doing what most of them were almost certainly desperate to do, yet I was the one feeling envious. They were out on the lash, pulling girls, doing what young lads do. I wanted to be doing the same. Mates from outside the yard would tell me that their old man had taken them down the pub for a pint the night before. I wanted my old man to ask me out for a pint and could not understand why he would not.

It is only now, with the benefit of hindsight, that I can appreciate and be thankful for what he was trying to do. When I look at some of today's young riders, I see in them what Dad saw in me then. Yet at the time, an underlying resentment was festering away inside, bubbling up and waiting to be brought to the surface. If only subconsciously, it stayed inside me and was not released until many years later when I confronted my demons.

4

SHOULD I STAY OR SHOULD I GO?

There was nobody more surprised than me when Dad said yes.

I had ridden for two seasons as an apprentice in Ireland and it was very much a case of so far, so good. It was in my favour that I was the son of a celebrated racing figure. Dessie Hughes had been a hugely successful jockey, and in his first decade since quitting the saddle had established himself as a talented trainer. That did me no harm, and nor did the fact that people liked Dad. As his son, they wanted me to do well and I was making the most of the chances that were coming to me.

What seemed a major opportunity came knocking towards the end of the 1989 season. I had become good friends with Johnny Murtagh, who had ended the year as champion apprentice. His star was in the ascendancy and it was obvious to everyone that he was going to make it. Like me, he was ambitious. Also like me, he was starting to get bigger. I was in the early stages of a growth spurt with both my weight and height increasing. Johnny, nearly three years older than me, had seen that happening to himself a few years earlier and had begun to take action to deal with it.

Inactivity was not an option. For a jockey who struggles with his weight, doing nothing is never advisable. When you're at your busiest during the height of summer, controlling weight is more straightforward than at any point in the year. It therefore follows that it's harder to keep weight in check when you're not regularly riding. Like other jockeys before him, Johnny had sought to rectify that by passing the winter abroad. The previous winter he had spent December, January and February in Australia. There were plenty of trainers out there who were keen to use his services in morning gallops and barrier trials, but there were also rides to be had once you proved to those trainers you were worthy of being given them. There were an awful lot of good reasons to head Down Under, not least the fantastic weather, which was also helpful to weight management.

As the Irish season began to wind down, Johnny told me that he was planning to return to Sydney. More importantly, as far as I was concerned, he reckoned he could get me a job working for the same trainer. Niall McCullagh, another of my best mates from the weighing room, had signed up for the trip and I became extremely keen to go with them. For a start, I knew it would be beneficial to me as a jockey. I would experience racing in an environment far removed from Ireland and I'd make new contacts. But that wasn't all. I was 16 going on 17 and the prospect of spending a few months away from home was a massive carrot. I loved Mam, Dad and Sandra dearly and I knew I would miss them, but I was growing increasingly frustrated by the limitations that were placed on me at home. Once I got to Australia I could do what I wanted, when I wanted, for as long as I wanted and with whoever I wanted.

First, though, I had to get permission. I might have been officially an adult but I worked for Dad and my apprenticeship was with him. I could not realistically scarper off to the other side of the world for three months without his blessing, and nor would I have wanted to. I was not overly confident. I felt sure he would say no, that he would want to keep a tight leash on his hormonal teenager, but he agreed almost straight away. Before I could explain to him the benefits of going out there, he told me them himself. He said it would do me good. I was amazed and delighted. I was going to Australia.

The day of departure was emotional. You might have thought I was emigrating. I was travelling on a flight that left in the middle of the night and Mam and Dad both came along to see me off. Mam was in floods of tears. Even Dad seemed a little upset. As I prepared to say goodbye I started to veer in the same direction as I realised that, for the first time in my life, I was going to be on my own, without my parents to look out for me. What had been an exciting thought suddenly seemed a bit scary.

My new boss was Peter Miers. Through the early part of his riding career, Peter had been a relatively successful journeyman jockey. He did well as a lightweight rider, making the most of the opportunities that came his way when trainers needed someone who could get down to a weight that most others could not. However, it was not in his native Australia that Peter really made his name, but Hong Kong. In 1971 he secured a contract to ride under the licence of the then Royal Hong Kong Jockey Club. He stayed there until 1983, and enjoyed his biggest success when landing the 1978 Hong Kong Derby, but for much of his final year he was involved in a long, drawn-out court case with the territory's racing authority. Peter had become famous for being the man on board when gambling coups were landed. The RHKJC told him that his licence would not be renewed. Peter fought the decision but eventually returned home.

Back in Sydney, he resumed his riding career and did well enough, including once riding a 100-1 winner for Australia's most iconic trainer, Bart Cummings. However, by the winter of 1989/90 – or, in Australia, the summer of 1989/90 – he had switched to training. Based at Randwick racecourse, he kept a string of around 20 horses and carved out a respectable living. He was strict and very much of the old school, but although Australian from top to toe, he had an unusual fondness for Irish riders. Having once spent a season working for Pat Rohan in Britain, Peter had forged lots of relationships with British and Irish racing folk and he particularly admired Irish jockeys. He liked them as horsemen and knew that they were prepared to work hard. And Peter Miers definitely worked us hard.

He immediately made clear how he saw things panning out, telling me, 'By the time you leave here you'll hate my guts, but later you'll thank me.' To a degree he was right on both points. Every day started at 4 am, way earlier than would have been the case in Ireland and more than early enough to ensure that we couldn't get up to much the night before. Not every night anyway. We would ride about 20 horses every morning, not only Peter's but often other people's, including those trained by Bart Cummings. After working on the track we would head back to the yard to muck out, after which it was my daily task to wash and dry the towels that the horses wore underneath their saddles. The worst part of my time in Australia was washing those bloody towels. I hated it, and even when it was done the day's work wasn't: we had to be back at the yard by no later than 4 pm for evening stables.

This was serious graft, but it was also a steep learning curve, and one on which I learnt plenty. Every morning we were spending time with some of Australia's top riders, all of whom rode with shorter reins and stirrups than I had ever seen. They also seemed to have been born with stopwatches in their brains. If a trainer asked them to complete a workout covering each furlong in 14 seconds, they managed it to the second. I was taught to do the same and became significantly better at understanding exactly how fast I was travelling on a horse – something that has become a priceless asset, not least when I'm making all the running on a Monday night at Windsor. We took part in endless barrier trials, which were a little like pretend races and allowed trainers to gauge where they stood with a horse. What became obvious was that Australian horses were trained to race in a very different manner to back home. In Britain and Ireland you tended to wind the pace up gradually. In Australia, tactics were much more like those employed in France. In a barrier trial over a mile, we would replicate how a real race would be run by hacking for the first five furlongs and then sprinting the final three. It took some getting used to and at first I was left miles behind by Shane Dye, who was able to get an unbelievable turn of foot from his horses at the push of a button.

The experience gained from those mornings was valuable, as was the experience gained from the afternoons. I was not promised many rides and I did not get too many, but from the ones that I did get I realised very quickly that it was not only race tactics that differed from those in Ireland. Jockeys also rode much tighter to each other. If you take a wide route in Australia you are deemed an idiot and vilified. Nobody wants to be even three horses deep. With everyone fighting to take the shortest route from start to finish, jockeys on the inside are constantly squeezed up as riders on their outer seek to make the best of their bad situation. Australian racetracks are not places for the fearless.

Nor was the place I lived in while in Australia. Landlord to Johnny, Niall and myself was Peter's head lad, Tony, a man even stricter than Peter but without the good bits. It would be wrong to say that I warmed to him. Had it not been for Ron Quinton, a superb Australian jockey who invited us into his home for Christmas, our festive season would have been anything but festive. Tony liked to talk the talk and conducted himself like an army sergeant major. Together with his wife, he was responsible for making my time in Australia less pleasant than it otherwise would have been. I was also unimpressed with him professionally as well as personally. While I was there, Peter was plotting a bit of a coup. He had identified a horse who could win at a big price and he made it his mission to sting the bookies. We did everything possible to keep his ability hidden from the eyes of others. It was impressed on me by everybody, not least Peter and Tony, that we were to say nothing to anybody about the horse, but on the day of the race at country track Kembla Grange, Tony kept telling everybody that ours was a cert. He just couldn't keep himself from opening his mouth. 'What the hell are you doing?' I asked him. 'Carry on opening your big trap and we won't get a price.' Needless to say my advice did not go down very well.

The horse won, and the gamble was landed.

I too won in Australia, hitting the mark twice at Kembla Grange. That was the icing on the cake of a great trip. It was no picnic. We worked our guts out for very little reward. We got our wages on Friday and by Monday we were broke, but that was in part because we went on the lash and got pissed. Beforehand, though, we always made a phone call home – the only one of the week we could afford to make because we used to have to pay Aus$5 for the privilege.

After three months the Australian adventure ended. I returned home with new ideas and fancy jodhpurs, and a fair bit heavier than when I'd left. I also came home thinking that I could ride with stirrups and reins as short as Australian jockeys. But when I tried to do that on some of Dad's huge chasers and found myself being all but dragged over their heads, I decided that when in Ireland, do as the Irish do.

Not much changed in 1990. In 1989 I had ridden 16 winners from 229 rides. In 1990 I rode 19 winners from 339 rides. It was a year of consolidation, one in which my progress continued, albeit steadily and without any fireworks.

The rides that Dad was able to steer my way largely disappointed. Only two of my winners that year came from home. Dad's fortunes were starting to wane and would continue to do so for the rest of the decade. Michael Grassick remained an enthusiastic supporter, while Mick O'Toole continued to use me on Smoggy Spray, who won a couple of handicaps at Leopardstown and the Curragh with me in the saddle.

It had been a good year but I was hugely ambitious and felt that things were not happening quickly enough. It was at this point that I first considered moving to England. Countless Irish jockeys had made the same move in the past. For some it had worked out, for others it had not. With Britain staging so many more meetings, the sport there was not as competitive and I felt that meant it could offer me more chances than I was getting in Ireland. Dad and I spoke about it at length but he was adamant that now would not be the right time to cross the water.

He believed I was too young and inexperienced to make a permanent move to Britain. There was a chance that such a switch could reap dividends but there was arguably an even bigger chance that it would yield nothing, and if that turned out to be the case my career could be damaged for good.

I stayed put, although not over the winter. Having spent the previous one in Australia, this time I opted for India, largely because Johnny was heading out there. In effect, I was his chaperone. It was a frustrating and largely fruitless visit. As had been the case with the winter in Australia, I returned a better jockey, but rides in India were few and far between and a lot of time was spent twiddling thumbs. I was glad to get home, but the experience, although unsatisfactory, did not sour my view of India, to which I've subsequently returned on numerous occasions.

Through 1990 my weight had remained easily controllable. I was able to ride at 7st 3lb, which meant that no mounts had to be turned down. That was clearly beneficial to me, and it continued to be so in 1991, when I came close to becoming Ireland's champion apprentice.

For most of the year I was involved in a rare old scrap with Willie Supple. It was in miniature form a little like the champion jockey battle I would fight with Paul Hanagan 19 years later. The racing media enjoyed seeing two young lads billed as the future of Irish Flat racing going head to head for the title, and their coverage fuelled interest in the final few weeks of the season.

In some ways I was fortunate because I was being employed by a wide variety of trainers, including Noel Meade and Declan Gillespie. There was even a ride for none other than Vincent O'Brien – although by this stage he was edging closer to retirement – and Zamanayn became my first winner wearing the colours of the Aga Khan. More significantly, Zamanayn was my first winner for the trainer John Oxx, whose horses I would link up with an awful lot more during the autumn of 1992 and spring of 1993. There were also two wins at Tramore within the space of three days on a three-year-old filly called Choisya, trained by

Anne-Marie Crowley, the wife of Aidan O'Brien, who would take over the licence from his other half two years later.

Unfortunately, what I did not have, and what I really needed, was a yard that could guarantee me a steady and guaranteed supply of winners. Willie Supple had that in Jim Bolger. Jim employed Christy Roche as his stable jockey but, sensing that his apprentice was in pole position to become champion, reallocated many of the rides that would have been Christy's to Willie. In that sense, the two of us were not competing on a level playing field, but at the same time I wasn't complaining because if I had been in Willie's position I know that I would have bitten off Jim's hand.

In the end, Jim's support proved crucial and the championship was won by Willie, who ended the season with 33 winners compared to my 30. I would never get the chance to be champion apprentice again for I would never again ride as an apprentice. After four years my apprenticeship was at an end. Things were about to change, not only professionally, but domestically as well.

All of a sudden I became a wealthy young man. From having next to nothing, I was loaded, certainly for a young lad on the verge of his 19th birthday. A windfall had come my way and brought with it an opportunity that was too good to miss.

My rise to riches was wholly as a result of the Irish apprenticeship system. Perfectly understandably, the sport's governing body, The Turf Club, did not think it a good idea for 15-year-old boys to be earning excessive amounts of money. During an infant jockey's early years it was deemed better for him to be paid a reasonable wage, but no more than that. As a result, for the last four years I had been receiving only half the official riding fee for every mount I had taken, which roughly equated to about £50 a ride; the other half went to the trainer by whom the apprentice was employed, which in my case meant Dad. Neither Dad nor I had seen any of what was owed to me in prize money earnings. Every jockey is paid a small percentage of the prize money their mounts accrue for winning or being placed. These days in Britain riders receive in the region of seven per cent per race, and when winning races boasting serious purses there is clearly good money to be made. I had not been winning those sorts of races but over four years I had still ridden enough winners, seconds, thirds and fourths to have built up a kitty of about £20,000. Since the day I took my first ride in 1988, each and every penny that my mounts had earned me had, under Turf Club rules, gone into a special pot that could not be opened by me or anybody else until my apprenticeship had been served. At the end of the 1991 season my apprentice days were over. It was time for The Turf Club to show me the money.

On reflection, I feel pleasantly surprised at how responsibly I reacted to my new situation. I could have dashed into town and returned with a shiny sports car or blown a huge chunk of it on an exotic holiday. Had I done either I would have received the mother of all bollockings from my parents, but that was only one part of the reason why I decided to invest my money elsewhere. The opportunity to get on the property ladder had arrived.

On land adjacent to ours a developer had been building a house from scratch. Land around the Curragh is highly prized and he knew he would have no trouble selling the house. He also knew that there was a young jockey living next door to the house who might fancy living in a place of his own. For both of us it was a win-win scenario. Also happy were Mam and Dad. They could see that investing in property was a sensible and mature move. They also knew full well that a man of my age would want to fly the nest, but as I was moving literally next door they were still close enough to keep an eye on their son.

Practically every penny of the £20,000 was needed for the deposit. Maintaining the mortgage payments was going to be difficult but not nearly so difficult if the property was earning me money. I therefore decided to take in lodgers. It was once again a perfect move because it enabled me to earn a few quid and also to live with some of my mates. My first housemates were Niall McCullagh, James Collins, then an apprentice and stable lad based with Dad, and another apprentice, P. P. Murphy. Over the next three years we would be joined by Jamie McGee, now a pre-trainer but then Dad's conditional jockey, while at weekends we often took in a few extras, including Stephen Nolan, then a jockey but now a trainer, Adrian Regan, a mate who lived just down the road from us and today runs a stud farm in Kentucky, and another mate, Frankie O'Connor, who has also since emigrated to the States.

Moving out of the family home was a wonderful feeling, one comparable to the day I left school for the last time. Then, as now, I adored Mam and Dad, but I was a young man who craved independence. I now had it. Every day I still walked around the hedge that separated me from them and came into work, but I wasn't like one of those students who gets his mother to do the washing at weekends. We cooked, we cleaned and we supported ourselves. For the first time ever, I was in control of my own life and in a position to make my own decisions. I was in charge.

I had a good time as well. In January 1992 I turned 19. I was earning decent money and had a place of my own. There was craic to be had and I was intent on having it, including with some of the young ladies of Kildare town. What I didn't want was to be tied down. These were supposed to be fun years, and for the most part they were exactly that.

Women were not infrequent visitors to the house. I remember riding out for Dad one morning alongside James Collins. Dad was also on horseback at the front of the string when he led us past the large window that ran along the front of my house. At the precise moment that Dad was going past the window and admiring the front garden, a young woman walked across the other side of the window, a bowl of cornflakes in her hand and not a stitch of clothing on her body. It was like a scene from a situation comedy. Dad seemed not to notice her at first and almost did a double take on the horse, putting it into reverse to make sure his eyes weren't deceiving him. They weren't.

'What on earth are you doing in there?' he said. 'Running a whorehouse?'

I blamed James.

I also had James to blame for another unfortunate incident. We had been out in Kildare town one Saturday night and James had brought back a girl he had picked up in the pub. After James and the girl had spent a bit of time together in his bedroom, the girl decided that she would prefer to sleep at her place and not with the guy she had just been getting to know quite intimately. James, however, had no intention of driving her home. She took umbrage and went off in a huff. What none of us knew at the time was that she had picked up my car keys from the kitchen table and decided that she would use whoever's car it was to return home. Sadly, she wasn't a very good driver and managed to reverse the car into the garden, where its wheels became embedded in the lawn. That one took some explaining.

So, too, did the consequences of a lads' day out at the Punchestown Festival. As a young man with an eye for the latest fashions I was delighted to be wearing a pair of tight cowboy boots. They looked very smart but were real ankle huggers, and as the day and night went on they began hugging my ankles with an ever-increasing dedication to the cause. We ate a lot and drank even more that day, and by the end of it I was struggling to get the boots off. It probably didn't help that I was pissed out of my head. All my efforts to pull the boots off came to nothing. My body had expanded within them and they seemed to have shrunk. In the end it was all too much like hard work. I pulled my trousers and pants off over the boots and, shameful as it is to admit, then got into bed and slept in them. Very regrettably, I slept for longer than I should have done and duly failed to turn up for work. Dad, who knew where I had been the previous day, put two and two together and stormed into the house, up the stairs and into the bedroom.

What followed will stay with both of us for ever. No parent should ever have to pull back the duvet of his son's bed to discover his own flesh and blood wearing nothing but a pair of cowboy boots. My Dad suffered that fate. Luckily, I was too bleary-eyed to catch the expression on his face but I did hear his reaction as he walked down the stairs to see Mam, who had come into the house to see what was going on. 'Eileen,' he said, 'I think we've raised a tramp!'

Sometimes, though, the tramp was the victim. That was certainly the case when I was at the centre of another bed incident. The lads and I came back from clubbing one night and, while talking and drinking in the lounge, Frankie and Stephen declared that they were capable of catching one of the sheep that were farmed on the Curragh. I like a good time as much as the next man, but I couldn't see that there was much craic to be had from chasing a sheep in the middle of the night. I left them to it and went to bed. About an hour later I was woken up in no uncertain terms when a kidnapped sheep was flung on to my bed. The sheep, no doubt confused and a little concerned, proceeded to cause carnage, darting left, right and centre around the house, searching for a route to freedom and shitting wherever it went. Luckily, I managed to keep that one from the eyes, ears and noses of Mam and Dad.

Almost from the moment I moved into the house I knew for certain that deciding not to quit Ireland for Britain had been a wise move, not least because in 1992 I cemented my connection to Noel Meade. Although best known for being a top jumps trainer, Noel has always enjoyed success on the Flat and in 1998 sent out Sunshine Street to finish fourth as a 150-1 outsider in the Derby. At the start of 1992, Noel's best Flat horse was Street Rebel, like Sunshine Street owned by Pat Garvey. The horse had won two of his starts at three the previous year and put up his best performance when fifth at 50-1 in the Irish 2,000 Guineas. With another winter behind him he was expected to do well at four, and he fulfilled a fair bit of the promise while also giving me two significant moments.

The first came at the Curragh in May when we teamed up to win the Greenlands Stakes. Although worth less than £11,000 to the winner, it was the first Group-race victory of my career. A Group 3 sprint over six furlongs, it was contested by only five horses, but we were outsider of the five at 12-1 and not expected to beat a field that was headed by British raider Chicarica, sent off at 11-10 under Walter Swinburn. While Walter attempted to make all, I employed tactics that had served me well since my days in pony racing. I put Street Rebel to sleep, although on this occasion almost literally. He was soon struggling to keep up with the leaders, but as he got closer to the horses in front he gained confidence. Entering the final furlong, Chicarica, running on the rail, had been joined by Christy Roche on the second favourite Maledetto. Street Rebel was the one going forward with momentum and, as the line drew near, I could see that there was enough room separating the two leaders to make a daring bid for glory. We squeezed in between Chicarica and Maledetto, sliced them in two and surged ahead, passing the judge with a half-length advantage.

Not only had I won, but I'd won cleverly and stylishly in a Saturday race shown on Irish state broadcaster RTE and Channel 4. It brought me to the attention of people to whom I had previously only been a name on a racecard. It also thrust me into the thinking of some of Ireland's leading trainers. It was a big win in every sense.

Less than a month later Street Rebel gave me another big day when Noel asked me to ride him at Royal Ascot. I had never previously had the opportunity to ride in Britain, but this wasn't only just a first ride in Britain, it was a ride at the most important meeting staged not only in Britain but anywhere else. In the end it was a bit of a let-down. As at the Curragh, Street Rebel found things happening too quickly in the early stages of the Cork and Orrery Stakes but also this time he found things happening too quickly for him at the end of the race. We finished ninth, which was disappointing, but I had made another little breakthrough. It had been a positive experience.

My fortunes continued to rise in the second half of 1992. Johnny Murtagh's went in the opposite direction. What happened to each of us was directly related.

My growth rate had increased. I had soared to 5ft 9in and my weight was moving in the same direction. The light weights I had once been able to make in handicaps were becoming a thing of the past. My minimum riding weight had nudged up past the eight-stone mark and it was inevitably increasing all the time. However, I was far from the only one in that position.

Everything had been going so well for Johnny. After becoming champion apprentice he had caught the eye of John Oxx, who offered him the job of stable jockey. John's string was one of the very best in Ireland, and to make it as a top-level rider there you had to have a position with a top trainer, of which there were very few. Johnny had struck lucky. He wasn't ready for it. Like me, Johnny is a big lad. He was finding it desperately difficult to control his weight. The constant battle with the scales was affecting his mental state and, like many others before him, he turned to alcohol. As he got worse, John Oxx found himself feeling obliged to part company with his stable jockey. I was a beneficiary and became one of John's regular riders through the autumn. I won a trio of Listed races for him, two on fillies owned by the Aga Khan, and I was the one selected to partner the two-year-olds that John was hoping could turn out to be Classic contenders at three.

I didn't know what to feel. I was on the verge of landing the job that could transform my career but only because one of my best friends had thrown that job away.

Johnny had gone badly off the rails, and forfeiting his position with John Oxx had hardly helped. To his credit, he decided to do something about it. Over the winter he checked himself into St Patrick's University Hospital in Dublin. St Pat's, situated close to Phoenix Park and the old Kilmainham Gaol, is Ireland's largest mental health hospital and among its patients are those suffering from alcohol dependency. I was one of those who went there to visit him. That visit is carved deep into my memory. St Pat's was a depressing place because the people in there were in such desperate situations. I found Johnny in an awful state in a tiny little room. It was encouraging that he was doing something to sort himself out, but to see him in a place like St Pat's was heartbreaking. As I left the hospital I cried.

I knew that I was also drinking too much at the time. When Johnny came out of St Pat's he showed me a leaflet that asked you various questions about your drinking habits. Based on the answers I gave, I was classified as a problem drinker as well. I laughed it off. I told myself that, unlike Johnny, I was able to control my drinking. Seeing Johnny had given me a fright, but it didn't change my lifestyle.

But Johnny had changed my working life. As preparations gathered pace for the 1993 Flat season it became obvious that I was now John Oxx's first-choice rider. I was never offered a formal position but I hoped that in time I would be. I was obviously concerned for a friend, but the greedy, self-interested voice in my head was telling me that I had to make the most of the chances that were being handed to me and that I shouldn't feel guilty about taking advantage of the situation. When Johnny told me that he was considering switching to jumping, on the basis that it would allow him to ride at a much heavier and more manageable weight, part of me was delighted. If Johnny switched codes and made a success of it, I could ride what would have been his mounts for John Oxx and not feel awkward. I even pointed him in the way of Dad and suggested that he should start riding out for him. He did, but at the start of February he also began riding out for John Oxx. It sounds horrible, but I hoped it would come to nothing. I also know that Johnny was hoping that I would do badly when I began partnering John's leading horses in the spring.

For both of us, it felt like we were sticking pins into a good friend's voodoo doll. Sometimes, that's exactly what being a jockey is like.

The season could not have started much better. At a big Leopardstown fixture in mid-April I won both the 1,000 Guineas Trial and 2,000 Guineas Trial on three-year-olds trained by John Oxx. Three weeks later I was back at Leopardstown and won the track's Irish 1,000 Guineas Trial for Michael Grassick on a lovely filly called Danse Royale. We scored snugly, but only by a head, and the stewards felt that I had interfered with the runner-up, Eurostorm. They amended the result and placed us second. A few days later we got the race back following a successful appeal, but Danse Royale's owner-breeder, Patricia O'Kelly, let it be known that the whole experience had been far too traumatic for her and she'd apparently decided that I was to blame. I was told I would not be riding Danse Royale in the Irish 1,000 Guineas. The man who took my place was Lester Piggott.

I didn't really know what to feel. Lester was my boyhood idol, and having retired and spent time in prison he was now back riding. There was barely a top jockey in the business who at some point had not been jocked off in favour of Lester – in fact Lester was very often the one telling trainers to do the jocking off – but it was still a rotten feeling to know that somebody else would be sitting on my filly in a Classic.

Danse Royale did not win the Irish 1,000 Guineas, but I believe that if I had been riding she would have done. That sounds like an immensely big-headed thing to say but I mean it, not because I was a better rider than the best there has ever been, but because I knew Danse Royale well and Lester did not. At Leopardstown I gave the filly a couple of smacks early in the race, as if you didn't she had a tendency to drop herself out the back and therefore out of contention. Lester seemed unaware of this and at the halfway point of the Guineas had her in an impossible position. As Lester got stuck into her she began making up ground hand over fist, but it was too little, too late and she advanced only into third, two lengths behind the winner, Nicer.

I was gutted, as I had been the previous Saturday when Massyar, one of my Leopardstown trial winners for John Oxx, was beaten little more than a length in the Irish 2,000 Guineas. That was a blow, but not as big a blow as when John once again started using Johnny on many of his horses. I had never been appointed stable jockey, and it wasn't even the case that John was stopping using me, but I sensed that things were heading in the wrong direction. That became very apparent a month later on Irish Derby day. John was increasingly employing Mick Kinane, who many years later would become his stable jockey, and in the Irish Derby it was Mick who was selected to partner my Guineas mount Massyar. John's other runner in the race, the 25-1 outsider

Mam, Dad and me, aged eight, at home at Osborne Lodge. Dad had just started to train there. I'm in need of a haircut.

Me and my first pony, Dino. I was only aged four at the time but I clearly knew I was destined to be a jockey!

Early days with a nine-year-old budding jockey riding out at Dad's yard.

Practising my style on my poor sister Sandra.

Waiting for my hero to sign his autograph aged 13.

Me, aged ten, sporting Monksfield's colours after winning a 13-hand pony race at Wexford. With me are my mates Micky Clarke (middle) and Muredach Kelly (right), with the sponsors of the race.

My first winner as a professional apprentice, on Viking Melody at Roscommon in 1988.

Dad was over the moon – and so was I.

Getting stuck in, aged ten. Dad would not have approved of the gloves!

Me, aged 13, and Muredach Kelly pony racing in 1986 at Maynooth. Muredach had the letters 'RVD' printed on his silks. That was intended to scare us. It didn't scare me!

In Australia with Niall McCullagh, Johnny Murtagh and Eddie Leonard (below) looking very cool on my first visit Down Under in 1989.

Scath Na Greine, the horse who gave me my first ever ride in a real race, at Naas in March 1988.

31 December 1993: my first win over hurdles at Punchestown on Amari Queen, trained by Dad. I'm with Sandra. Dad was absent as my granny had passed away the day before.

Stephen Nolan, Frankie O'Connor (on board) and James Collins, around my mechanical horse in 1993. When I started to stretch my style had to change, so a mechanical horse was really helpful. All three are enjoying taking the mickey out of me.

Dotrecuig, trained by Dad, wins at the Curragh in 1989. Tornabuoni (Christy Roche) was second.

The Mick O'Toole trained, Smoggy Spray, wins at the Curragh in 1989.

Another win on Smoggy Spray, this time at a wet Leopardstown in 1989. The saddle was the one that Dad had used to win the Champion Hurdle and Gold Cup. I've got a bit bigger since then and now use a much smaller saddle that weighs no more than two pounds.

Dotrecuig wins his fourth race of 1989 at Leopardstown. I only weighed 5st 7lb at the time – a pea in a haystack!

A dream come true: beating my boyhood hero, Lester Piggott, as Massyar defeats Fatherland in the 1993 Leopardstown 2,000 Guineas Trial.

Dad joins me in 1989 to receive the prize given to the year's most improving apprentice at the Jockeys' Awards in Dublin. It was a proud moment for us both.

A callow youth in 1990!

Foresee, performed better than his more fancied stablemate and stayed on into third, but I was not the one on his back. That was Johnny. And that seemed to signal where I stood.

As the weeks went by it became ever more obvious that John and Johnny were getting back together. I continued to ride winners, but far fewer of them were for John. Moreover, opportunities in the big races were sparse. Ireland's Group races are something of a closed shop. These days Aidan O'Brien dominates. Back then, the same was true of Dermot Weld, John Oxx and Jim Bolger, with the likes of Tommy Stack, Michael Kauntze, Kevin Prendergast and Con Collins all fighting for their own small slice of the pie. If you were not attached to one of those stables it was practically impossible for a jockey to be involved in the top races. Moreover, without the backing of a major yard, just making a respectable living was difficult.

My season ended with 38 winners. It was the biggest total of my career, but I still felt frustrated and severely lacking in optimism. I began to consider my options. Weight was becoming a bigger and bigger issue. I now viewed 8st 6lb as my minimum, but getting down to that required effort and planning. Over the winter I decided to try my hand at jumping. It was not an unsuccessful experiment and I rode winners over hurdles for Dad at Punchestown in December and Tralee in March 1994, but at no point had I been seriously considering quitting the Flat.

There was a different, far more tempting option. The time had come to quit something else. I was about to leave Ireland.

5

A NEW BEGINNING

I was not approaching the new season in a positive frame of mind. Having tasted, however briefly, how it felt to be first-choice rider to a major stable, I was miserable at the thought of spending another year picking up scraps and watching from the weighing room as other jockeys, to whom I thought I was at least the equal, competed in Ireland's Group 1 races.

My problem was finding a way out of the situation. It seemed increasingly clear to me that you simply had to hold a senior position with one of the leading Flat trainers to stand any chance of competing at the sport's highest level. I had shown during my brief stint as John Oxx's preferred rider that I was more than capable of delivering in the bigger races, but that did not seem to be enough. There were too many good jockeys seeking opportunities from too few top trainers and I was one of the jockeys who was missing out. Even more worryingly, I saw no prospect of that changing.

It wasn't even as if I was doing anything wrong. I was confident in my ability as a jockey. I viewed myself as an all-rounder, someone who could happily dictate a race from the front but also someone who had a flair for bringing horses from off the pace. I knew I could easily mix it with the big boys, but only if I was sitting on the right ammunition.

It had reached the stage where I was prepared to try anything. Dad knew how I was feeling and one morning mentioned an idea that had been suggested to him by another Irish trainer, Liam Browne. Liam had heard of a course in positive thinking that was about to begin not far from us at the Ambassador Hotel in Kill. Given that I was hardly optimistic about my future, a few lessons in positive thinking sounded like they might be beneficial, so I signed up.

From 14 March to 3 May 1994 I became a paying student at The Phoenix Seminar on the Psychology of Achievement. The course was billed as 'an integrated programme in professional development' and its tutors set out to help us with our individual problems. The first thing we had to do was decide what we wanted to gain from the sessions. I explained to them my feelings. I wanted to climb out of the second division of jockeys and thereafter to fulfil my potential. I also explained that I didn't see a way of doing that in Ireland unless something changed that was out of my control, such as a leading rider retiring. In a nutshell, I knew what I wanted but I could not see a way of making it happen. It was therefore decided that my aim at the end of the course was 'to be able to put my thoughts into practice'.

But come May, Irish racing looked just as it had looked at the start of the course. I had ridden only three winners that season, all of them in maidens, and while two of them were for John Oxx, they were mounts that Johnny Murtagh had not been available to partner. I needed more than ever 'to put my thoughts into practice'. I needed to get on better horses, and better horses were not going to come along for me in Ireland. I needed to do something drastic.

By the middle of June my total for the season had risen to just seven winners. The additional four wins had come in four more maidens. Even more depressingly, there had been no involvement for me in any of the major races. On Irish 2,000 Guineas day in mid-May I watched the Classic and the chief supporting event, the Tattersalls Gold Cup, on television. The only action for me that day was in handicaps and maidens. Things were worse still on Irish 1,000 Guineas day when I took part in only one race, the opening maiden, on an unfancied 14-1 shot. I might as well have gone home after that. For the rest of the afternoon I could have stood in the crowd and watched from the stands. I had no more part to play in proceedings than the paying customers.

A week before the Irish Derby, and with no obvious hope of a ride in the country's premier Flat race, I decided that enough was enough. I spent a late night in Kildare town with mates, only a fraction of my brain thinking even remotely about riding out for Dad the next morning. My enthusiasm for the job was at rock bottom. The prospect of going up the gallop on three of Dad's jumpers held zero appeal. I slept in late – something I had got into a habit of doing. When I finally rolled in to work, Dad wasn't happy and he let me know it. More than anything he wanted me to be a success, and he had always drummed into me that to be a success I had to be disciplined. There and then we had a major row. He told me what I was doing wrong and I responded by telling him that even when I was doing things right it was doing me no good.

'There's feck all here for me,' I said before blurting out that I intended to move to Britain.

Dad's first reaction was that if I was going to do that I would need to start putting my alarm clock inside a steel bucket. He felt that my behaviour was letting him down, but as we both calmed down he started to hear me out.

I had reached the point at which the arguments in favour of a move were more numerous and persuasive than those for staying in Ireland. There was so much more racing in Britain, so many more trainers and so many more horses that I considered it almost impossible for me not to have a better shot at success there. I felt disillusioned with my own country. I was putting in the hours and the effort but it was giving me little in return. The prospect of a new start in Britain was tantalising. For all Irish racing fans, British racing was at least as familiar to us as our own sport. We saw little Irish racing on television, but we saw British racing every weekend and on plenty of weekdays thanks to the coverage on the BBC and Channel 4. I might have only ridden on one British racecourse, Ascot, but I already felt as if I knew more than enough about Britain's tracks, trainers and horses to feel comfortable about relocating.

The only question was, where should I relocate? If I was going to do it, I had to do it properly. I could hardly just take a flight to Heathrow and then hope for the best. I needed a plan of action.

Dad agreed with me that the time had come to leave Ireland. He also agreed that I had to arrange in advance a source of rides. Any jockey who restarts his career in a new country has to hit the ground running and build instant momentum. Early winners would be essential if I was to stand any chance of establishing myself away from home.

Dad had an idea. His old head lad Jimmy Gallagher was now working for Richard Hannon, one of Britain's leading trainers. Richard had won Classics at home and abroad and, just as importantly for me, had sent out an astonishing 182 British winners from 1,214 runners the previous year. Even better, he did not really employ a stable jockey. The likes of Pat Eddery, John Reid, Michael Roberts and Richard Perham were all regularly legged up by Richard but none had a retainer. Richard seemed an extremely attractive option – but only if he could be persuaded to use me.

After speaking to Mick Kinane, who had ridden plenty for Richard, I began to convince myself that this could happen. The prospect seemed even more real after Dad spoke to Jimmy, who agreed that Richard Hannon would be perfect for me. Dad also spoke to his friend, the legendary bloodstock agent Jack Doyle, whose son Peter bought and still buys many of Richard's horses.

It was arranged for me to meet Richard Hannon at the Curragh on Irish Derby day. Unlike me, Richard had an involvement in the big race. He was due to saddle his French Derby third Alriffa, who would on this occasion go on to finish fourth. As I had expected, there was nothing for me in the Irish Derby. Equally depressingly, there was nothing for me on the whole of Irish Derby day. Six other races took place that afternoon, three Group contests, two handicaps and one maiden. In none of them had I been able to get a mount. It had been almost as bad the previous day when on the Saturday of the fixture I had managed to secure only two rides in minor races, one on a 20-1 outsider, the other on an almost equally without-hope 16-1 shot. Staying in Ireland was no longer a sensible option. I went to the Curragh knowing that, while I would not be riding, I would be doing something that could have enormous implications for my future.

If I'm absolutely honest, I'm not sure that I knew at the time what Richard Hannon looked like. I had never met him. What I had in my mind was the image of an old-fashioned English trainer, very probably someone who spoke with a plummy public school accent. I think I was expecting a proper English gent, someone who would sound something like John Dunlop. It transpired that Richard sounded nothing like John Dunlop.

When I introduced myself to him he was stood alongside Peter Doyle. I explained who I was, we made a bit of small talk, and then I handed him a cv I had put together in the belief that a professional approach would impress him. 'I don't need to see a cv,' he said, 'I've seen you ride.' I wasn't in the least bit sure that he would have done, but I saw Peter winking at me, which I took to be a good sign. 'Get yourself across to my place, start riding out, and we'll see what happens,' Richard added.

I liked him straight away. He was friendly, relaxed and very clearly without any airs and graces. He had told me he would give me a chance. There was nothing to stop me moving to Britain.

All that was missing was somewhere to live.

Pat Healy had the answer. Pat, one of Ireland's very best racing photographers, was a good friend and one with excellent connections in Britain. I rang him in the hope that he might know of someone who had a room to let. As ever, Pat came up trumps.

At that stage I only knew Norman Williamson to the extent that we would exchange hellos on the racecourse. Pat knew him much better and told me that Norman was looking for someone to help pay the mortgage on his house in the Berkshire village of East Garston. Situated between Newbury and Lambourn, East Garston would make a perfect British base, so I rang Norman very much hoping that he would agree to having me as his lodger. He took no convincing and told me to move in whenever I wanted. Everything was falling into place.

Norman's profile as a jump jockey was already high but it was set to get much higher in the very near future. He had made a big impact since moving from Ireland, totalling 104 winners in the 1993/94 jumps season. Life, however, soon got sweeter than that for Norman. In the months that followed he enjoyed a dream period in his role as stable jockey for Kim Bailey, who had in his care the horses who would be crowned the season's leading chaser and hurdler. Master Oats progressed from winning the Welsh National to bagging the Cheltenham Gold Cup, while just two days before that Norman would storm to victory in the Champion Hurdle on one-time Flat star Alderbrook. I remember Norman telling me weeks beforehand that Alderbrook would take a lot of beating in the Champion, which says a lot for his judgement. What a shame jockeys aren't allowed to bet.

For all that he was a successful jump jockey, Norman could easily have ridden on the Flat had he wanted. He was the most petite, sparely made man I had ever seen. The biggest part of him was his neck. I have skinnier legs than anybody I know, but one morning when I tried to put on Norman's riding boots I found that I couldn't zip them up. Norman Williamson has the legs of a ballerina. His legs are as thin as his wallet is thick, because he so seldom opens it. Norman and I instantly became great pals and he was a wonderful friend; he was good for me and helped to give my life order and structure. As such, I don't think he'll sue me when he reads that some might have described him as ever so slightly tight. On cold days – and I kid you not – Norman would often sit inside the house wearing a winter coat rather than put on his heating. Living with Norman was fun but I did sometimes fear that I might succumb to hypothermia.

Fortunately, I moved to East Garston during the middle of summer so there was no need for Norman even to contemplate activating his radiators. It was also a time of the year when there was a plethora of meetings being staged in Britain. Whereas in Ireland there would sometimes be racing only three or four times a week, in Britain there was Flat action every day and almost always at three or more meetings. That was certainly the case on 9 July 1994, when I had only my second ever ride in Britain and the first of a stint that has lasted for just shy of two decades.

That first ride, on a colt called Jackattack in the second division of a Salisbury juvenile maiden, came not for Richard Hannon but Mick Channon. My long-term Irish agent Ciaran O'Toole had given his complete backing to my decision to head to Britain. In fact, he was so helpful that he told me he would do his best to find me a way into Mick's yard, whom he evidently already knew. Mick is not only a great friend of Richard's, he is also a very similar person, extremely likeable and easy-going. When Ciaran rang him with the request, Mick said that he would be happy to have me on board and suggested that I begin riding out at his place on Tuesdays and Fridays. I had already promised Richard that I would ride out for him five days a week, which meant that I was going to have plenty of access to two yards that were strong both in terms of quality and quantity.

I quickly discovered that riding out for a trainer in Britain did you far more good than riding out for a trainer in Ireland. Back home, you often got up at the crack of dawn, drove miles to a trainer's yard and then rode out three lots, more in the hope of getting a racecourse ride than with any great expectation of it happening. You practically had to beg for rides in Ireland, but in Britain, if you showed commitment to a trainer by riding out – a job that jockeys never get paid for – you were invariably rewarded with rides. Those rides might not be particularly exciting to begin with, but they gave you another chance to impress, not only that trainer but other trainers as well.

Jackattack led for the first couple of furlongs at Salisbury but then weakened out of contention. It was an inauspicious start, but I had at least made a start. What was also pleasing was the reception I received from the British riders. I knew a few of them from my winter stints in India, but even those who were new to me were friendly and welcoming.

I recently looked at the result of that Salisbury race and was surprised to see that only two of the jockeys who rode in it, Dane O'Neill and myself, are still riding. All the others, including Brent Thomson, Ray

Cochrane and Richard Quinn, have since retired. I'd say Dane might outlast me as well!

One jockey who was particularly helpful at the time was Billy Newnes. I didn't have a clue how to get to most of the tracks but Billy often drove me around and offered advice as to how to make the most of Britain's motorway network. Lorna Vincent, who worked for Mick Channon, was another who took me under her wing. But I wouldn't be telling the whole truth if I didn't say that some of my riding colleagues were in no way averse to taking advantage of the new Irish import. There was many a time when I was about to leave the weighing room without any knowledge of what the trainer I was riding for in the next race looked like. When that was the case I had to ask other jockeys who I should be walking towards. More than one were not entirely truthful in the answers they gave. Embarrassing scenes often followed.

You live and learn, though, and I soon found myself visiting tracks and riding for trainers for the second, third and fourth times. What I needed was a winner, and the wait ended in the 7.30 p.m. at Wolverhampton on the Saturday of the King George VI and Queen Elizabeth Diamond Stakes. I was not at Ascot that day (although I would be enjoying happy days there in the not too distant future), but Wolverhampton seemed a special enough place that evening when Scissor Ridge, a 9-4 favourite trained by Mick Channon, powered to an all-the-way four-length win in the Essanelle Hair and Beauty Selling Stakes.

I was thrilled to bits. It was only a seller and it was only Wolverhampton but it was a winner, a winner in Britain, and, I hoped, the springboard to many more. While driving home I got a phone call from Mam and Dad, who said that they had come home early after going out to dinner especially so that they could watch the race. For them it was special on two counts. One, they had never seen their son riding a winner in Britain before. Two, they could never remember watching a televised horserace on a Saturday night. They went to bed happy, and so did I. The victory was made even sweeter a few days later when I opened a letter of congratulation and thanks from Kevin Keegan, who bred Scissor Ridge. He'd clearly bred a tough, hardy horse because Scissor Ridge carried on racing until the summer of 2002, at which point he was retired having run in 165 races.

The *Racing Post* report from Wolverhampton that night was clearly not huge – the King George was given quite a few more words than the Essanelle Hair And Beauty Selling Stakes – but they still led the report on me, generously describing Richard Hughes as 'stylish' in the copy. It was the sort of positive reaction I needed. I was also getting an increasingly favourable reaction from Mick Channon. My early impression of him was that he was a bit mad but every bit as good a racehorse trainer as he had been a footballer. He would often come close to spontaneously combusting on the gallops, and he couldn't half shout if he wasn't happy with someone or something. But after giving a bollocking there was no lasting resentment. He also seemed to like me. Richard Quinn was riding most of Mick's best horses at the time but Mick was also making clear to me that he wanted to use me as much as possible. That much was obvious in the build-up to my second British winner.

After riding a two-year-old colt called Sumoquinn in a piece of work one morning, I got off and told Mick that he was a really nice horse. Mick explained that he was owned by his mate and fellow ex-footballer Mick Quinn, who was keen that Sumoquinn should make a winning debut. On the day that declarations were made for the chosen race, a seller at Bath, Mick brought myself and another of his regular jockeys, Richard Painter, into the office. Mick was going to be running two horses in the race and he said he would toss a coin to decide which of us rode the fancied horse, Sumoquinn. 'Hughesie, you're heads,' he said, before tossing the coin high into the air and catching it. He looked at the coin and said, 'Ah, no, I tossed that wrong, I'd better do it again.' Up into the air went the coin again, and this time after it was caught and examined, Mick said, 'Heads it is. Hughesie, you ride Sumoquinn. Bad luck Richard.'

Mick is a tremendous racehorse trainer but he's not very good at covering up a porky pie. It was obvious that he had fixed the coin-toss and I felt awful for Richard, who was spared the ignominy of riding an unfancied horse in the seller and instead got to forgo the trip to Bath. He was extremely good about it and continued working for Mick for the rest of the year. He retired from the saddle a few years later and retrained as a stalls handler.

The favourable impression Sumoquinn had made on the gallops was confirmed at Bath, where he won easily. He won with just as much in hand when put into another seller at Folkestone eight days later, and then completed a hat-trick under me when upped in class to a nursery at Chepstow later in August. By the end of the season we had won six times together including in a Newmarket nursery and, finally, in the Listed Rockingham Stakes at York. As I had always suspected, Sumoquinn was far better than a selling-class juvenile. I wasn't the only one to think so either, as he was then bought to race in Hong Kong. He left owing me nothing. I owed him a lot.

Sumoquinn and Mick Channon played a huge part in giving me a great start to my new life in Britain. At the end of a year in which I only had my first British rides in July, I had notched up 19 wins in the country. Twelve of those were for Mick, but I had also been regularly used by Richard Hannon, whom I scored for twice. Other top trainers were also starting to ask for my services, including Luca Cumani, for whom I had a winner at Brighton, and John Dunlop, on whose Sheikh Hamdan-owned Luhuk I landed a Goodwood Listed race. I was even managing to pop back to Ireland for the occasional ride, and there was a winner for John Oxx at the Curragh in October when I won a handicap on a filly despite putting up two pounds overweight at 8st 8lb – yet another indication that keeping my weight down was becoming a major issue. But at least I had shown that should I ever want to return full-time to Ireland I could be confident of picking up some rides.

I had no intention of returning to Ireland, though. Moving to Britain was the best decision I had ever made.

6

'GO ON ME!'

I knew that Mick Channon liked me, and at the start of 1995 I found out just how much.

Never before had I been a stable jockey. Dad had always made me number-one choice for his Flat runners, but there were never too many of them. Michael Grassick and John Oxx had both, at times, made me their first pick but those relationships were always loose and ad hoc. This time it was different. Early one spring morning, just as we were getting the string – which then amounted to a not inconsiderable 80 horses – ready for the start of the turf season, Mick came out with the sort of sentence I had been waiting to hear from a leading trainer for years: 'You can ride all of mine this year, if you want.'

If I want? It was most definitely something I wanted. Mick was climbing the training ladder fast. The previous season, only his sixth with a licence, the former England striker had sent out an impressive 74 winners and many of those winning horses were returning for the new campaign. His yard, then in Kingsdown, Upper Lambourn, was situated perfectly for me and allowed me to ride out both there and for Richard Hannon in Wiltshire on the same day. Richard had given his blessing to my new enhanced status with Mick. He had told me it made sense, and it did, for although it was Richard who had effectively brought me over from Ireland, he had plenty of other jockeys to satisfy. I would be able to continue riding for him but he appreciated that my principal loyalties would rest with Mick.

As ever, I had kept myself busy over the winter. After a four-week stint in Mumbai during December I had spent Christmas with the family in Ireland before heading back to Britain and the all-weather circuit. As a treat to myself, I also rode in a few jumps races and partnered one of Dad's handicap hurdlers at the Cheltenham Festival, but that was mainly for fun. The Flat was what mattered, and having made such a good start to my new life in Britain I was adamant that I didn't want people to forget who I was or what I could do.

From the moment I rode my first winner of the season at Leicester in late March, a ball started rolling, gathering pace all the time. There was a first career treble at Brighton on 6 April with one of my three winners coming in a claimer on Shikari's Son, who would win a very much bigger prize during the height of summer. Nine days later there was a double at Kempton, with further braces following in rapid fashion at Carlisle, Chester, Salisbury and Goodwood. The vast majority of the victories came on horses trained by Mick, but not exclusively. I was in fashion, more so than at any point in my life.

In early June there was even a first Classic success – of sorts – when I landed the Spanish Oaks at La Zarzuela racecourse in Madrid on a daughter of Slip Anchor called Riaza. It was a distinctly odd experience. The first race on the card did not begin until 9 pm, which meant the Premio Beamonte-Oaks Español was not run until past my normal bedtime. We were sent down to the start a good 15 minutes before the race was due to begin and spent an age circling behind the stalls until we were finally loaded and released. My late night out yielded only second place, but just as I had got myself dressed and ready to walk out of the racecourse I was grabbed by a weighing room official and told I was needed in the winner's enclosure for the victory presentation. It turned out a stewards' inquiry had been taking place, in Spanish, for the last 30 minutes and that the first past the post, Lagoa, had been disqualified. The pesetas were coming home with me.

Winning in Spain was grand but, in the great scheme of things, it meant nothing. What happened just over two weeks later meant everything.

Sergeyev was not an easy horse to ride. Even Lester Piggott had struggled to master him, which hardly boded well for anyone else. In five starts as a two-year-old, Lester had ridden him four times but won on him just once. The problem was that Sergeyev was constantly in a hurry. He took a fierce hold, not only on the racecourse but also on the gallops. He wanted to do everything too quickly, and by engaging in a fight for supremacy with his jockey was using up valuable energy that could otherwise have been put to good use at the end of races.

Dad's former head lad Jimmy Gallagher was one of the few people who could ride him at home. Dad described Jimmy as the best head lad he ever had, and he was also fun to be around. Few people in any racing yard have ever enjoyed a laugh more than Jimmy, who only measured five feet from top to toe yet introduced himself as a professional basketball player whenever he met someone new. As well as being good for a funny line, Jimmy was also a superb horseman, as he showed on a daily basis when somehow managing to keep Sergeyev in check. Jimmy could not ride Sergeyev on the racecourse but he told Richard Hannon that I was the man who should be given that job. Richard took Jimmy's advice, and I was entrusted with the chestnut anarchist when he made his three-year-old debut in a conditions event at Brighton.

Brighton went well, but Sergeyev was still far from the finished article. When the other eight runners broke into a gallop, I purposely held Sergeyev back so that he faced a wall of horses through the early part of the race. That, I hoped, would lead him to drop the bit, but he failed to understand and still fought me through the first half of the trip. Even so, his ability carried him through, and we cruised to a facile victory. He did the same next time at Kempton, with Richard Quinn standing in for me on a busy Bank Holiday Monday when I was required elsewhere for Mick. I ought also to have been on duty for Mick when Sergeyev appeared next, at Newbury, as we were running Silca Blanka who had finished ninth under me as a 200-1 outsider in the 2,000 Guineas, but he released me to partner a colt who by now was making headlines and looking every inch a Royal Ascot contender. Winning easily at Newbury only served to heighten that impression.

We went to Ascot thinking that we had the likeliest winner of the Jersey Stakes. We were not alone in thinking that as Sergeyev was sent off 5-1 favourite to scoop the traditional curtain-raiser to the second-day card. A field of 16 went to post and we were drawn four horses away from the stands' rail. That suited me fine. My plan was to miss the kick, put him to sleep and bury him before waking him up entering the final two furlongs. It was a potentially risky manoeuvre and one that Frankie Dettori had been unable to execute the day before when he found all sorts of trouble against the fence while attempting to bring 2-1 favourite Sayyedati with a winning run in the Queen Anne Stakes. That was not perturbing me. I knew that Sergeyev was the best horse in the field and I knew that he had gears. However, we all agreed that he could only win if settled far back from the leaders and brought with a late run, which inevitably carried with it an element of danger.

Had I tried to write a script for what happened, I could not have penned it more perfectly. I managed to let everyone else get first start on us and, crucially, an older, more mature Sergeyev relaxed and settled in my hands. Approaching the final furlong I began to look for daylight, and when I found it the horse beneath me responded instantly.

It was the greatest moment of my life. Royal Ascot had always been my favourite meeting of the whole year. Just 12 months earlier I had been watching the BBC coverage feeling depressed about my situation in Ireland and with little hope for the future. Now, here I was, stable jockey to one of Britain's strongest trainers and winning a major race at Royal Ascot for another. Happy days.

They got happier three days later. Piccolo was an outsider for the King's Stand Stakes but not to me. He was probably the best horse in Mick's yard and had struck in Group 1 company the previous August when finishing second in the Nunthorpe Stakes, a race he was later awarded on the disqualification of Blue Siren. I had ridden him only once before when we managed sixth in Newmarket's Palace House Stakes. Mind Games, the horse who won that day, was an odds-on favourite for the King's Stand, but I felt that if Piccolo was ridden with confidence and dropped in like Sergeyev he was capable of springing a shock. As on the Tuesday, the plan was executed perfectly. Piccolo filled with confidence as the race went on and once sent to the front had the race in safe keeping in just a handful of strides. Rarely have I known a better feeling in the final moments of a race. Mick had put immense trust in me and I was rewarding him with a notable win at the season's most prestigious meeting. If you watch the race online you'll see that I was waving my whip in the air a good 50 yards before the finish!

I remember two things in particular about the postscript to the race. One is that the racecourse celebrations did not last long, at least not for me. After dismounting and posing for photographers, I was asked by journalists to return to the winner's enclosure for interviews after weighing in. 'Sorry, I can't, I've got to sweat,' I told them. In just over an hour I was due to partner the rank outsider in the meeting-ending Queen Alexandra Stakes and I knew that I would not make the allocated weight of 8st 9lb without a final spell in the sauna. More enjoyable was the party held that night at Mick's house. The tape of the race was being played over and over again and as I watched it I kept roaring 'Go on me!' That stuck with me for a while and whenever I saw anyone connected to the stable I was greeted with those same three words. I didn't complain.

Nor did I have any reason to complain as the year went on. Professionally and personally, there were plenty of reasons to be happy.

The Royal Ascot wins were certainly not the only victories of note that came my way during my first full season in Britain. The most significant came in mid-September when I tasted Group 1 success for the first time. Had I drawn up a wishlist for 1995, I would not have been bold enough to write down a Royal Ascot double, nor would I have dared to dream of a first top-flight triumph. In my head, days like that would come two or three years down the line, but they were instead happening to me in the here and now.

As had been the case with my job at Mick Channon's, there was a sense in which I had Richard Quinn to be thankful for when it came to winning the Gran Premio d'Italia at San Siro racecourse. Richard had been Mick's principal jockey before I came on the scene but he had a further and more important commitment to Paul Cole, whose stable was, at the time, among the strongest in the country. Richard's loyalty to Paul allowed me to ease my way into Mick's, and it was Richard's unavailability on the day of the Gran Premio that got me the call up for Posidonas. Luck was very much on my side. I only rode Posidonas once and Paul was at no point a regular source of rides but on this occasion we teamed up to great effect and took the prize with some ease.

A tougher assignment, but one still secured in some style, was the Cambridgeshire, which I won 13 days later on the Roger Charlton-trained Cap Juluca. Roger, who had sent out Quest For Fame and Sanglamore to win the Derby and French Derby in his first year as a trainer five years earlier, had just begun to put me up on his horses. I liked the way he trained and he liked the sympathetic way that I rode. He wanted to see a jockey let a horse find its stride and he was keen that his horses were ridden within their own comfort zone. Everything he said was music to my ears.

Roger was certainly keen that I looked after Cap Juluca. Then a three-year-old, the son of Mtoto had never run at two and was tackling the Cambridgeshire and 38 opponents on only his sixth racecourse appearance. Despite his inexperience, he was being asked to hump top weight of 9st 10lb as a result of two deeply impressive handicap wins at Newbury and York that had led the handicapper to force up the horse's mark.

At both Newbury and York, Cap Juluca had made the running, tactics that would not be so easy to execute on a horse seeking to smash the 20th century's weight-carrying record for a three-year-old in the famous cavalry charge. Moreover, he was running without his usual rider. Once again, fortune was favouring me. Jason Weaver, now a popular TV pundit, had been in the saddle for Cap Juluca's last two wins but his main trainer was Mark Johnston, who was running his star stayer Double Trigger at Longchamp on the day of the Cambridgeshire. Jason was claimed by Mark and went to France, where Double Trigger failed in his bid to make all and weakened into fourth as 1-2 favourite. With Jason absent, Roger needed someone else. I had three things going for me. One, my profile was rising; two, Roger liked the way I rode; three, Cap Juluca's owner Martin Myers was also Mick Channon's landlord in Upper Lambourn. After one, two and three were added together, the answer was that I got on Cap Juluca.

It transpired that I had been wrong to be nervous about asking Cap Juluca to lead from the start. When the stalls opened, we were out of them like a rail-running greyhound bursting from the traps. My horse established his own rhythm, and without me having to ask any sort of question that rhythm was faster than the other 38 runners were either able to go or wanted to go. It was the simplest of wins. Going into the dip I switched my whip from my right hand into my left and Cap Juluca responded straight away. We were pressed hard through the final furlong by Ball Gown, but at no point did I feel we were in the slightest danger of being denied. Handicap performances do not get much better than that.

There was no time to rest on my laurels. The day after the Cambridgeshire I was booked for four rides up at Haydock. That yielded two winners, which was no bad thing, but racing on Sundays back then, especially racing which demanded an early start and a long journey, was always part pleasure, part pain, because it interfered with my free time.

It had taken me no time at all to fit into Berkshire life. Living with Norman was a hoot, and so was socialising with him. Much of the fun came from where we went, which was almost always to the Queen's Arms. An 18th-century coaching inn, the Queen's was the Lambourn racing community's pub. As well as serving fantastic food in its restaurant, the Queen's bar was never short of craic, and the place also served as a hotel whose rooms we sometimes used if we were considered incapable of making the short journey home. Even when we were able to make it home, we were invariably in a sorry but merry state. If there was a drink to be had, it was a good bet that I would be having it. Long before I left Ireland I had begun to enjoy a few jars and I had not signed the pledge since moving to Britain.

Part of the problem – though at the time I didn't see it as a problem – was that the Queen's felt like a home from home. While I was living with Norman, we either stayed in at night and watched TV or we went down to the Queen's, often eating there as well. The place was run by a lovely Aussie guy called Tom Butterfield. A former air steward, Tom had done a marvellous job since taking over the Queen's. His place was the place to go. Brent Thomson, Adrian Maguire, Jason Titley and Graham Bradley were among the regulars, while Richard Dunwoody popped in now and again, as, a little later, did Tony McCoy, for whom Tom started driving after he sold the Queen's in 2001. These days he also drives regularly for me and, just as importantly, has become a great golfing buddy. Back then, it was far from uncommon for us to be in the pub long after midnight had passed, and a gang of us would often stay up late into the night for a lock-in, playing poker or pontoon behind closed doors and curtains. Eventually we would stagger home, although if either Norman or myself had pulled we would head back before that.

After a while, female company for me meant one female in particular. During 1995 I began dating Richard Hannon's daughter Lizzie. She was far from my first serious girlfriend but it didn't take long for me to realise that my feelings for Lizzie were stronger than for any girl I had known. One of triplets but far more attractive than her two brothers, Richard junior and Henry, she was not only beautiful on the outside but also on the inside. (I know that sounds corny but it's true.) I could see straight away that she was kind and gentle and, coming from a racing family, she knew how important my job was to me. She also put up with a lot. Right from the start I was not the easiest boyfriend in the world. I wondered at times why she stayed with me, and I had good reason to scratch my head over that much more in the future, but she kept the faith and I was never less than grateful.

Lizzie was not the only thing that was new in my life. So, too, was a house. As much as I enjoyed living with Norman, I could not impose on him for ever, so in the summer of 1995 I bought a two-bedroom terraced house in the nearby village of Great Shefford, just under two miles north of the M4's junction 14. I got it for £63,000, but paying for it was problematic because most of my money was still tied up in the house next door to Mam and Dad's, which I only sold later. Fortunately, I had an extremely understanding and friendly bank manager who lent me the deposit money, not out of bank reserves but his own savings. He was a keen follower of racing and could see that I would be good for the money.

So 1995 was a very good year in more ways than one. I met the love of my life, bought a home of my own and rode more calendar winners – 68, to be exact – than ever before. Equally importantly, there were not just winners but winners in big races. I mopped up the Jersey Stakes, King's Stand Stakes, a first Group 1 and the Cambridgeshire. In late July, to my surprise as much as anybody else's, I had also won the Stewards' Cup on Shikari's Son. It was another win that made people sit up and take notice of Richard Hughes. They also took notice of the fact that I won despite putting up four pounds overweight. I won at Goodwood in spite of a problem with my weight. Until the day I retire, that problem will not go away.

7

A WEIGHTY MATTER

There was more than a degree of misfortune behind me having to put up so much overweight in the Stewards' Cup.

Any jockey who struggles with his weight will tell you that there are good times and bad times, periods when satisfying the scales is easy and periods when it is hard. For me, this was one of the tough periods. I had only recently returned to riding following a short suspension. During my enforced absence I had been far less active than would otherwise have been the case and my weight had risen. I had returned during Glorious Goodwood, a meeting at which competition for rides is fierce, and for me, only a smidgen over a year into my British career, obtaining mounts was proving problematic.

I knew when Shikari's Son's trainer John White asked me to ride that I could be in trouble. The horse was due to carry 8st 9lb, which would normally have been perfectly manageable, but I have always known my body and I could foresee that shifting the requisite number of pounds might be a big ask. John, however, was adamant that he wanted me. I had won on the horse earlier in the year at Brighton and Shikari's Son, for similar reasons to Sergeyev, was a horse it helped to know. John believed that my style suited his sprinter, who had to be produced late. My suggestion to him that he book someone else fell on deaf ears.

Having twice ridden at 8st 12lb the day before, including when winning on a 33-1 shot, I left Goodwood with only three pounds to lose. When I woke up the following morning, there was more than that to shed. Even so, I remained hopeful. At that point I was doing plenty of my wasting in a sauna I had installed in the Great Shefford house. I planned to lose a few pounds in there, drive to Goodwood and then lose whatever else was needed in the racecourse sauna. The Stewards' Cup was not due off until 3.15 p.m. and I had no rides booked before then so there was every reason to believe that 8st 9lb was achievable.

Sometimes the fates conspire against you, and on that morning it seemed that they had it in for Richard Hughes. Not long after I got in my sauna a fuse blew and the heat disappeared. So, too, did I. Quick as a flash, I got myself suited and booted, got in the car and set off for Goodwood. The journey would normally take around an hour and 40 minutes. That morning it took a lot longer. The roads around Newbury were a nightmare and delays added at least an extra hour to the journey. By the time I got to Goodwood I had much less time to sweat than I had expected, and I found myself with even less when trainer Peter Chapple-Hyam asked if I could take the mount on Erin Bird, his runner in the Nassau Stakes, which immediately preceded the Stewards' Cup. No jockey would turn down a ride in such an important race and I readily agreed, even though I knew that it would almost certainly cost me a further 30 minutes of wasting time. Erin Bird ran respectably and finished third, but after I got changed out of her colours, into Shikari's Son's and on to the weighing-room scales, I saw that I was showing at 8st 13lb, four pounds more than the horse was supposed to carry.

For any jockey that would be embarrassing. I felt no different. It is a matter of pride that you ride at the weight your horse is supposed to run off. If you don't, you instantly penalise your own mount and also send out a signal to trainers that you cannot be relied upon. Worse still,

I was four pounds heavy in the day's highest-profile contest. The only consolation was that Shikari's Son was a 40-1 outsider and relatively unfancied, including by his jockey.

Nobody had told Shikari's Son. A field of 27 was contesting the Stewards' Cup and, riding a confirmed hold-up performer, I saw no point in giving my lad the hurry up too soon, particularly as on this sprinter you had to pass dead horses while still travelling on the bridle before you could dare to ask him a question. I had also come to the conclusion that those who set the pace in races such as this often went off too fast and usually paid the price in the closing stages. I was increasingly seeking to take advantage of that and set out to do so again, but with no expectation of success.

Our stalls berth against the far rail enabled me to drop in behind horses, so I did exactly that. My plan was simply to wait until the second half of the race and then pick off as many of those in front as I could. When I began to press some buttons I was taken aback by the response. The horse was ducking and diving, weaving this way and that, all the time navigating his way between tiring horses and loving it. It felt as though we had dropped into the race at halfway having expended no energy to that point. Entering the final furlong, those racing on the far side of the track held a narrow advantage over those on the stands' side and I had only the 9-2 market leader Top Banana under Michael Roberts to aim at. We were finishing with far more momentum and had very little trouble in sailing past the favourite and on to a bizarrely easy victory.

In the newspaper reports that followed, the racing writers paid plenty of attention to our last-to-first swoop. That, though, came further down in the articles. Almost all the headlines and introductions referred to the 5ft 9in jockey who had won despite putting up four pounds overweight. People already knew that I was tall and unable to do light weights. Now they knew that without the help of a sauna I could not manage the sort of weight that the vast majority of riders found easy.

81

What they did not know at the time was that I was often using more than just a sauna. I was constantly trying to beat my body into submission. Riding was easy. Controlling my weight was the hard bit.

I used to say that the only weight problem I had was people constantly talking about my weight. That was not strictly correct.

It's true that I had become increasingly annoyed by people talking about my weight, asking questions about my weight, and making forecasts about my weight. From the moment I arrived in Britain the subject seemed to go with me wherever I went. It did not help that people quickly began making comparisons between me and my boyhood idol, Lester Piggott. They highlighted how we positioned ourselves on a horse in a similar fashion, my backside always high in the air as his used to be. They made reference to my preferred style of riding, from off the pace, patient and confident, and pointed to how Lester had for decades done the same. They also compared how we looked, both of us long and lean with little flesh on the bones. At 5ft 9in, I was exceptionally tall for a Flat jockey, taller even than Lester, who had famously survived on a diet that largely consisted of champagne and cigars. I preferred cigarettes.

The names people called me did not help. Lester had been 'the long fellow'. I was 'the window cleaner' or 'the coat hanger'. Both names left little to the imagination. I was sparely made, all bone and not much meat. When I was riding at what for me was a light weight, I looked gaunt and ghostly. Compared to anybody else of my height I was almost unbelievably light, but that was only because I was a jockey manipulating my body. It's what I had to do. I still do it. The motivation remains the same. It's just the methods that have changed.

I did what all jockeys facing a similar situation do: I watched what I ate, and when I ate it I kept myself busy and the calories burning. And I made myself sweat. Constantly. In a sauna, if necessary, but preferably in a hot bath.

But I did more than that. Like so many jockeys facing up to a weight battle, I drank. I drank regularly and often. Not tea or coffee or cola or fruit juice. I drank alcohol, and especially, whenever possible, champagne. Alcohol, as any doctor will tell you, has a dehydrating effect on the body. The more you drink, the more dehydrated you become. Not only does it dehydrate, it slows the rate of rehydration while also increasing the need to pee. Given that up to 60 per cent of a person's body is water, getting rid of that water will inevitably trigger weight loss. For a jockey, that's bingo.

Alcohol, unfortunately, is addictive. The more you drink it, the more addicted you get. I was becoming hooked, although back in the 1990s that reality had not dawned on me. Given what I had seen Johnny Murtagh do to himself, that might seem unusual. Sportsmen, however, are adept at focusing on what they need to focus on while at the same time putting to the back of the mind anything they either don't need to think about or don't want to think about. And I was no different.

Champagne was effective on its own but it worked better in partnership with something else that had a dehydrating effect. I had started taking piss pills at the age of 19. It's what almost all jockeys had been doing on and off for decades. If someone rang Dad the night before a race and asked him to do ten stone, he too would resort to the pills. They were a quick-fix solution, the lazy way out of a predicament. When I moved to Britain loads of the jumps lad were using them because they worked, but only to a point, and only for so long. The knack to them was to wait for as long as you possibly could before peeing for the first time. You had to try and make the first one a good one. When you could hold it in no longer you would pee, but it was only after about half a minute that you started to feel any real relief. That's how much they made you pee. The problem with piss pills was that they did what it said on the tin without doing anything else. You got rid of water but nothing more than water. As soon as you started putting liquid back into your system, the weight went straight back on. When you woke up the following morning you were immediately back to square one, but at least you had made the correct weight the previous day. And to deal with the day ahead you could just open the pill bottle again.

I remember getting my first diuretic from a chemist back in Ireland. I had to beg for one. I pleaded my case and stressed that the tablet was essential for me to do my job. I would be given the odd piss pill but that was no long-term solution. That came when I started to visit India, where you could easily buy diuretics over the counter.

Unsurprisingly, there were side effects. Most of the body's vital organs need water to function. Sixty per cent of the brain is water, the blood is around 83 per cent water, the lungs not far off 90 per cent. Water is essential for the body to work properly. Suddenly and unnaturally forcing the body to extract water from itself does it no good. Piss pills used to make jockeys feel nauseous, woozy and weary. They could leave you with severe cramp. They could suck out every last drop of energy from your body. But they also made you lighter, albeit not for long.

During my first three years in Britain I became increasingly fond of using a mix of champagne and piss pills. The day of the 1996 King George, when I took 14 in that desperate attempt to drop a few pounds, was an extreme example, and one that terrified Lizzie and my parents. Dad's words were influential, but just as big an influence was the memory of losing consciousness in an Ascot toilet.

Stopping taking the pills initially caused me a major headache. Champagne still had a dehydrating effect but I was finding it increasingly difficult to make weights that would in the past have been easy. In a *Racing Post* interview in May 1996 I tried to pour cold water on the topic. 'I'm delighted with my weight,' I said. 'I'm eight stone five pounds stripped and Dad reckons I ride better when I'm at my lightest. It would be nice to wake up eight stone every morning, but I'm not complaining. People were telling me four or five years ago that I'd be too big to ride on the Flat. But I'm here, I'm happy, and I don't regard it as a problem for the future. I'm riding good horses and that's all the incentive I need.'

But there was a little more to it than that. I might have been 8st 5lb stripped some mornings, but on other mornings I was far heavier. I had ridden in one hurdle race at Thurles early in 1996 and stopped the scales at 10st 4lb. Even during the height of the summer I was often waking up at 9st 2lb, knowing that I had six or seven pounds to lose before racing. I was putting up overweight on a regular basis.

Racecourse clerks of the scales noted that I was continually failing to make 8st 9lb and produced a report expressing concern about my situation to Dr Michael Turner, the Jockey Club's senior medical adviser. I was sent a letter, asking me to come and see Dr Turner on 8 August for a private chat. I declined the offer, thanked him for his concern and told him that I was doing fine. He wasn't going to take no for an answer. I was assured that the meeting would be held in the strictest confidence and that it was being sought merely for the benefit of my own health and safety. When I saw Dr Turner he told me that I should not be losing three pounds at a time and certainly not so often. I told him that most jockeys had to do the same. I also rejected his suggestion of a high-protein diet and told him that I knew that would not suit me. I left, hoping I had made my point.

Not long after the meeting I was contacted by the *Racing Post* asking for my reaction to how the meeting had gone. Dr Turner was quoted in the following day's *Racing Post* saying, 'Weight is one of the areas that I cover and it would be a fair assumption that the meeting was called to discuss that area.'

This infuriated me. The Jockey Club told me that the *Racing Post* had telephoned and clearly knew something was happening. They said that, in the circumstances, they had an obligation to give a quote. In the *Racing Post* article about the meeting I stressed again that 'I am fine with my weight', and pointed out that some of the instances in which I had failed to make 8st 9lb were due to trainers giving me heavy chamois leathers to use under saddles. In my head I believed I did not have a weight problem so much as a press problem, in the sense that they kept covering and, I was convinced, inflating an issue that I had under some sort of control. I still feel that the widespread reporting of my weight was not helpful at the time; the impression it created in the minds of trainers and owners very possibly prevented me from being offered one of the very top riding jobs. But with hindsight, it is clear that I was having difficulties maintaining my weight at a sensible and manageable level.

Many years later, I still have to wage war on my own body. I keep it at a level that is far below what nature intended. But things have got easier and I no longer put up overweight to anything like the extent of old. Even what I do now will be deemed excessive by some and it will make others squirm, but it works for me. I do what I do for a reason. I love being a jockey, and to be a jockey I need to restrict my weight. For me it is worth it, and as long as I continue to feel like that, I see no reason why I should not continue doing what I need to do in order to live the life I want to lead.

Over time I have realised that saunas and I are not happy bedfellows. They work extremely well for some people but not so well for me, save for one day at Ayr when, with the help of a masseur's pummelling, I lost seven pou. ' e space of an hour. (The thought of that still makes me shu... don't like running, either. Johnny Murtagh runs like a lunatic, trainers on his feet, gloves on his hands, woolly hat on his head, whenever he feels the slightest need to shift a pound or two. Like the majority of Irishmen, I don't do running. I hate it, can't do it, won't do it. I'd much rather save my energy for the racecourse. I would also much rather sit in the bath than a sauna. When you're in a sauna you go through a dry sweating process that, for me, does not have the beneficial effect of a bath. If I spend time in a sauna, I find it relatively useless as the weight goes back on so quickly. Not so with a hot bath, and nor does it leave me with the irritable dry mouth that saunas tend to produce.

I can't imagine that many people spend as much time in the bath as me. More days than not I will need to lose two or three pounds before leaving for the races. I do it by lying deep in a hot bath, not for five or ten minutes but for what most would consider an eternity, sometimes as long as a full hour. I often try to get through a couple of chapters of a book, or I might spend the time making phone calls. It seems normal to me now, part of my daily routine.

That routine almost always starts with a short drive to one of Richard Hannon's two yards, where I'll work a few horses and drink two to three cups of coffee with two artificial sweeteners and a drop of milk in each. If Richard's wife, Jo, has been cooking for owners, I might grab a sausage from the oven, or failing that, maybe a slice of toast. Then it's back home and into the bath. The sound of the taps running is now enough to start the sweat beads trickling off my body. In a room full of steam, I get in the tub and top it up with hot water whenever the temperature begins to cool. I can easily lose two to three pounds in just half an hour. But people trying to lose weight for more conventional reasons would be wrong to get excited about the idea. All I am losing is water, and that water – and therefore the weight – goes straight back on once I start drinking. When out of the bath, I put on a dressing gown, stick a towel around my head and lie on the bed, recuperating while also continuing to sweat. I'll lie there for up to 15 minutes before peeling off the gown and towel. As my body returns to room temperature I dress for the races, get in the car and start driving.

Once at the racecourse I tend to spend the afternoon grazing. I eat little and often, nibbling away on chocolate more often than not. Matty the Tea Boy – everyone in the weighing room knows him only as Matty the Tea Boy – feeds us at about a third of the tracks and he is always very good at giving us what we want. That's not necessarily skinless chicken or vegetables. It's sugar. Matty seldom comes to work without a hefty supply of Haribo goodies – sweet, sticky and a great supplier of energy.

Assuming I'm not riding at an evening meeting I'll head home, where Lizzie cooks dinner. And if I'm having dinner, I'll usually have the sort of dinner I like. For me, that means anything that is not bland. I like my food spicy, the spicier the better, not least because the heat increases the metabolism. Hot curries are a favourite, but even food that would normally be relatively quite mild can be given a little fire. I manage that by putting Tabasco sauce on things that most people would never dream of putting Tabasco sauce near. Crisps and smoked salmon both get the Tabasco treatment, and are all the better for it. You'll be pleased to know that even I wouldn't put Tabasco on toast. I put pepper on that.

Pepper on toast probably sounds wrong to you. It will also sound wrong when I say that I smoke, but I do, and among British and Irish jockeys I'm not alone. Jockeys are the only breed of sportsmen who in large numbers smoke. For the majority, cigarettes are an alternative to food. Some jockeys, such as Ruby Walsh, have poured scorn on that notion. Ruby is honest enough to admit that he smokes because he enjoys smoking and he has no desire to give up. If I'm being similarly honest, I would say that I fall into the same category as Ruby. I started smoking when I was a young lad because that's what young lads, especially young lads in racing, seemed to do.

There's no doubt that cigarettes do help to fend off the hunger pangs. Jimmy Fortune always says that he is lighter when he's going through one of his smoking periods, but that is not the principal reason why I continue to buy cigarettes. I do it because I love smoking – the smell, the taste, everything about it. Silk Cut is my brand of choice, but if I don't have those to hand I'll smoke pretty much anything. Seb Sanders would be another weighing-room smoker, while the Hills twins, Michael and Richard, are sporadic smokers, in that one week they smoke and the next they've given up, at least for a while. Not many of the French riders smoke, and guys like Ryan Moore, Kieren Fallon and Johnny Murtagh don't either. Frankie Dettori does, although you would only classify him as a social smoker, someone who enjoys the odd cigarette with a drink.

I can enjoy a cigarette with anything. I do accept that it can't be doing me any good, and I'm sure that when I give up riding I'll give up smoking as it would be impossible to maintain a good level of fitness not doing one but still doing the other. At the moment, though, there's no point me even trying to give up because I'm just not ready for it. When in India last year I had an MOT done on myself and the doctor told me that he could see I was a smoker because there was a line on my lungs. He also said that I didn't have anything to worry about. I ran at high speed on a treadmill for 20 minutes and he could not believe my level of fitness. Even when I return to racing after a long injury break, I don't feel at all breathless following my comeback ride.

I did once try to give up, back when I was living with Norman Williamson, another enthusiastic smoker. We came to an agreement that we would both attempt to reject the evil weed and that whoever succumbed first would have to pay for a holiday in Spain. As part of the deal we agreed that we would allow ourselves the odd cigar during times of stress. I discovered that I don't like cigars, but Norman developed a bit of a taste for them. He would wake up in the middle of the night and light one up. He practically started chain-smoking the things. The smell was making me feel ill so in the end I gave in, lit a cigarette and told him he could have his bloody holiday.

I know my body extremely well. I seldom need to use scales, and when I do it is only to confirm what I already knew. I know when I'm heavy. I can tell by how loose my watch feels on the wrist. I know that if I can't get my hand around my ankle I'm heavy – or, more precisely, heavier than I can afford to be to ride in Flat races.

But having ridden as a professional jockey for 24 years, I know exactly what I need to do. I know how my body will react in different circumstances. I know how to manage my day and I know what I can and can't get away with doing. As I go through the day, eating and drinking in small quantities, I get heavier, even when I'm riding and burning off much of what I'm taking in. If my last ride of the day is at 8st 9lb, I know that I'm in for a horrible time. I won't be able to eat and I won't be able to properly drink, only to sip. Just half a can of cola would put on another pound. There are days when I cannot allow that to happen. It's for that reason that I cannot do 8st 7lb at an evening meeting without plenty of rides beforehand as I know that I have no chance of keeping at such a rock-bottom weight. To do so, I would have to go through an entire day without drinking.

That's the worst part of it. Jockeys in my situation get used to not eating. Indeed, I couldn't imagine riding a horse on a full stomach. Being hungry becomes a way of life and it's no more than a case of mind over matter. Not being able to drink for hour after hour is by far the hardest part. For jockeys on a strict weight regime, thirst is the killer. You never see a guy marooned in the desert desperately looking for a sandwich. In those circumstances he needs water. I know how he feels.

Never, though, do I moan about it. Few things irritate me more than hearing jockeys griping about their weight. What annoys me most is hearing complaints from jockeys who seldom have to sweat. They should see what life is like for some of us. However, I am sensible and I only take a ride at 8st 7lb or 8st 8lb if I think the horse has a serious chance of winning. In fact, I invariably ride at my best when I'm at my lightest. I suppose subconsciously I'm thinking that if I've had to starve and sweat to take a ride I had better make it count. To starve and sweat for nothing would be stupid. I won't do it.

That, then, is the story of me and my weight, past and present. I don't ask for any pity because the only person making me do it is me. My lifestyle sometimes drives me insane but I get so much satisfaction from my job that all the rough stuff that goes with it is worth it. Well worth it.

8

HONG KONG PHOOEY

With hindsight, I might not have been wise in agreeing to an association with David Loder. Sometimes a relationship with a trainer does not pan out quite as you'd hoped, and this one did not. David, however, was a vastly superior trainer and a far better person than the man who persuaded me to temporarily quit Britain for Hong Kong. Even now, 15 years on from my lucrative but still miserable time as stable jockey to Andy Leung, the merest mention of his name makes me shudder.

Leung would be no loss to the training ranks. Loder is. That he no longer trains is to be regretted, for in his relatively brief time with a licence he showed himself to be a trainer of rare talent and astuteness. That's why, when he made me an unexpected offer towards the end of 1995, I decided that he was someone who it was better to be riding for than against. Unfortunately, he did not give me nearly as many chances as I had hoped. And therein lay the problem.

The approach came towards the end of 1995, a year that, as I've described, had gone incredibly well for me. Even though I was enjoying success in Britain far sooner than I had dared hope, I remained every bit as ambitious as ever. David had the same mindset.

He had only begun training in 1992 but was already a leading name without quite yet having broken into his profession's upper echelons. In a way, that explained why he wanted me. Frankie Dettori was his favourite jockey – unsurprisingly given that his principal patron was Sheikh Mohammed – but Frankie's first commitment was to Sheikh Mohammed's Godolphin stable. Realising that he was going to fail more often than he would succeed in securing Frankie's services, David wanted to know that he would generally be able to call upon another top rider. In turn, I was keen to strengthen my firepower, as while Mick Channon was providing me with plenty of winners, few of them were coming in races of note. Mick understood my point of view, so we came to an agreement whereby I would continue to ride as his first jockey but that I would be permitted to jump ship to one of David's horses if it seemed to have a better chance.

It quickly became apparent that on those occasions when I wanted to jump ship to one of David's horses, David had already appointed a different skipper. All too often for my liking, I was not the one being jocked up when Frankie was unavailable. That was not the only thing that annoyed me. David's yard was situated in Newmarket, which is a long way from Great Shefford, where I was living at the time. Twice a week I had to leave home at 4 am – not great news any day but particularly if there had been evening racing the night before – and be at his yard by 6 am sharp. I have no idea why he made me arrive for six o'clock. I don't recall many occasions when I ever sat on a horse until 6.50 am, yet David remained insistent that I should be ready to start at six.

Richard Hannon had warned me about joining forces with David. With a fortune teller's foresight, he told me that it would be a largely one-way relationship with David using me in exactly the way that David wanted to use me, whether that suited me or not. I should have listened, but in my defence, my connection with Richard at the time was largely built around Lizzie. I was getting rides for him but I was still only a squad player and a long way off being his star striker. The fact that Mick seemed happy for me to ride for David was much more relevant in my thought process. Now I feel guilty about the way I treated Mick. He showed enormous faith in me and could not have been a better ally. I thanked him by looking for what I thought might be greener grass.

For all that my time working for David was frustrating and largely disappointing, it did have its ups as well as its downs, two ups in particular. The first came when Bahamian Knight gave me a second Group 1 success when landing the Derby Italiano in a country where I landed another Group 1 win on the Sean Woods-trained Mistle Cat later in the year. Bahamian Knight carried the colours of Edward St George's Lucayan Stud, and so did Lucayan Prince, who was responsible for me completing back-to-back victories in the Jersey Stakes when springing a 50-1 Royal Ascot shock the following month.

This might sound like I am stretching being truthful to breaking point, but I told Edward in the paddock that his horse was going to win. Like Sergeyev 12 months earlier, Lucayan Prince was an extreme hold-up horse, exactly the sort of horse I love to ride and the sort of horse I was by then already famous for excelling on. David's mantra when it came to Lucayan Prince was that 'the jockey has to wait until he thinks he has waited too long'. I waited even longer than that.

I could see the reasons why he had run races that resulted in him being dismissed as a no-hoper. His two previous defeats had come in unsatisfactory events made up of small fields in which early pace was minimal. That was no good to him. However, I felt sure that a 16-runner Jersey, conducted at a proper end-to-end gallop, would be exactly what he needed. Edward laughed when I described his outsider as 'a good thing' but I was convinced that the race would pan out to his benefit and that the contest would fall into his lap.

After watching Lucayan Prince slice through the field for an easy win, Edward was smiling once again. He had not only won the Jersey, he was also about to collect on a £2,000 each-way bet.

When Lucayan Prince returned to Ascot in September, I was not on board, although this was of my choosing. I was being regularly overlooked by David, who, for whatever reason, did not seem to have confidence in me. When Lucayan Prince had run three weeks earlier in the Haydock Park Sprint Cup, Frankie had been on board, which I could just about tolerate. However, the second-string Blue Duster, who had been 1995's champion two-year-old filly, was being partnered not by me but by John Reid, which I could not tolerate. Not that I was surprised as in her two other starts in 1996 she had raced under Mick Kinane and then Pat Eddery. When the Diadem came along, I therefore chose not to ride Lucayan Prince, even though he was a strongly fancied 15-8 favourite. Instead I stuck with Yorkshire trainer Karl Burke's much less fancied 8-1 shot Daring Destiny, on which I had won Group races at Leopardstown and Baden-Baden. Karl had shown me loyalty and I wanted to repay that loyalty. Sadly, Daring Destiny disappointed at Ascot, but I was spared the discomfort of seeing Lucayan Prince win after he was beaten a short head by the Frankie-ridden Diffident.

I found that riding for David was bringing back the feelings I had experienced in Ireland, where other jockeys were regularly selected in front of me. Perhaps the most irksome rejection had come on a Lucayan Stud juvenile called Bahamian Bounty, whom I steered to an easy win in a Yarmouth maiden. His next two starts both came in Group 1 races. He won both of them and on both occasions was ridden by Frankie. It gnawed away at me.

My association with David ended not in a Group 1 race but with victory in a maiden at lowly Wolverhampton. That somehow said it all. Things had not worked out between myself and David Loder. However, compared to what was to come, we were a marriage made in heaven.

The money was good but not much else was. Professionally, 1997 was all about Hong Kong. What was supposed to be a nine-month stint in what was then still a British colony instead lasted for just over three months. It was short and not particularly sweet. In many ways, I could use the same words to describe Andy Leung.

Richard Quinn, Kevin Darley and Ray Cochrane can all count their blessings. Leung had tried to sign up Richard and Kevin but both had turned him down, while the hugely powerful and incredibly strict Hong Kong Jockey Club had, for reasons unknown to me, rejected the bid to ensnare Ray. They were all spared the misery of working for a trainer who is rock bottom in my personal rankings.

The early signs had been promising. The proposal had been made in late spring and was attractive for a number of reasons. I would be based in Hong Kong for the duration of their season, which began in September, primarily to ride the 55 horses trained by Leung. For doing so, his owners would combine to pay me a very generous sum of money. How on earth could I turn that down? Leaving Britain would mean severing my position as first jockey to Mick Channon, but I didn't feel that my job with him was big enough to warrant me saying no to the Hong Kong offer. (Once again I was showing myself to be horribly ungrateful for what Mick had done for me.) I would also not have to leave until August, meaning that I would miss less than half of the British season, and I would be back the following year in time for Royal Ascot. It was also an attraction that the minimum riding weight in Hong Kong was 8st 3lb, which meant that my basement weight would be far closer to the minimum there than in Britain. The risk was that being away for so long would take me back to square one when I did return to Britain. However, if I did well in Hong Kong I might want to return there anyway. And even if I didn't, a successful season in an increasingly high-profile racing territory would surely do my reputation as a jockey no harm.

I could not say no, and I didn't. The news was announced in early May, Leung describing me to the local press as 'a top young rider who comes highly recommended'. The HKJC seemed pleased as well, Philip Johnston, their director of racing, quoted as saying, 'He is up there at the top in Britain and is tremendously stylish. He could have a lot of success out here.' Shortly before the news broke I had been to Hong Kong to meet Andy, view his facilities and have a look at Hong Kong's two racecourses, Happy Valley and Sha Tin. As I knew little about racing there, having never previously set foot on its soil, I had to take on trust much of what Andy told me but he assured me that he had some progressive horses and was expecting to do well in what was set to be his third season with a licence.

I was at the centre of a second announcement in May when Lizzie and I made public our engagement. We had been seeing each other for some time and I had no doubt that she was the person I wanted as my wife. Over the coming weeks we set about convincing Lizzie's father, in whose office she was working at the time, that he should give his blessing to her moving with me to Hong Kong. To our delight, he did exactly that. Richard and Jo had both been exceptionally good to me since I'd arrived in Britain, not only by bringing me into their racing stable but also their family. Since I had been dating Lizzie they had been nothing less than supportive and I was often invited to be part of family occasions. They made me feel at home, which was exactly what I needed at the time. For Richard and Jo, there was probably a sense of deja-vu about Lizzie and I getting together as Lizzie's older sister, Fanny, was engaged to Richard's assistant, Sylvester Kirk, now a trainer in his own right. I suppose by having his daughters paired up with his assistant trainer and one of his jockeys he could at least keep an eye on his two intended sons-in-law!

Just over a week before our scheduled departure, we held a farewell party at the new house I had bought in Burbage, Wiltshire, situated not far from Richard's yard, which was handy for riding out at Richard's and, even more importantly, enabled me to see Lizzie most days. All the Hannons came along plus loads of jockeys, and quite a few of us, including Tony McCoy, Dane O'Neill, Paul Eddery and myself, ended up soaking wet after being thrown, fully clothed, into what, for August, was a surprisingly icy swimming pool. Lizzie, ever the shrewd and sensible one, remained dry at all times.

Hong Kong was anything but icy when we arrived on 19 August. Both the weather and the reception we received were wonderfully warm. Getting off the plane I felt like a footballer or movie star. As we walked into the airport's arrivals hall, journalists and photographers swarmed around me. My eyes had to adjust to camera flashes going off one after the other. Everyone seemed to want a piece of me, to know what I was feeling and just how much I was looking forward to being a part of Hong Kong racing. Nobody could ever accuse the Hong Kong racing press of not being interested in jockeys. I came to learn that it was more an obsession than an interest.

Around three weeks passed between touching down in Hong Kong and the first meeting of the season in early September. I was supplied with a lovely apartment close to Sha Tin and a car, which was handy as Sha Tin was a good way from the centre of Hong Kong. Slap bang in the centre of the city is Happy Valley, where I made my Hong Kong debut on an unforgettable Saturday night.

Happy Valley is one of the wonders of the modern racing world. It truly has to be seen to be believed. In terms of the quality of sport it offers it very much plays second fiddle to Sha Tin, which stages all Hong Kong's feature events, but that does nothing to detract from the Happy Valley experience. Once a week, generally on a Wednesday night, it opens its doors and the place quickly becomes a heaving mass of racegoers. Seen in daylight it is an astonishing sight, but at night it is even more incredible. The racecourse itself is less than a mile in circumference, a bit like Chester but right-handed. However, whereas Chester is situated just outside the city, Happy Valley, bold, brassy and in your face, lies within its beating heart. From the grandstands you are confronted by skyscrapers all around you. Everything you see is lit up, creating a stunning effect against the black sky. It's like having a racecourse in London's West End.

The atmosphere for the season's opening fixture was electric. There must have been 40,000 people either sat in the racecourse's restaurants and hospitality boxes or stood on the grandstands' steep steps as the build-up to the first race gathered pace. Anybody who wasn't was almost certainly queuing by a Tote window. Hong Kong's largely

Chinese racegoers love to place a bet. Racing in Hong Kong is very much viewed by the locals as a vehicle for having a punt, and the bets are made in enormous numbers. The HKJC takes in vast sums in betting revenue and is therefore able to pump millions of dollars back into racing. More than that, though, it supports numerous projects in the city, so that when you drive around Hong Kong you see hospitals and schools that have all been built and maintained thanks to HKJC funding. It really is an amazing money-making organisation.

I had five rides that first night, when the visiting 'British' riders – myself, Alan Munro, Wendyll Woods, Brett Doyle and David Harrison – all wore black ribbons as a mark of respect to Princess Diana, whose death was still all over the news. My five mounts were all for Leung, who was by then well into his forties but still somehow managed to look like a fresh-faced twenty-something. Before racing began, he escorted me to his biggest owner, a man who was no doubt paying a significant chunk of my salary. The owner wanted to know what he should be putting his money on. Andy told him that four of our five runners had great chances of winning but that the other was a no-hoper.

It did not bode well for my view of Andy's judgement that the four with great chances were all stuffed and that the no-hoper, Heavenly Wind, my very first ride at Happy Valley, won the Chongqing Handicap at odds of 23.9-1. Even so, it was a huge relief to make a winning start. The Chinese are famously superstitious and Chinese punters believe that if a jockey does not ride an early winner he is not lucky. And if a jockey is not lucky, he will not be given rides.

Luck then left me. I went weeks without a winner. The horses I was riding for Leung were not winning and all the spare rides I was picking up were on 100-1 shots. After about three weeks, he started behaving oddly. He began riding work on the horses himself and leaving me to watch. When he looked in the mirror he saw what he thought was a tasty work rider, but, in truth, he couldn't have ridden a rocking horse. He said that he wanted to know how the horses were feeling and that the best way of doing that was by riding them himself. That I didn't like.

I was also feeling ill. Since not long after arriving in Hong Kong I had been suffering from fierce pains in my ribs. At first I thought I had broken one. I had suffered a fall while riding out one morning at Sha Tin and I half thought that might have left me with an injury. The pain became so excruciating that I was finding it impossible to sleep at night. Lizzie, who was very worried, insisted that I go to see a doctor. I did so and went through a host of tests, at the end of which the doctor sat me down and said that, in his judgement, I either had tuberculosis or cancer. I nearly died on the spot. The only word I heard him say, and the only word that stayed in my head, was 'cancer'. Lizzie tried to reassure me by saying that doctors had to give a patient the worst-case scenario as a precaution but I remained convinced that the worst-case scenario was coming at me like a speeding bullet.

I can't tell you how delighted I was to be informed that I had tuberculosis. As part of the treatment I had to temporarily give up cigarettes and take 14 tablets a day. I was also supposed to stay off alcohol as drinking while taking the pills made you violently sick. That was not enough to stop me drinking. I preferred to be sick than not to drink. That was clearly a telltale sign as to the direction in which I was heading.

The illness was not the only thing that was getting me down. I managed to ride another winner but it was only the smallest sort of relief or consolation for everything else that was going on. I forgot my riding boots one morning so rode out in my trainers. Amazingly, such a tiny little thing triggered a story in the newspapers. The headlines said that my feet were too big for the stirrups and that I was too tall to be an effective jockey. The amount of crap I read and heard was unbelievable. Most of it came from Leung and his assistant, who one day told me that I had to ride our second string in a race. I told the assistant that I didn't fancy the horse and that I wanted to ride the other one. 'No, no,' he said. 'The boss says this one has a better chance. You must ride this one.' I went back on the fags there and then.

When I first arrived in Hong Kong, Ivan Allan, a legendary owner and trainer in the territory, had warned me about Andy Leung but I had not heeded his advice. Ivan had told me to be careful. I had not been careful enough, but I now decided that the time had come to draw stumps. Since the day of that first Happy Valley winner, my tally stood at one success from 103 mounts. When we had two runners in a race, Leung was attempting to put me on the wrong one. I was getting fewer and fewer outside rides because other trainers and owners were branding me as useless.

I decided to use the tuberculosis as my passport out of Hong Kong. At that point I had received almost half of the money that was owed to me. I confronted Leung and told him that I was off. I said I would take what I had already been paid and that he could use my illness as the reason for my premature departure. He agreed to terminate my contract and I left on 2 December, not a day too soon. Leung was the furthest thing from a horseman I have seen. He did not have a clue what he was doing and he was not a nice man either. He was, however, only a single bad apple in what is a fascinating place. Anybody who wants to experience racing like they have never seen it before should go to Hong Kong. I was only there for a short time but I left it with many friends and some vivid memories.

The following year was all about rebuilding – contacts, relationships and trust. Trainers who had been disappointed by my decision to leave Britain, albeit very temporarily, had to have their faith in me restored. Horses that I had ridden before leaving had since been ridden by other jockeys. I had to try to get back on them. Some I did, some I did not.

What quickly became apparent was that there was now no doubting the identity of my principal stable. Of my 55 British winners, 33 were for Richard Hannon, for whom I was riding as first-choice jockey. Mick Channon brought me back into the fold and I was on board a few winners for him, but if Richard had previously played second fiddle to Mick when it came to my commitments, it was now very much the other way round.

Disappointingly, neither Mick nor Richard was able to provide me with much firepower in the top races, and the vast majority of my successes in 1998 came in maidens and relatively low-grade handicaps. Two notable exceptions coincided within minutes of each other on the Saturday of Arc weekend when I completed an enjoyable double on the Peter Chapple-Hyam-trained two-year-old Bienamado in the Group 3 Prix de Conde and James Fanshawe's Invermark, who gave me arguably the most prestigious win of my career to that point in the two-and-a-half-mile Prix du Cadran, France's equivalent of Ascot's Gold Cup.

Winning the Cadran was satisfying on numerous levels. I had ridden Invermark only once before, taking a Chester Listed handicap on him towards the end of August. I had been offered the chance to get on him again at Longchamp but to do so had to turn down a number of rides on Newmarket's Cambridgeshire card the same afternoon. The percentage call suggested that France was the sensible one, and so it proved. Invermark was a textbook 'Richard Hughes special', in that he had to be switched off, buried and brought with a late challenge. In France that can sometimes be difficult, as in an average field you tend to find that at least 50 per cent of the riders are employing exactly the same tactic. That was never more so than in this marathon. The early gallop was more of a canter. We were going so slow passing the enormous Longchamp grandstands the first time around that I feared we were going to stop. I remembered from watching the Arc on TV as a kid that if you kicked on down Longchamp's false straight you were often collared, so I delayed making a move until inside the final furlong. Invermark gave me everything I wanted and won well. Passing the post, I punched the air with glee. That was not something I usually did, but it was an opportune victory. It meant I went into winter quarters on a high and having refreshed people's memories about my ability. I hoped it augured well for 1999.

And the last year of the millennium did indeed turn out very nicely. By the time it had been wrapped up I had ridden 95 winners, by some margin my biggest total. Among the year's highlights were plenty more successes for Richard Hannon, a second Stewards' Cup victory (this one achieved in trademark last-to-first fashion on Harmonic Way) and a return to Australia to ride in the race that stops a nation.

Mark Johnston had put me up on Yavana's Pace only once before, when we joined forces to win the Listed March Stakes at Goodwood in late August. Mark asked me to ride him for a second time in the Melbourne Cup, a request to which there was only ever going to be one answer. Mark had also been considering Darryll Holland and Joe Fanning, both of whom had won on the horse, but he pointed to my previous experience of riding in Australia as being a major reason for selecting me.

The Melbourne Cup was every bit as big an occasion as people make it out to be, but at no point did I look like winning it. Yavana's Pace raced in mid-division pretty much from start to finish and at no time landed a blow.

Going from one side of the world to the other for just one race had yielded nothing, but I was at least back home to ride on the final day of the British season at Doncaster, where I notched a double. It was on the following day that I got a phone call from Mark asking me to go back to Australia. In a significant change to the original plan, he and the owners had decided to extend the horse's stay in Australia and run him in a valuable Group 2 contest at Melbourne's Sandown racecourse the following Saturday. I duly flew back to Australia, once again for just one race, and once again for nothing. This time I set out to make all but we were swamped inside the final furlong and dropped back into sixth place. Prize money was paid out only to the first five.

I had been to Australia and back twice in a fortnight. It had been an exhausting experience, but Mark Johnston was one of the country's top trainers and I felt flattered that he asked me. Within the space of a year I was set to be left both flattered and flabbergasted when someone else came seeking my services.

9

A PRINCELY MEETING IN McDONALD'S

The most important business meeting of my life, the one that shaped my career for seven years and resulted in me getting a lucrative job for Saudi Arabia's Prince Khalid Abdullah, took place in a branch of McDonald's on the A34. I was sat on one side of the table. Sat on the other side was Prince Khalid's trusted racing manager Lord Grimthorpe. Both of us decided against a milkshake and instead drank coffee. No burgers were eaten.

That was in October 2000. The meeting represented a fantastic end to a largely wonderful year, one in which I rode a century of winners for the first time, landed a third Stewards' Cup in typical Richard Hughes fashion, delighted punters more than once, and upset a few now and again as well.

To say that the Abdullah approach came as a surprise would be something of an understatement. It was a complete bolt from the blue, particularly as my name had not long since been rejected for one of the biggest jobs in racing. In the summer of 1999, Henry Cecil sensationally dispensed with the services of his stable jockey Kieren Fallon, who almost immediately joined forces with Cecil's arch rival Sir Michael Stoute. With Cecil now without a high-profile rider, the gossip grapevine inevitably cranked into motion. A number of names were talked about and plenty of the racecourse whispers suggested that mine was one of those in the frame. At no point did I ever receive an approach from Cecil and I have no concrete evidence that I was on his wanted list, but numerous newspaper reports suggested that I was his second choice. Unfortunately for me, his first choice, Richard Quinn, accepted the job.

That meant more of the same for me as the new season started. Once again I had first call on everything trained by Richard Hannon, but while his string was strong numerically and contained tons of horses who were capable of winning races, there were no obvious superstars in his squad. Richard, aided by his long-term bloodstock agent Peter Doyle, was a genius at buying the right horse at the right price, very often at less than the right price. He has always had a wonderful eye for a bargain, but the cream of Flat racing's equine crop tended to have classier pedigrees than his owners could afford, or were the property of breeding giants such as Dubai's Maktoum family, Ireland's Coolmore operation, the Aga Khan or Khalid Abdullah. And it therefore followed that if Richard was seldom competing with a serious shot at winning in the very biggest races, nor was his main jockey.

Not that I had much reason to complain. The season still brought me much cheer, not least in two of the calendar's biggest sprint handicaps.

Races such as the Wokingham Stakes and Stewards' Cup were made for me. Contested by around 30 horses, they are always run at a furious pace, one that very few animals are capable of maintaining. Races like this were ideally suited to my finely honed tactic of coming late and burgling a prize inside the closing stages. That is exactly what I did on Harmonic Way and Tayseer.

Harmonic Way, on whom I had won the previous year's Stewards' Cup, was sent off one of the main fancies for the Wokingham at 12-1 having run well on his previous outing. He stepped up a notch on that at Ascot but he needed luck on his side, as you so often do in the big-field sprint handicaps. The far side was definitely the place to be in the 2000 Wokingham and we were berthed on the favoured side of the track. I also felt sure I was on the best horse in the race, a horse whose penchant for exaggerated waiting tactics was a seamless fit with me and the race. I told his trainer Roger Charlton in the paddock that I planned to drop him back into last place, as I had done at Goodwood. 'Maybe not quite last place, Richard,' said Roger. The grin on my face told him all he needed to know. 'OK,' he agreed. 'You're the driver.'

I was also a driver making a bit of history. The BBC wanted to jazz up their coverage of the royal meeting and had the idea of giving viewers a different perspective when watching the races. I was therefore asked if I would wear a small camera on the top of my riding helmet so that people sat at home would be able to get a jockey's-eye view of how it feels to ride in a race. I'm pleased to say that the BBC picked the right man in the right race. Almost as soon as the Wokingham was over, Clare Balding and Willie Carson talked over shots taken from the top of my head that showed me steering Harmonic Way in between tiny gaps that one after the other opened up for us exactly when I wanted them to. It was dramatic, innovative television, akin to the helmet-cam shots now common in the coverage of F1, and it brilliantly captured us coming from last to first.

Just over a month later I employed almost identical tactics to win my third Stewards' Cup and second in consecutive years on Tayseer, trained by the sprint handicap king Dandy Nicholls and owned by a pair of fearless gamblers, Henry Rix and Jonathan Ramsden, who had played a large part in Tayseer being backed down to just 13-2.

But I would be lying if I said that I impressed everyone in 2000. When you regularly choose to come late in a race you can fall victim to misfortune, more often than not in the form of trouble in running. Riders like myself and Jamie Spencer, who likes to ride in a very similar style, have often been vilified by punters, pundits and those who spend their time in internet chatrooms. When we get it right we can look brilliant, but when things don't quite unfold as we had hoped we can be made to look incompetent, at least to the uninformed and ignorant.

There were plenty who fell into the last two categories on show on a June afternoon at Salisbury, where I rode what Richard Hannon and

I both thought was one of our better three-year-olds, Mana-Mou Bay, in a four-runner conditions event. We were expected to win by most people and were duly supported into 4-6 favouritism. But this was the horse's first run since he returned home sick after disappointing in the 2,000 Guineas and I was conscious not to beat him up. I rode him confidently, as you would ride a 4-6 favourite, and sat him just on the heels of the front-runner Hopeful Light. Entering the final two furlongs, I allowed him to move alongside the leader, but when I asked him to quicken and assert he just emptied underneath me, which was not altogether surprising as he had pulled very hard through the first half of the race. It felt like I was driving a car that was suddenly without fuel. I pushed him out with hands and heels but he was not responding, and we failed by a head to overhaul Hopeful Light.

As I guided the colt back into the unsaddling enclosure, we were met with jeers and heckles. The same noises were heard when the stewards later announced that they were taking no action. Richard Hannon leapt to my defence and said the horse was probably not as fit as he should have been, but, just as importantly, Mana-Mou-Bay turned out to be nowhere near as good as we had thought, ending his career contesting handicap hurdles in the north of England. In fact, on Racing Post Ratings the Salisbury run was the best of his life, which suggests I could not have ridden him that badly.

Without wishing to sound cocky or arrogant, the reaction of that disgruntled minority at Salisbury did not bother me in the least. I'd felt far worse a few years earlier when I completely messed up in a two-mile handicap at Wolverhampton and rode a finish a circuit too soon. On that occasion I held up my hands and accepted the suspension I quite rightly received.

It was not even as though I were a one-trick pony. Yes, I loved, have always loved and continue to love the thrill of stealing a race in its final stages, but I also get a huge buzz out of dictating a race from the front. That is the tactic I often use to win races at Windsor, where Richard Hannon and I have been cleaning up on Monday nights for years. Around Windsor's figure of eight circuit it is absolutely the right thing to do. You take plenty of bends at Windsor, and if you're in front leaving one you can ask your mount to quicken at a point when everything else is still on the turn and therefore unable to instantly respond. It works time and time again.

Front-running was also my modus operandi on Persian Punch when we teamed up to win the 2000 Jockey Club Cup at Newmarket, the victory that brought up my first century of winners. Many jockeys enjoyed the pleasure of winning a race on Persian Punch, who was one of the most popular stayers ever to race in Britain, and rightly so. I am never convinced when people try to suggest that horses can display human characteristics so I don't necessarily go along with the view that he had a huge will to win. However, what I will say is that he was immensely game and always responded to a rider's urgings. He was a horse whose mind had to be made up as soon as the stalls opened. I can't think of many Flat horses who have had the size or scope of Persian Punch and, as such, he took a lot of driving, but if you got him motivated he would give you everything you wanted and a bit more. He almost tried too hard for his own good. I had ridden him two weeks earlier in the Prix du Cadran when we attempted to lead from start to finish and at one point held a lead of six lengths. He deserved to win that day but was ultimately collared just yards from the line. He had given so much that in the unsaddling enclosure he went into a spasm and wobbled, at one point looking as though he might collapse, which, as everyone knows, he did on a desperate day at Ascot four years later. This Newmarket afternoon was an immeasurably happier experience, and the old lad gained compensation for Longchamp, once again setting off in front but this time staying there for a superb five-length win. On days like that he was a relentless galloping machine. The public adored him and it was a pleasure to be associated with such a much-loved horse, albeit only briefly.

The Jockey Club Cup success, my 100th of the season, was a magical moment for me and a landmark day. Yet as important as it was, something even more important was going on behind the scenes.

I was driving back from the races early in October when I got the phone call from Prince Khalid Abdullah's racing manager, Lord Grimthorpe, then still known as Teddy Beckett. I had ridden a few horses for the Prince in the last couple of years, mainly for Roger Charlton, but there had been nothing of any note recently and nothing of any note was expected in the near future so I was surprised to hear Teddy's voice on the other end of the phone. And of course what he said after pleasantries had been exchanged surprised me even more: 'Prince Khalid is looking to retain a jockey next year and your name is at the top of the list. Would you consider it?' I nearly crashed the car into a ditch. Nothing that had happened in the previous weeks, nor anything that had been said, had given me the tiniest inkling that something like this was coming. I was in the final stages of my best ever season but only a handful of the horses I had ridden during that season had been owned by Teddy's boss.

Needless to say, I made it quite clear to Teddy that I would very happily consider the offer, which led to our meeting two days later. Teddy would be coming from Newmarket and I was setting off from home in Wiltshire, so we decided to meet somewhere in the middle and settled on the A34. The meeting was taking place early in the morning so neither a restaurant nor a pub was going to be any good, which is why we plumped for a roadside McDonald's.

As you might expect, the tone of the meeting was serious and businesslike. Teddy told me that the job, which was mine if I wanted it, would be to ride all the Prince's horses trained in Britain by Barry Hills, John Gosden, Roger Charlton and Amanda Perrett. But there was somebody missing: Henry Cecil trained the best of the Abdullah string but he had not been mentioned. I asked Teddy why. 'I'm afraid they won't form part of the retainer,' Teddy replied. 'Henry insists on using his own jockey.' The wind was taken out of my sails. The Cecil horses, which tended to descend from the best of the Prince's Juddmonte families, were the jewels in the Abdullah string. For them not to form part of the job offer was a significant blow.

We went our separate ways with me assuring Teddy that I would phone him with a decision in a few days' time. On the one hand I was genuinely gutted that I would not have access to Cecil's horses. On the other hand, Gosden, Hills, Charlton and Perrett all trained lovely horses for the Prince and could potentially provide me with the sort of firepower that I had been lacking on a regular basis. Moreover, if I did well on those horses, in time the Cecil horses might become available.

I decided to go for broke. Teddy had offered me a handsome financial package that included a chunky retainer and a five per cent cut of whatever prize money Abdullah himself earned from the horses I rode. I said to Teddy that the retainer he had offered would have been fine had the Cecil horses formed part of the package; as they were not, the job was less attractive and I therefore needed more of an inducement. I asked Teddy for double the retainer. No negotiation followed. It was not needed, because Teddy agreed. I was given a one-year contract to be retained jockey to Prince Khalid Abdullah. I did not tell Teddy that I would have done the job for nothing had the Cecil horses been included.

Right from day one I never truly felt as though I was Prince Khalid's jockey. He had agreed with Henry Cecil's wish to use someone else, the inference being that I was not considered good enough to ride those horses. A further blow came just before Christmas when Teddy told me that the Prince was sending five yearlings to Sir Michael Stoute, and that they would be ridden by Stoute's stable jockey Kieren Fallon. The Prince had agreed to the same request that Cecil had made, all of which meant that I was going to begin 2001 as retained jockey to one of racing's biggest owners without being retained to ride for that owner's two highest-profile British trainers.

Richard Hannon nevertheless felt that I had done the right thing. He was adamant this was a job I had to take. He also said that he would continue to give me first refusal on his horses whenever I was available to ride them. That pleased me as Richard had a nice bunch of animals for the 2001 season. However, I was hoping that I would not be available to ride his on too many occasions. I was hoping that Prince Khalid would have more than enough top horses to keep me busy.

It became immediately clear that the Prince's squad for the new campaign was not lacking in talent. For me that was crucial. I wanted to hit the ground running. I considered it essential to ride at least one Group 1 winner in what I hoped would be the first of many years as his jockey. My opening winner for him augured well. The Barry Hills-trained Perfect Sunday, who had been placed in three starts at two, had no difficulty in winning a maiden on the first day of Newmarket's Craven meeting. On its second day, John Gosden's Clearing, who had won the Group 3 Horris Hill Stakes at two, made a winning three-year-old reappearance when carrying 9st 6lb to success in the European Free Handicap, one of the spring's noted Classic trials. Earlier on the card I had landed a handicap on the Roger Charlton-trained Welcome Friend when once again sporting the Prince's green, pink and white silks. In two days I had ridden winners for three of the trainers I would be teaming up with, and, as icing on the cake, I landed the following afternoon's Craven Stakes for Richard on King's Ironbridge. The season could hardly have got off to a better start.

It continued largely in the same vein. With the Prince unrepresented in the 2,000 Guineas I partnered Richard's Tamburlaine to beat everything but Golan, and then four days later landed the Chester Cup for my new employer on Rainbow High, who became the first horse in the race's more than 100-year history to carry a weight as big as 9st 13lb to glory. At the end of that week I was legged up by Rainbow High's trainer Barry Hills on to the back of Perfect Sunday, who duly emerged as a major contender for Epsom on the first Saturday in June when winning the Lingfield Derby Trial from the front.

The following afternoon I went to Longchamp and came face to face with the Prince for the first time. Clearing was taking his chance in France's 2,000 Guineas, the Poule d'Essai des Poulains, and the Prince had come to Paris to see him run. We did little more than shake hands and say hello, although that was to be expected as the Prince is famously a man of very few words. To my great disappointment, I was unable to win him a Classic that day as Clearing, not helped by a wide draw, could manage only a close third, although he was later promoted to second. Better was to come at the same course the following Sunday when I broke my Group 1 duck in the Abdullah colours.

Like Clearing, Observatory was trained by John Gosden. He had signed off an excellent three-year-old season by conquering the unbelievably tough Giant's Causeway, by then known throughout racing as the Iron Horse, in the Queen Elizabeth II Stakes. He was one of the horses I had been most looking forward to riding, and I got my first chance to do so in the Prix d'Ispahan. John had planned to start him off in the previous day's Lockinge Stakes but changed his mind after walking the track at Newbury and deciding that conditions would be too testing. He feared that the ground at Longchamp could be quicker than ideal, but most importantly it was safe, and Observatory was allowed to run. Sent off 11-10 favourite, he justified his position at the head of the betting despite, according to John, being only 85 per cent fit. I sent him into the lead midway down the Longchamp straight, and although harried by a very good horse in Hightori all the way to the line, he never lay down and dug deep to hang on by a short head. 'Observatory is the new Iron Horse,' I said to journalists. I meant it as well. He had outfought the ultra-tough Giant's Causeway at Ascot and he had now done the same to a race-fit rival on his first start of the year. The rest of the season was his for the taking.

He did not take it. Indeed, the rest of the year, while far from miserable, was something of an anti-climax. Observatory raced only once more, finishing fourth of nine in the Prince of Wales's Stakes at Royal Ascot. Clearing never raced again, and Perfect Sunday, about whom I had been getting extremely excited in the days leading up to the Derby, disappointed both me and the many punters who backed him in to 9-2 from 7-1. Like so many horses before him, he failed to handle Epsom's unique camber and faded into sixth behind an outstanding winner, Galileo. In truth, he was simply not good enough and did not win another race.

In two of those subsequent races that year I was not even the one riding him. A series of suspensions left me unavailable for a number of important days. Worse was to come: I was wiped out for the remainder of the year after breaking my left leg in a fall at Newmarket on Cambridgeshire day. That reverse was timely for all the wrong reasons as it came at an incredibly difficult period in my personal life, of which more later. Encouragingly, however, I had already been offered and signed a new contract for 2002 when, in a significant change to 2001, I would have the Prince's Sir Michael Stoute horses included among my battalion. That was a major boost, and I hoped to build a relationship with Sir Michael similar to the ones I had developed with John, Barry, Roger and Amanda, all of whom had been helpful and supportive in my first year. As in 2001, I would not be riding the horses trained by Henry Cecil, but that no longer bothered me so much. Cecil had entered a period of decline. His fortunes were falling, and they would fall alarmingly steeply over the years that followed. Horses that should have been winning no longer were. Had I been riding them I might have been the one to be blamed. It seemed to me that they were perhaps best left for someone else to lose on.

John Gosden remained very happy to use me. However, with John I did more than just ride the horses. He wanted to know what I thought about them, and where I had recommendations to make, he would often act on what I had suggested.

Zenda was a case in point. After two runs as a juvenile she was still a maiden but we were convinced that she had much more ability than she had so far shown. Her spring homework was exceptionally positive and all the signals left us confident that we had a filly capable of holding her own in Group races. We were even surer of that after her reappearance in a Monday-night maiden at Windsor, where she made all the running to win with any amount in hand. As I got off her, I told John that I could never remember moving at such speed down Windsor's home straight. The impression she made on me was electric.

John then asked me if I thought he should run her in the French 1,000 Guineas. I was flattered. John made me feel part of his team and I was grateful for it. My response was that I definitely felt we should head to Longchamp. John then had lunch with Prince Khalid at Saint-Cloud racecourse and the Prince agreed that a Classic tilt was in order. With everyone of one mind, we took the bold step to run a Windsor maiden winner in the Guineas, known in France as the Poule d'Essai des Pouliches.

As at Windsor, I bounced her out of the stalls in front, which seemed a sensible move as we knew she enjoyed racing prominently and, unlike 12 months earlier with Clearing, we had a decent draw near the inside rail which seemed too good to waste. Zenda was magnificent that afternoon. I would like to think that I was not bad either. Turning into the false straight with just over half a mile to run, I steadied the pace, mindful, as in the past, that you do not want to commit too far from home at Longchamp. For a furlong or so we were headed, but when I asked Zenda to accelerate she found an extra gear that took her back to the front. It was hard work through the final 150 yards, but she fought bravely and held on to give me my first Classic as the Prince's rider.

Zenda was unable to win again but she continued to cover herself in glory, save for one disappointing effort on horrible ground in the Irish 1,000 Guineas. In the Coronation Stakes she was caught in the shadow of the post by Sophisticat – who had finished third to her in France – while she was also grabbed with the winning post within touching distance when sent to the States for a Grade 1 contest at Keeneland. John kept her in America and ran her two weeks later over a mile and a quarter in the Breeders' Cup Filly & Mare Turf at Arlington Park, where she ran honourably without ever quite managing to land a meaningful blow.

Although Zenda was our only Group 1 winner that year she was not our only high-class performer. One who made an appearance more than once was Amanda Perrett's best horse Tillerman, on whom I had one of the most embarrassing moments of my career, and later notched one of the most controversial victories.

First the embarrassing bit. The problem was that I thought I had won the Queen Anne Stakes, but I hadn't. This was one of those races in which some might have viewed me as foolish for coming with a late swoop, but it was not that I failed by a short head to get up that caused my mortifying moment. Just when I wanted to be going forward, Tillerman was checked for a stride or two, which meant I had to angle out to the right and throw everything into the final furlong. With the horse beneath me thundering down the straight, I was homing in on Johnny Murtagh on No Excuse Needed and, bang on the line, I nabbed him. Or so I thought. Unfortunately for me, I didn't just think I had won. I was convinced of it, so convinced that I waved my whip high into the air for several strides.

'Did you win, then?' Johnny asked as we started to pull up. I told him I had definitely nicked it on the line, after which he looked intently at me and asked, 'Are you sure? My lad's head was down on the line. I thought I'd just held on.' A seed of doubt had been sown in my head.

As we turned around to canter back, that seed began to germinate. I could see Tillerman's stable lad waiting for me and shaking his head. 'Oh, shit,' I thought to myself. I knew there and then that the lad must have seen a freeze frame of the finish. He had. It suggested that No Excuse Needed had won. And it suggested right.

Now, it would be wrong to say that I didn't make a great big cock out of myself. Celebrating a win when you haven't actually won is never advisable for a sportsman, particularly when you do so at the biggest meeting of the year, live on terrestrial television with 600,000 viewers watching at home and another 40,000 sets of eyes fixed on you at the racecourse. One witty journalist said that I had been guilty of premature jock-elation, and I became the butt of quite a few jokes for the rest of the day. That said, it could have been worse. I had only begun my ecstatic display after the winning post, so I had not caused Tillerman's defeat, and I did at least get to enjoy winning the race, if only for about 30 seconds.

Fortunately I was able to see the funny side of what had happened, which could not be said for the trainer Terry Mills when he spontaneously combusted in my direction after I rode Tillerman to victory in the Group 2 Celebration Mile at Goodwood in late August. The finish could not have been closer. Only a neck and two short heads separated the first five home, but what left Mills fuming was that I had finished first and his beloved Where Or When, a horse he also part-owned, was only one of the fourth-place dead-heaters.

There is no doubt that Where Or When was the best horse on the day, but the best horse on the day does not always win. Approaching the final furlong I was cantering, but so too was Where Or When under Kevin Darley. In a tightly packed field I was able to keep Kevin hemmed in with nowhere to go, so I did. I made sure he was locked up until I kicked on with 75 yards to run. By then there was no time for Kevin to do anything about it.

After the race Kevin offered not one word of complaint or criticism. He knew that I had won the race through jockeyship. I had done what I was obliged to do, namely give my horse the best possible chance of winning. Terry did not see it that way. As I returned to the winner's enclosure down the chute that takes you back from the racecourse, Terry came running at me, fury written across his face.

'If you hadn't held my horse in we would have beaten you!' he shouted at me.

'I know you fucking would, why do you think I did it?' I said back at him.

This caused Terry to go completely bananas. First he lodged an official objection with the stewards – which the stewards quickly dismissed – before shouting his mouth off to the press. 'I really am annoyed,' he said to anyone who would listen. 'All our hard-earned money is lost. He stopped us from winning. All we wanted was a fairly run race and when we didn't get it, we objected. They had a stewards' inquiry and we got absolutely nothing. I tell you why we never get nothing here – it's because we're a small stable from Epsom. I talk like

I talk. I ain't got a silver spoon in my mouth. That horse should have been slung out. He should not have won the race because he held the favourite in. All those punters have done their money because he was allowed to get away with it.'

I was allowed to get away with it because I had done nothing wrong. As I said at the time, that's what I was being paid to do. I think I might have said 'If they don't like it, tough.' In fact I'm sure I said that. I might have been just a little guilty of winding Terry up. I saw the funny side of the situation, which Terry did not, at least not there and then. He probably didn't afterwards, either, but that was Terry. He wore his heart on his sleeve. He could shout louder than most people but he cared, and you cannot criticise a man for that. Sadly, he died from cancer far too young and his death robbed the sport of one of its real characters. I don't regret stopping his horse from winning at Goodwood but I do regret the fact that we don't get to hear Terry's chuckle, or Terry blowing his top, any longer.

10

AN OASIS AND A TORNADO

My role as retained rider to Prince Khalid Abdullah lasted for seven years. It began promisingly and ultimately petered out, but if one year stood out from all the others it was 2003, our third season together.

In my seven years riding as the Prince's jockey I won nine Group 1 races on his horses, five of them secured during the sparkling months of that 2003 campaign. It was the year in which I enjoyed two major sprint triumphs on the fastest horse I have ever sat on and also the year in which I conquered France and forged associations with two of its premier trainers. It was also a year that ended with one of the Prince's principal British trainers being confronted with my slump into serious alcoholism. By that point, however, I had already more than secured my future in the Abdullah silks.

Inevitably there were disappointments along the way, none greater than when Trade Fair, our big spring Classic hope, failed to make it to the 2,000 Guineas having suffered an untimely setback in training. Come the Newmarket Classic I had little chance of success on the 50-1 outsider Saturn. He ran way above his odds to finish a fine fifth, but I was left with a sense of what might have been, feelings that were enhanced when Trade Fair subsequently unleashed an electric turn of foot to win the Criterion Stakes on Newmarket's July course. The 1,000 Guineas came and went without me getting on a horse, and although I got a spare in the Derby, my mount, Strength 'n Honour, was a 100-1 shot and ran like one. On paper I had more of a chance in the Oaks, but although the Prince's High Praise was deemed worthy of a 16-1 starting price having won a Group 3 prize on her final juvenile start, she was miles below her best on the big day and finished 35 lengths behind Martin Dwyer's first British Classic winner, Casual Look.

Fortunately, the tide was about to turn. Epsom apart, June proved to be an extremely successful month.

It began in earnest for me at Chantilly on the month's second Sunday when I received an unexpected call to ride for the Prince in the Prix de Diane, France's version of the Oaks. My contract with the Prince did not, never had and never would encompass his horses trained outside Britain. That had never particularly irked me as the majority of the Abdullah string in France was trained by the legendary Andre Fabre, not a person who would easily be told who could or could not ride his horses, not even by the Prince. Moreover, Fabre had as his stable jockey one of Europe's very best, the outstanding but far from controversy-shy Christophe Soumillon. Christophe could have ridden Nebraska Tornado in the Diane, but he understandably preferred the claims of stablemate Musical Chimes, who went into the race with much more obvious and persuasive claims. While Nebraska Tornado had run just twice, winning a newcomers' event in May before following up in a Longchamp Listed heat, Musical Chimes was already a Classic winner thanks to her success in the the Poule d'Essai des Pouliches. The bookmakers thought she had the better chance of Fabre's two runners, and so did Soumillon. With Christophe opting for Musical Chimes, Nebraska Tornado needed a jockey, and as the Prince had a retained rider in Britain, namely me, it was suggested to Fabre that I should take the mount. Fabre agreed, and Teddy Grimthorpe phoned me to pass on the good news that I would be required to work in France that Sunday.

My work that afternoon received widespread acclaim. For a while it seemed as though I might not have any work to do as the filly proved very troublesome at the start, stubbornly refusing to enter the stalls until finally consenting just as the patience of the starter must have been beginning to wear thin. Once out of the stalls, she behaved immaculately. Looking at the race beforehand, it seemed clear that, as with so many of the major French races, there would be little early pace. Only ten fillies had been declared and none was a confirmed front-runner. In such circumstances it nearly always pays to race close to the leaders as the last place you want to be when a sprint finish ignites is out the back and out of your ground. Knowing that, I got Nebraska Tornado into her running quickly and parked her right on the heels of the pace-setting Arvada. Musical Chimes was positioned in mid-division with favourite Fidélité, already a Group 1 winner, even further back in the field. As we turned for home, the uphill Chantilly finishing straight lay before us. Having taken a perfect stalking berth, there seemed little point in waiting for those behind to negate the advantage I had gained, so with two furlongs still to run I kicked for home. Nebraska Tornado responded instantly, poaching a lead that never looked likely to be relinquished.

Outside Arc day, the Prix de Diane regularly attracts the biggest crowd of any major French Flat fixture, so winning the Diane itself, one year on from taking the French 1,000 Guineas on Zenda, gave me a huge thrill. It also opened up the possibility of new avenues coming my way. Given how I had ridden Nebraska Tornado, I thought I would be unlucky not to be offered the seat when she made her next outing. I had also impressed Fabre, a trainer who is notoriously hard to excite. Just as importantly, I had produced the goods for my boss on a horse that was, contractually, not mine to ride.

Just over a week later at Royal Ascot I enjoyed wins on three of the Prince's horses that did count among my squad. The Prince was still relatively new to having horses with Sir Michael Stoute. I was also relatively new to being allowed to ride them. Having been told that

Stoute's Abdullah-owned horses would be partnered by Kieren Fallon in 2001, I got on them for the first time in 2002 and did well, winning seven races on horses trained by Stoute and owned by the Prince. One of those was Spanish Sun, a leggy filly who had readily won a backend maiden on Kempton's now defunct Flat turf track. She was now due to run for the first time since that debut strike in the Group 2 Ribblesdale Stakes. At 9-2 she was evidently fancied to run a big race and she more than lived up to her tall reputation, bridging a sizeable deficit down the straight, grabbing the lead 150 yards from the finish and then responding to pressure to hold on for a diminishing head victory.

The Ribblesdale was the biggest race I had won for Stoute and I hoped it might earn me a more elevated place in his estimations. However, I already knew that Roger Charlton was a fan, and it was he who supplied me with two other winners at Royal Ascot. One of them, Deportivo, looked a Group winner when making all under the stands' rail to land the now axed Balmoral Handicap by two lengths. The other looked both a Group 1 and Classic winner in the making. Six years later I would win the Coventry Stakes by six lengths on Canford Cliffs. Three Valleys won the same race by eight lengths in incredibly impressive fashion.

He went to the Coventry with a good chance but nothing more than that. On his debut at Nottingham a month earlier he had been backed into 4-5 favouritism, his price recognition of some pleasing performances up Roger's Beckhampton gallops. Everyone was delighted with the manner of his Nottingham success but the jump from that to Royal Ascot was considerable and it would be wrong to say he went to the Coventry, always the hottest juvenile race of the season to that point, with his connections expecting a follow-up win.

To the man on his back, all that changed in the handful of minutes it took me to take him to the start. I had not sat on the horse in the four weeks between Nottingham and Ascot. He was a changed animal. There had been nothing wrong with him first time out, but second time out there was so much more right about him. He positively floated over the ground. To this day I have never been so impressed by a horse during the preliminaries of a race. I knew at the start that he would not only win but win with something in hand. Quite how much he would have in hand surprised even me.

Not since Mill Reef in 1970 had a horse taken the Coventry by the eight lengths that separated Three Valleys from runner-up Botanical. Had he not shifted right as he accelerated, the margin might well have been greater. When kicked in the belly two furlongs out, he unleashed a turn of foot that left quality opposition trailing in his wake. How disappointing, then, that he never quite built on that display. Next time out at the Curragh he flopped when a red-hot 4-6 favourite for the Phoenix Stakes, finishing third to One Cool Cat. It transpired he was a colt prone to getting mucus in his lungs, so he had a valid excuse, but even when he won the Middle Park Stakes (a victory he subsequently lost after a prohibited substance was found in his urine sample) the brilliance of Ascot was missing. It was again absent when he rounded off his two-year-old campaign by finishing a head second to rank outsider Milk It Mick in the Dewhurst Stakes. From the dizzy heights of Ascot, Three Valleys' juvenile season ended in anti-climax.

That, however, was as nothing to the anti-climax that smacked me the moment I first sat on him at home as a three-year-old. He did not seem to have grown an inch. You always want to see horses develop from two to three, and he had not. A five-length drubbing by Haafhd in the Craven Stakes confirmed that he would not take a high ranking in Europe, and following a dismal effort in the 2,000 Guineas, he was sent to continue his career in America, where he won a couple of stakes races but never worried the US elite.

On the strength of his Royal Ascot tour de force, Three Valleys still deserved to be called the best horse I had ridden. Bizarrely, that label was soon to be assumed by a horse who was beaten in the race staged just 35 minutes after the Coventry.

Although Oasis Dream ran four times at two, I had only ridden him in the first of those outings. On that occasion he finished fifth of 12 in a six-furlong Salisbury maiden after which he ran out of puff and weakened into second when upped to seven furlongs at Sandown. It was third time lucky at Nottingham, from where he was sent by John Gosden to the Middle Park Stakes, which he won in clear-cut fashion under Jimmy Fortune, in the process doing enough to be crowned champion juvenile. I had missed out that day due to a suspension, but I was determined not to miss out when Oasis Dream returned as a three-year-old.

Bookmakers gave him flattering quotes for the 2,000 Guineas but, hands on hearts, we knew that he would struggle to see out the Newmarket mile. I remember seeing legendary punter Jack Ramsden during the winter and he told me that he was 100 per cent certain that Oasis Dream was not a miler but a sprinter. John Gosden evidently thought the same and, after a minor niggle prevented him being tested over Longchamp's easy mile in the French 2,000 Guineas, we set out our stall and sought to exploit his speed.

All the top sprints are staged from June onwards, and it was only in June that Zenda's Green Desert half-brother made his three-year-old return in the King's Stand Stakes, a five-furlong contest that at that point had still to be promoted from Group 2 to Group 1 billing.

Homework reports from John's Manton base had set plenty of tongues wagging and Oasis Dream left the Ascot stalls as 6-1 favourite to win a 20-runner event that was intriguingly playing host to a 25-1 Australian raider called Choisir. Although dismissed as a no-hoper by the British punters, Choisir turned out to be anything but. Out of the stalls like a flash, he was guided to the stands' rail by Johnny Murtagh and never saw another horse, winning in electrifying fashion. We took third, but despite being beaten could hardly have been more encouraged. John had been open in saying that for us this was a preparatory race, a means to an end, the end being the Group 1 sprints that would soon follow. Oasis Dream had been working well, but he was not quite ready to shine. Approaching the furlong pole I got close enough to Choisir to start thinking about reeling him in, but it was at exactly that point that he took a heave and blew up.

We had not beaten Choisir but we knew from what we had seen at Ascot that we could. Choisir had completed a famous Royal Ascot double when supplementing his King's Stand win with victory in the final day's Golden Jubilee Stakes. His exploits had been extremely well received back home, where reports of the Pommy-bashing sprinter led many of his fans to stay up until the early hours for his next race, the July Cup, traditionally regarded as Europe's premier sprint. Choisir's stay-at-home supporters went back to their beds with the smiles rubbed from their faces.

To his credit, Choisir ran a super race. His misfortune was simply that Oasis Dream was a better horse. At Ascot he had been fat. At Newmarket he was lean, honed and trained to the minute. Choisir once again surged through the gears at frightening speed but my horse matched him every step of the way. Choisir was burning off all those behind him except one. We were the one. Approaching the two-furlong pole Johnny was having to ask his mount some increasingly serious questions. Oasis Dream was still tracking his every move on the bridle. With Johnny clearly anxious, I asked for more and was rewarded handsomely. A few smacks were needed but Oasis Dream was value for more than the one and a half lengths by which he belittled the giant Choisir. On the day, ours was much the better horse.

From Newmarket, the obvious place to go next was York for the Nunthorpe Stakes. While the July Cup is staged over six furlongs with a climbing finish that can sap stamina reserves, the Nunthorpe is run over a trip a full furlong shorter and on a perfectly level racecourse. None of that bothered us in the least. Oasis Dream was faster than any horse I had ever ridden. In some ways he was the opposite of what you would expect a champion sprinter to be. Not overly big or muscular, he was a kind, quiet, gentle individual. In the stalls he would stand like a lamb, but once the gates crashed open he would burst into life and hit the ground running. He also hit the ground extremely hard. Also unusually for a sprinter, he had a tendency to bend his knee quite noticeably, so that the impact of every stride was significant on his limbs, particularly on fast ground. Utterly honest and genuine, he shrugged off any discomfort he might have felt and ran like the wind.

Punters and purists expected a win. The pre-race talk was not of whether or not he would win but how easily and by how far. We felt the same. I remember meeting John in the York paddock before the race and telling him that I planned to go as fast as possible from start to finish with the intention of breaking Dayjur's course record. John smiled, but added a word of caution. Not long after York's winning post is a covered road crossing. I've known more than one horse break down on it and we were fairly sure that few horses would ever have crossed it as fast as Oasis Dream was about to cross it. John was nervous about Oasis Dream sustaining an injury and asked me to bear the road in mind.

John was absolutely right to be cautious. Had he not been, Oasis Dream would undoubtedly have smashed Dayjur's record, but we might not have had a horse for the rest of the season. Even without the record, his performance was breathtaking. In front from the off, he quickened two furlongs out and then quickened again entering the final furlong. He was able to do everything so effortlessly, without any fuss. He was so fast that it was hard to judge at what speed you were travelling. The horse liked to change his legs at full speed and every time he switched leads he seemed to accelerate once more. Through that last furlong he pulled further and further clear until, with John's advice at the front of my mind, I started to apply the brakes about 50 yards from the finish. We coasted past the judge, stopping the clock at 56.2 seconds, 0.04 seconds outside Dayjur's track record.

The top-flight European sprint season heads next to Haydock for the venue's Sprint Cup, where Oasis Dream was back up to six furlongs and, for the first time in his life, asked to perform on testing ground. Heavy rain fell at Haydock in the build-up to the track's premier event and the race-day downpours turned ground that had been described as good to firm to ground that was described as good to soft. We knew the conditions would not suit him. We were not alone, and the season's outstanding sprinter drifted from 4-11 to 8-11 in the minutes leading up to a race that panned out almost exactly as we had feared. Knowing that he might not see out the distance on gruelling ground, I attempted to hold on to him for longer than at York or Newmarket. When racing on the bridle, all seemed well, but once off the bridle he floundered and gave best to the admirable mud-lover Somnus. Naturally we were disappointed, but we felt we'd had nothing to lose by running. John's long-range plan had been the Breeders' Cup, which then was still nearly two months away. The colt had also been beaten in the past, so one more defeat was not going to drastically detract from his value or reputation. We took a chance. It was a chance that did not quite come off but it had been worth taking.

There had also been a defeat for Nebraska Tornado. As with Oasis Dream's Haydock reverse, the loss was taken on the chin. Indeed, it was expected.

Just over two months on from her Classic triumph in the Diane, she was brought back to the racecourse by Andre Fabre for the Prix Jacques le Marois, the first of France's two late-summer Group 1 mile contests. Twelve horses had been attracted to Deauville's flagship race, the dozen including Godolphin's runaway Queen Anne Stakes winner Dubai Destination, the previous autumn's Breeders' Cup Mile hero Domedriver, and France's unlucky 1,000 Guineas runner-up Six Perfections. In the circumstances, Nebraska Tornado was only one of many in with a chance, but when I spoke to Fabre in the paddock he made it blatantly obvious that her chance was minimal. 'She is not fit so be kind to her,' were his only pre-race instructions. I did as he said and she ran as he had predicted, quickening up to lead entering the final quarter of the journey only to then weaken dramatically into sixth place behind Six Perfections.

Three Sundays later, I returned to France for the second leg of the Paris mile double, the Prix du Moulin de Longchamp. Having run what, at face value, was a disappointing race in the Jacques le Marois, the Prince's filly was largely ignored by the local Pari-Mutuel punters, who allowed her to go off at just under 15-1. Much more popular in the 14-runner field were the 2002 Diane heroine Bright Sky – a Group 2 winner in her trial for the Moulin – Dermot Weld's 2,000 Guineas winner Refuse To Bend, and the Christophe Soumillon-ridden Clodovil, who, at nearly half the odds of Nebraska Tornado, was viewed by most observers to be Andre Fabre's first string. Fabre was of a very different opinion.

Once again he was sparing but insightful with his paddock conversation. When I asked how he wanted me to ride her, he said, 'Do what you like. She will win.' I couldn't believe it. There was a heap of Group 1 winners in the Moulin field and my filly was running just 21 days after being summarily dismissed in a similar event at Deauville, yet Fabre was sufficiently confident not to even contemplate the possibility of defeat. Monsieur Fabre was not wrong. In a race run almost identically to the Diane, the early pace was no more than moderate so I sat one off the lead before asking for an effort over a furlong from home. This time she ran all the way to the line and had enough in reserve to hold off the front-running Lohengrin and Bright Sky, who had also raced prominently.

Some journalists were kind enough to suggest that I had stolen two Group 1 races on Nebraska Tornado thanks to me showing exactly how to make the most of slow early fractions. I do regard them both as two of my better rides but the praise should have been directed at Fabre for his insightful understanding of the filly he was training. He is a man who always seems to know exactly how his horses are going to run. For Fabre, what happens on the racecourse tends to bring little in the way of surprises. He is a truly exceptional trainer but perhaps better at his relations with horses than people, something I'm sure he would readily admit to. Pat Eddery, who rode numerous big-race winners for him, including on the Prince's outstanding miler Zafonic, always said that Fabre was not an easy man to get on with, even after years of knowing him. I think that, when it comes to jockeys, that indifference is largely because he does not need us. Fabre likes to develop his own young jockeys – Mickael Barzalona and Maxime Guyon are his two most recent star riders – because he is happier keeping everything inside his own team, a team he knows and manages incredibly well. To ride one of his top horses in a major race is therefore a real privilege.

But for the Prince I would not have enjoyed that privilege. And it was after Nebraska Tornado's Moulin triumph that I had what was only my second proper conversation with the man who paid my wages. Even more surprisingly, I never had another. As I have said before, the Prince is not a chatty man so his reluctance to say much to me was not taken as a direct snub – he has Teddy Grimthorpe and his trainers to voice his opinions – but it was still a bit odd to have so little direct contact with my boss.

To his great disappointment the Prince had not been able to get to Longchamp, but on the way back from the racecourse I had a call from Teddy who told me that the Prince was about to ring me. A few moments later, the call came in. The Prince congratulated me on the ride and said how impressive she had looked. I replied that the filly had been brilliant, and he then explained that Nebraska Tornado's dam, Media Nox, was his own personal favourite. That, he said, was why the Moulin win had excited him so much.

The first time he had called was in my first year in his employment, 2001, not long after I had broken my leg on Cambridgeshire day. I was back in Ireland recuperating when Teddy rang my mobile to say the Prince was planning to ring as he wanted to pass on his best wishes. I gave Teddy my parents' landline number, but before I could tell them what was about to happen, the phone started ringing and my mother answered. When the voice at the other end announced himself as Prince Khalid, Mam thought it was a wind-up. It was only when I looked at her and made very clear that she was talking to the real Prince Khalid that the truth dawned on her. Correcting herself, she put on her best Sunday voice and said, 'Oh, hello Prince.' Not many people in racing, even those who have worked for Khalid Abdullah, have ever had the chance to say that.

My connection with the Prince's French string continued into the autumn. I got another chance to ride for Fabre when winning the Group 3 Prix Thomas Bryon on his Apsis, but more significant was my booking to partner American Post in the Prix Jean Luc Lagardère on Arc Sunday. Criquette Head, American Post's trainer, had requested that I ride at Longchamp even though Olivier Peslier had been in the saddle for the colt's first two runs. Criquette is a beautiful lady in every sense. She is thoroughly decent from head to toe and also a real horsewoman who allows jockeys to ride her animals as they think best. She is my sort of trainer, so I was chuffed when Teddy let me know I would be aboard American Post in France's most prestigious two-year-old prize.

Criquette had asked for my services because she felt I would suit the horse. He was a playboy who liked to try it on. He had no malice in him but he was naughty and it took some persuading just to get him to set foot on the Longchamp's racecourse. He then reared up repeatedly down by the stalls before finally consenting to load, only doing so after a smack around the arse left him in little doubt who was in charge. In the race, he was the one in charge – total and complete charge. He looked a serious Classic contender for 2004.

American Post ran once more in 2003 but I was unable to ride him. Criquette sent him to Doncaster for the Racing Post Trophy, in which he beat Richard Hannon's Fantastic View into second after being tempted into the stalls by a carrot. While Christophe Soumillon was being shown a root vegetable in South Yorkshire, I was in California for the Breeders' Cup at Santa Anita, where Oasis Dream was bidding to end his year in fabulous fashion with a famous win.

John Gosden had been keen to up him in trip for the Breeders' Cup Mile. It was a bold move, but there was a notable precedent as Last Tycoon, another champion European sprinter, had stretched his stamina and triumphed in the 1986 Mile under Yves Saint-Martin. John, who was training in California at the time, had saddled the very first Breeders' Cup Mile winner, Royal Heroine, in 1984. He believed he could win the race again with Oasis Dream and, as part of his planning process, gave me a video of Last Tycoon's victory. The race on that cassette showed that a sprinter could thrive around the two turns of an American oval. Our hope was that Oasis Dream could follow Last Tycoon's example.

There is no point riding a horse believing that he will not stay so I rode Oasis Dream believing that he would. Sadly, he did not. Although slightly slow to kick in a country where horses start faster than anywhere else, he was nevertheless quickly into stride and had made up a huge chunk of the lost ground by the time we got into the first bend. Taking the turn proved to be an odd experience for a colt who had spent almost his entire career galloping in a straight line, but we were soon back on an even keel and in a promising position heading out of the back straight. From there, it all went wrong. Taking the final turn he lost both front shoes, which inevitably caused his stride to shorten. I have no doubt that had a bearing on his tame performance up the straight but, in all probability, he also ran out of stamina.

He never ran again, but since retiring from the racecourse his reputation has soared at stud. In Oasis Dream, the Prince now stands one of Europe's best stallions, a horse who produces outstanding sprinters, milers and middle-distance athletes. Perhaps the best horse he has sired is one that the Prince retained, the fabulous mare Midday, who gave her father and breeder some Breeders' Cup consolation when taking the Filly & Mare Turf in 2009, winning around the same Santa Anita oval on which the racing career of Oasis Dream had ended six years earlier.

But for the kindness of John Gosden, my career, or certainly my job with Prince Khalid, could have come to an end in America. Through 2003 I enjoyed more success than I had ever known, yet I failed to appreciate much of it. I found myself getting angry when not winning races I felt I should have won and annoyed when I did not get rides I thought I deserved to get. When I was winning races, even prestigious races, I enjoyed none of the thrill that should have come with such moments. My problem was that by then I was hopelessly alcoholic.

I had not admitted it to myself. I just drank a lot. On the flight out to America I drank an awful lot. I travelled over with John and, in his company, downed two vodka and tonics before lunch, during which I drank an awful lot of wine. To John's astonishment, I was still sober by the time I went to bed. After landing, we went for dinner in Pasadena, where I again got through more than my fair share of the local liquor. John said nothing. It was back in Britain when he first mentioned what he had seen in the States. He called me into his office at Manton and told me that he could not believe how much alcohol I had consumed during the Breeders' Cup. I admitted that I had a problem. John offered to help in whatever way he could. He spoke to me as a friend. He did not talk to Teddy Grimthorpe or the Prince and instead kept the matter between us.

John may have been astonished by my behaviour, but little in my life had changed. I was drinking too much before America and I drank too much after America. I write these words as a sober alcoholic. Getting to that point has taken me on the most turbulent ride of my life.

11

THE LONG ROAD TO SOBRIETY

John Gosden was far from alone in detecting that I had an unhealthy relationship with alcohol. My dependency on booze had an impact on every part of my life and scarred almost all my most important relationships. It changed the way I saw myself and the way others saw me. To my enormous regret, it caused me to inflict the most terrible pain on the people I love, nobody more so than Lizzie, who showed a degree of loyalty and commitment to me far greater than I could ever have asked. And now I have come out the other side, I realise how blessed I am.

I well remember one of my first drinking experiences and the ill omens associated with it. I was 17 and was with a few of the lads on a night out in Tipperary. We ventured into the small village of Fethard and its pub, McCarthy's, once famous for its ghosts, now famous for being regularly frequented by those working at Coolmore and Ballydoyle. It was in McCarthy's that I put beer to my lips for the first time. I probably drank six or seven pints. I'm not sure I actually enjoyed the taste much, but I wanted to be the same as the lads and if they were drinking six or seven pints, I was as well. I woke up the next morning without the faintest idea of where I was or how I had ended up there. I had gone through my first blackout.

You might think that not being able to remember many hours of your life would serve as a warning call. It did not. I was a young lad and I was hungry – or, more accurately, thirsty – to behave like one. Dad continued to impress on me that I was a jockey and that as a jockey I could not do what some of my non-racing mates did. His advice was frequently ignored. As my rides in Ireland dried up, I chose to soak myself in something else. Without the prospect of quality mounts to look forward to, my feeling was, why shouldn't I enjoy myself? I ended up going out on Friday, Saturday and Sunday nights, plus twice more during the week, especially Mondays, which was the evening we went to the pub to watch football. At first, my tipple of preference was vodka and lemonade – largely, and ironically, because it did not taste of alcohol – but my range soon widened as my threshold for consumption increased. Night after night I was out on the lash, but news of my behaviour somehow went below the radar of the local gossip mongers. I was largely ignored, save for bollockings from Dad if I was late to ride out the morning after the night before.

Not even the sight of Johnny Murtagh looking sad and pathetic in his tiny room at St Pat's deterred me from the path I was to take.

In my defence, I do not believe I first became hooked on alcohol because of a love of alcohol itself. Through my growing years it became a means to an end. The end was not to get pissed but to control my weight. For a number of years, the combination of champagne and diuretics enabled me to ride at weights that I did not consider achievable in any other way. I would drink copious amounts of champagne, confident in the knowledge that it would begin a dehydration process that could be completed the following morning with piss pills. In my head, there was nothing inherently wrong with what I was doing. In the end I stopped drinking champagne, not because of anxiety over what it was doing to my health but because I was sick of it. It was successful in sucking out of me every last drop of water and, after a while, the feeling became intolerable. It had turned into a sort of medication, whose side effects were too much to handle. I switched to lager. I found it an altogether happier drink.

Moving to Britain was a major factor in the acceleration of my alcoholism. The culture among British jockeys was very different to the one I had known back home. In Ireland, jockeys often interrupted their return journeys from the races by stopping off for an ice cream. In Britain, jockeys also liked to interrupt their journeys home, but they went to an off licence. For me, that was heaven. It was an invitation to drink, and one that suggested no stigma was associated with alcohol. Unwittingly, my first British boss gave me the same sort of invitation. After I was late for work one morning, Mick Channon called me into his office. He said that he knew what it was like to be young. He told me he couldn't care less what I did out of work as long as I fulfilled all my duties on the gallops and at the racecourse. I believed, wrongly of course, that Mick was giving his approval to my behaviour. In my distorted impression, he was saying that I could do whatever I wanted in my free time on the proviso that I didn't let it interfere with what he was paying me to do. My answer, therefore, was to have a driver live across the road from me. Put simply, I was employing someone to drag me out of bed in the morning. In my head, I now had it sorted. As long as I did everything that Mick expected me to do, I could drink as much as I wanted to drink.

Norman Williamson, landlord and housemate during my first year in Britain, tried to help. He was a calming influence on me and sought to ensure that I did not allow my busy social life to hamper my progress as a jockey. Yet even Norman sometimes gave out the wrong signals. After one seriously heavy session at the Queen's Arms I only made it back as far as my car, inside which I fell asleep. When Norman discovered me the following morning he gave me a stern lecture and told me I was jeopardising everything I had worked for. He made a 5ft 9in man feel small. I promised to take on board what he had said. Then, a couple of days later, I came out of the house and found

Norman, stubbly, dishevelled and dirty, lying sound asleep in his car.

Therein lay part of the problem. I have nobody to blame for my behaviour but myself, but I was living in a culture of excess drinking. The Queen's was just down the road and it was there that most of my Lambourn mates could be found on a nightly, sometimes daily, basis. The pub was like a second home. And we did have a great time.

One story in particular sticks in the memory. During one of my stints riding over jumps I was booked to partner a horse trained by Brian Meehan called Quelque Chose in a selling handicap hurdle on a Monday at Fontwell. I had ridden him a few days earlier in a better race at Wincanton, where he blew up after travelling well for a long way. Down in class and with his fitness enhanced, I felt sure he was capable of winning with ease. Unfortunately, I spent most of the weekend in the Queen's and got paralytic. In one of my more sober moments I told the proprietor of the pub, my great friend Tom Butterfield, that Quelque Chose was a certainty and that he should have a meaty bet on the horse. Tom has always enjoyed a punt and he became ever more excited as the weekend went on.

Given how much I had put away on Sunday, Tom let me stay in one of his bedrooms that night, and it was on the bed that he found me lying face down, dead to the world, on Monday morning. Tom told me I had to get dressed. I told Tom what he could do with his suggestion. 'I don't do Mondays,' I said and made very clear my intention to continue sleeping. Tom, anxious that everything should be in Quelque Chose's favour, rang a local jump jockey, Jimmy McCarthy. Jimmy was not even riding at Fontwell that day but Tom paid him £100 to drive me there. I was dragged down into the bar. I insisted on downing a pint of Guinness before we left.

Once at Fontwell, I got myself changed and headed out to partner Quelque Chose in the Pagham Selling Handicap Hurdle. The race was as easy as I had forecast. Although almost certainly well over the permitted alcohol limit for riding racehorses, I had little to do and merely steered the 2-1 favourite to a simple 11-length success. The race took place at 1.40 p.m. Less than three hours later I was back in the Queen's with another pint in my hand.

As I became more established in Britain, my dependency on alcohol became ever more deeply rooted. From drinking to control my weight, I began drinking for the sake of drinking.

Despite spiralling into a situation that seemed ever more out of my control, two positive strands were developing in my life at the same time. One was my career. My profile as a jockey rose through the late nineties and into the new millennium, so much so that I had landed the retainer with Prince Khalid Abdullah. Secondly, my relationship with Lizzie Hannon had blossomed. I fell completely in love with her. We had been an item for almost as long as I had been in Britain. The logical next step was marriage, and in April 2001 we went public with our plans to tie the knot on 1 September that year.

That Lizzie agreed to marry me might have surprised anyone who knew the intricacies of our relationship. Being the partner of any jockey can be a difficult, thankless task. The hours we work are long and punishing and the amount of quality time a couple gets together is minimal, certainly during the midsummer height of the Flat season. With Lizzie and myself, that was not necessarily the big problem. I was. And I was only a problem because of my drinking.

For much of the time I was great fun to be around. We had some great laughs, some as a direct result of my reliance on booze. During our time living together in the Wiltshire village of Collingbourne Ducis, Lizzie once found me literally hanging in the front door. As she approached the house all she could see were my legs and arse sticking out of what had been a glass panel. I had been on a bender and somehow managed to stagger back home, but between heading out and heading back I had lost my keys. I'd decided I had to think of a different way of getting in the house. My solution was to break through one of the door's glass panels. In a state of sobriety I would have smashed the panel, put my hand through the empty space and opened the door from the inside.

This, though, did not occur to me. In my confused state, I thought it best to scramble through the broken panel and get into the house that way. Unfortunately, at the point where I was half in and half out I became trapped. I did not struggle for long. Instead I fell asleep.

We were able to look back on this incident and laugh. Not so some other incidents. My behaviour was frequently appalling. More often than not I was a funny drunk, but there were also occasions when I would turn nasty – never physically, but verbally. I would call Lizzie some deeply unpleasant names and unleash a torrent of abuse when all she was doing was trying to help. Lizzie had to be not only my girlfriend but also my babysitter. She was seeking to protect me from me. When I was under the influence of drink I did things I would never normally do. Morals were swept aside. I would chat up other girls while Lizzie was in the same room watching. Her presence had no influence on my actions. She once intervened while I was blatantly writing down my phone number for a girl.

And if I was prepared to flirt with other women when Lizzie was with me, I was prepared to go a whole lot further when she was not. More than once I cheated on Lizzie. When I had been drinking I seemed to have no grip on what was right and what was wrong. With a drink inside me it was as though I felt I was both invisible and invincible.

While I was working on this chapter, Lizzie and I discussed what I should and should not say. To her enormous credit, she agreed that I should be open and honest about my failings. What I do not want people to think is that Lizzie was a doormat who meekly accepted her man's behaviour. She says now that she always knew that if I could give up drinking I would become the man she knew I could be. She says that she could not believe that a son of Dessie Hughes was not inherently decent. She gave me more chances than I deserved.

In a sense, that almost made me feel worse. For years I was ravaged with guilt. I could see what I was doing to the woman I loved, but I carried on doing it. I had the same feelings whenever my Dad rang me up to congratulate me on a good win. I felt a fraud. In my head I was not behaving like a person who deserved to be congratulated. I became trapped in a vicious circle of deceit and alcoholism. Yet at that point I did not see myself as an alcoholic, merely someone with a drink problem. What I was doing left me in a state of personal torment, and in that state I was ever more vulnerable to my own demons.

It had been partly through guilt following my actions with another woman that I first asked Lizzie to marry me. I was terrified of losing her and felt that a proposal of marriage would solidify our relationship. However, even after she accepted my proposal, I carried on misbehaving. In the weeks leading up to our planned wedding I was embroiled in an affair. I spent a lot of nights in Newmarket, and Lizzie understandably became suspicious. People who should not have known about the affair started talking about it. If they knew, I realised that Lizzie would soon find out as well. I panicked. I concluded that the only sensible course of action was to call off the wedding. My head was also telling me that, once freed from the demands of a loving relationship, I would be freed of responsibility. I would not have to feel bad about my drinking. I would be free to act as I pleased. The fact that I was in the first year of my job with Prince Khalid was not impacting on my actions. The only person doing that, out of love for me, was Lizzie. I convinced myself that I would be better off without her and that she would be better off without me.

About six weeks before we were supposed to marry, I told Lizzie that I could not go through with it. Unforgivably, I said that I no longer loved her. It was a terrible thing to do. She said that I did love her and that there must be another reason. I told her there was not. A few days later, we went to speak to her parents. Lizzie told Richard that I had called off the wedding. He started laughing because he thought it was a joke. Then it started to sink in that Lizzie was telling the truth. Richard did not take the news very well. He and I had forged not just a good working relationship as trainer and jockey but also a more personal bond. He was desperately upset. Jo Hannon is a practical lady and she took the news slightly better. She looked at me and said that if I did not want to marry her daughter it was best that I should not.

Not long afterwards, Lizzie discovered what I had been up to. Itemised telephone bills listed one number again and again. I had caused her terrible humiliation.

Things then took an unexpected twist during racing at Newmarket on Cambridgeshire day in early October, which was when I broke my left leg after being unshipped before the first race. The timing of the injury served as a major wake-up call. I was not only in pain, I was also miserable. At no point had I ever stopped loving Lizzie, even when my behaviour was at its worst. I did not deserve her but I needed her, and my parents could see that. Dad, who has always adored Lizzie as much as she has always adored him, phoned her. I was not aware of this at the time but Lizzie later told me that he had asked her if she would see me. Her private reaction was, quite rightly, that she owed me nothing. Nevertheless, she swallowed her pride, subdued her anger and came to see me in the Cambridge hospital that had become my temporary home. More than that, she checked into a nearby hotel so that she could visit me every day. I think part of the reason she did it was out of love for Dad, but she was also, if not directly, giving me another chance. I resolved to take it.

Secretly, we began to rekindle our relationship. We saw plenty of each other over the Christmas period, including in Ireland when Lizzie came to my parents' house. Not long after she had returned home I rang her and told her I was coming over and wanted to see Richard and Jo. She asked why, and I, in a way that I hoped would sound romantic, replied that it was because we were going to get back together and I wanted them to know. Her response took me by surprise. 'We're not just getting back together,' she said. 'If we're going to do this again we're going to get married. It's that or nothing.' The thought of that sounded much more preferable than the thought of nothing so I agreed, and suggested that we went out to Barbados early in the new year and got it done.

First, though, I had to get through another encounter at the Hannons' home. I walked into the kitchen and saw Richard and Jo, plus Lizzie's brothers Richard junior and Henry and two of her sisters, Julie and Fanny, all lined up in front of me. It was probably the scariest moment of my life. I had hobbled in on crutches and was stood there before them like a defenceless animal. Lizzie announced that we were not only once more a couple but that we planned to get married a few weeks later in Barbados. I was too frightened to say anything, but Jo walked up to me, kissed me and said, 'Welcome back.' The ice had been broken; Richard smashed through it when he approached me and playfully boxed me on the head.

It was not the first time, and it would not be the last time, that I saw face to face what wonderful people Richard and Jo Hannon are. They had also shown their decency a few weeks earlier when my parents had attended a friend's wedding at Luttrellstown Castle in Dublin. They were horrified to see that Richard and Jo were among the other guests. Given what I had just done to their daughter the Hannons could have said any number of unpleasant things to my parents, but they were characteristically lovely. They really are the very best of people.

I was still far from being their equal. Lizzie says that she could smell drink on me the day we told Richard and Jo of our reunion. On the day of the wedding my most dominant thought was not the wedding itself but that I should not get drunk and ruin it for Lizzie. I paced myself from morning to night and drank an awful lot of cola, just so that I would not embarrass Lizzie on her big day. On that occasion I managed it, but my uneasy relationships with alcohol and my new wife were both soon to hit new lows.

Marriage did not make me a better person. At least not at first. It certainly did nothing to curtail my love affair with alcohol. I drank, and then I drank some more, increasingly at the expense of everyone and everything that mattered in my life. Racing started to become an inconvenience. In the years that followed my wedding to Lizzie I won some of the biggest races of my career but the buzz those successes gave me was very often minimal. My job was getting in the way of my drinking. I remember being in action at Newmarket on a Friday night having ridden earlier in the day at Royal Ascot. When we got to Newmarket we learnt that the sport's alcohol testers were taking random samples. They did not pick me but I managed to get hold of their equipment. I recorded double the permitted limit. It was a sorry state of affairs.

At the time I did not care. My feelings towards racing were almost wholly negative. It was only later, when I looked at myself in the mirror and set about changing myself, that I realised that drinking was affecting my abilities as a rider. I could see that Ryan Moore, then a young up-and-coming jockey with Richard Hannon, was riding considerably better, and far sharper, than the jockey to whom he was supposed to be deputy. That annoyed and eventually motivated me, but not for a while yet. For at my lowest ebb I was thoroughly and helplessly dependent on alcohol.

By 2004 the situation had reached a point where I could not remember the last day on which I had not downed a drink. That's not to say that I was getting pissed on a daily basis. There were long periods when I remained sober, but not a day went by when I did not have at least one or two beers. I was trying to get every day over as quickly as possible and I was using alcohol to make that happen. There were occasions when I was inexcusably rude and unpleasant to Lizzie, but I had no positive feelings towards myself, let alone anyone else. It was a regular occurrence for me to drink and drive. There is a long stretch of road near home that I use almost daily. I would often speed down it at 120 miles per hour. I used to ask myself, what would happen if a deer suddenly jumped out on to the road? I decided that I didn't care. I would just carry on regardless. At no point did I ever directly contemplate suicide but nor did I ever think twice about smashing speed limits whilst pissed or the consequences, to myself and others, that might come from my actions.

Towards the end of 2004 the situation was reaching crisis point. My wife and my job were playing second fiddle to alcohol like never before.

I have an addictive personality, and I had never been more addicted. I therefore reacted with inner glee when Lizzie told me that she had to go to Australia. Henry, who had been out there on holiday, had been taken into hospital and needed surgery so Lizzie was heading over to offer love and support. Shamefully, I saw the news as a way of getting rid of her for a while. I had my plan organised within minutes of her telling me the news. I would drop her off at Heathrow and then drive to west London, where my old friend and occasional drinking buddy James Collins was living with his wife Fiona. When I rang James, who had worked alongside me for Dad when we were much younger, he readily agreed to me staying with them for a few days. What I did not know was that James planned to use the visit to tell me a few home truths.

As soon as I got to his house, I was dragging him off down the pub. We spent most of day one in O'Riordans Tavern, a popular Irish pub situated near Kew Gardens in Brentford. I drank myself into the ground and was dragged home by James, who, now not just older but wiser, remained in one piece. The following morning I was fine because on following mornings I was always fine. I never once suffered from a hangover. And now, as ever, I wanted to be down the pub. I kept urging James out of the door. Finally he relented and we returned to O'Riordans. By one o'clock I had already finished off three pints. James had barely touched his first. I wanted him to join in the fun and was annoyed by his reluctance to keep up with me. Then he came out with it.

'You're an alcoholic,' he said.

I told him to fuck off.

'You're a fucking alcoholic,' he said.

The words seemed cruel, unnecessary, and absolutely accurate.

I shouted back at him, 'I know I'm an alcoholic, but just leave me alone.'

He left the pub.

Many hours later, I got back to his house. I was not prepared to listen, but the following day I was given no choice. He told me once again that I was an alcoholic. He said that every time he rang me I was in a pub with a drink in my hand or, worse still, driving home from the races with a can in my hand. He said that I was half the jockey I should be and that I was throwing away my career and my life. He said that he was certain that I knew every word he was telling me was true. Given where the words were coming from, I did. I had been best man at James's wedding. I thought the world of him. Lizzie had told me until she was blue in the face that I needed to sort myself out. I had always blocked out her words. When the words came from a more dispassionate source they somehow carried more weight.

I listened to what James said, then packed my bag, got into the car and drove home. Once inside and with the door shut behind me I broke down and wept. I can't explain why, but it was only when James confronted me that I confronted my problem. Maybe I was reaching that point anyway, but I shall always be thankful to him for making me see myself as others were seeing me.

James had threatened to ring Dad, but I did not need him to. I phoned Dad and told him I was coming home. I waited until I was sat with him and Mam before explaining why I was back. When I did I broke down and wept all over again. Mam burst into tears as well, but Dad put his arm around me and told me that everything would be all right. He told me where I needed to go. The person he knew could help me was Johnny Murtagh.

When I rang Johnny he told me to come and see him that afternoon. For months I had been avoiding even eye contact with one of my greatest friends. Johnny had once been exactly where I was now. He had sunk further than he thought it possible to sink but he had risen back to the surface. But it was because Johnny had won his battle with the bottle that I had made such efforts to keep out of his way. I feared that seeing Johnny in his new sober state would magnify just how far I had plummeted. However, when he opened his door to me there was no lecturing or reprimands, merely comfort and support. 'I was wondering when you were going to come,' he said. He knew this moment had been drawing closer. He said he was relieved it had finally arrived. He talked me through the journey he had been on and how he now felt a happier, healthier and better person. He told me that the only way I could rid myself of alcohol was if I truly wanted to be rid of it. I told him that I did.

Dad also rang Lizzie and explained what had happened. Like Johnny, she was relieved.

That, however, was not that. It would be wonderful to say that I saw the light there and then. In a way I did, but in other ways I did not. Part of me still felt that I could live my life with alcohol in it. I believed that if I took Johnny's advice and sought help from counsellors and Alcoholics Anonymous I could find my way to a situation in which I could enjoy alcohol without being ruled by it. I attended numerous AA sessions, some of them in Ireland with Johnny. I listened to what I was told without ever really feeling a connection to the people there or the advice they were giving me. I could not see in what way I was the same as a plumber who used to drink neat vodka from a brown paper bag. I convinced myself that I could win this race my way.

Three months into sobriety I attempted to test that theory. I was away riding in India and was due to head off to Dubai a couple of days later. It had been a bad day, I was feeling terrible and I was desperate for a drink. It was at that point that my sister Sandra rang. Not long after putting the phone down on her Johnny called, and then, almost immediately after that conversation ended, Lizzie's number showed on my mobile. In my head I wanted to know why they couldn't all just leave me alone. I then did what I had always done at times of stress: I reached for a bottle, opened it and poured myself a drink. I emptied my glass, refilled it, then refilled it twice more. I had finished off four drinks by the time I got into a taxi and returned to my hotel. As I walked in through the main door I could see the residents' bar. I wanted to go in but I didn't. Instead I went up to my room, got into bed and slept.

In my head, that was a monumental victory. I had proved that I was no longer an alcoholic. I rang Johnny and told him what had happened the night before. I related how I had enjoyed a few drinks but resisted the urge to have a few more. He told me I was a lucky lad. Mistakenly, I interpreted his reaction as one of approval. I was ecstatic. I told myself that I had turned the corner and that I was now a responsible drinker.

To celebrate, I flew to Dubai and got pissed for a week.

During that week in Dubai, the Richard of old made an unwelcome return. In the past, when I drank I let go of my morals. Nothing had changed. On my first night in Dubai I started flirting with a girl who was staying in the same apartment block. It quickly developed into a holiday fling. Looking back on the episode, I am full of remorse and guilt. I was texting the girl to tell her I was on my way down to her room and then, with the send button just pressed, I was texting Lizzie to tell her how much I loved her and that I was so looking forward to getting back home.

It was not long after I got back to Britain that the truth came out. Lizzie had been suspicious of the messages I had sent. They seemed too affectionate and she'd feared that something lay behind them. She found out exactly what one night while we were in bed together. As I slept she got hold of my mobile and started scrolling through some of the messages I had sent to a man called Stan. It was obvious that the man called Stan was not a man called Stan but a woman. Lizzie read messages that were horribly graphic. They must have felt like daggers to her heart. I had brought back all the pain that she had once grown used to suffering.

Her reaction was totally understandable. She woke me up, devastated, angry, and demanded an explanation. There was no point in lying. I started crying, in part because I knew what I had done to her but also because I was petrified at the thought of her walking out.

We had been here so many times, and the reason why dawned on me in a way that it had never dawned on me before. When I drank, I behaved appallingly. I had drunk heavily in Dubai and the consequences were enormous. Before going to India I had got through three months without alcohol. That showed I could do it. What had subsequently taken place in Dubai showed that I had to give up drinking. I was astonished how quickly I had returned right back to square one. After only one day of drinking I was once again at the mercy of alcohol. The compulsion to drink had totally left me over the previous three months. How quickly the compulsion was reignited stunned me.

I was riding at Lingfield the day after Lizzie's discovery. I spoke to her from there and promised, with full sincerity, that I would cut alcohol out of my life. She agreed to give me another chance. By doing so, she gave me the extra motivation I needed. Save for the distress I had caused Lizzie, I was also glad that I had tried for one last time to have alcohol in my life. By so spectacularly failing to cope I had seen, once for and all, that we were not compatible. But for that, I would always have been wondering if I could flirt with the bottle.

A few days later, on Easter Sunday 2005, I had a pint in The Shears pub. My intention was that it would be the final drink of my life. I have kept to my word. For the last seven years of my life, I have been sober.

Do not for a second think it was easy. I attended Alcoholics Anonymous sessions for ten months before I fully understood why I drank, what happened to me when I drank, and the ramifications that followed. It was then, almost a year into my second attempt at sobriety, that I completely 'accepted' that I was an alcoholic. I started getting a little better every day thereafter.

I was a very sick man. The longer I stuck with AA, the longer I realised just how sick. I learnt that alcohol is cunning. It baffles and confuses its victims. Alcoholism is the only disease that tells those who suffer from it that they don't have an illness. If you have cancer, you know you have a condition with the capacity to end your life. When you are an alcoholic, you live with a little devil on your shoulder. As you go through the day, it tells you that you can cope with a drink and that a few sips will make you feel better.

For me, the problem was that I was not equipped to cope with life. Dessie Hughes was born with the tools to deal with a problem. Richard

Hughes was not. My solution was always to drink the problem out of my mind. One drink was all that was needed because it is the first drink that gets an alcoholic drunk, not the sixth, the seventh or the last. I know now that if I put a drink to my lips I won't stop. When I drank, I drank to secure my passage into oblivion, to force out of my head whatever was in it. Now, if I have a problem that I'm struggling with I don't turn to a glass or a bottle. Instead I turn to Alcoholics Anonymous, its Big Book and the 12 steps that the group recommends members take to rebuild their lives. The serenity prayer, long ago adopted by AA, sums up those aims:

> *God, grant me the serenity to accept the things I cannot change,*
> *Courage to change the things I can,*
> *And wisdom to know the difference.*

Those words never fail to help me. As an alcoholic, you are always fretting about the future and worrying about the past. The prayer has taught me that there is no point tearing myself up over something that has already happened. If I cannot change something, whether in my personal or work life, I should let it go and instead concentrate on making today the very best it can be.

At times of stress I take solace in the prayer and AA's 12-step plan, in which alcoholics admit they are powerless when it comes to alcohol and seek help from a higher being, which for me, as a practising Roman Catholic, is God. I constantly remind myself of the 12 steps, not only when I'm not feeling great but also when, for instance, I'm having a sweat in the bath. Each and every one has helped to reshape my life.

These are the 12 steps, and how I interpret and respond to them:

1. We admitted we were powerless over our addiction – that our lives had become unmanageable.
I had to accept that I could not control my drinking. After going clean for three months, I came off the wagon in India and Dubai and quickly

realised that I do not possess the capacity to drink responsibly. I also accepted that my drinking had major consequences in my life, and the lives of others, and that to regain control of my life I had no option but to remain sober.

2. Came to believe that a Power greater than ourselves could restore us to sanity.

On this front I was fortunate. I don't think it would be right to describe myself as religious, but I have always believed in God and never had a problem about bringing him into my life. Mam is very religious and Dad has always said that a man without faith has nothing. Alcoholics Anonymous backed that up by stressing that it helped alcoholics to entrust themselves to the care of a higher being.

3. Made a decision to turn our will and our lives over to the care of God as we understood him.

In the past, my relationship with God had been one-sided and horribly selfish. All I wanted was for him to do things for me. I asked him to help a certain horse win or to get me out of any trouble that drinking had led me into. Alcoholics Anonymous made me realise that I needed to develop a closer-knit relationship with God. I have come to realise that there has always been someone up there looking after me. The number of times I got home safely when driving under the influence of drink were too numerous for me not to think that someone had been keeping watch over me. Now I go to church regularly. Even when on one of my winter stints in India I have tried to attend Mass on Sundays. I now thank him for what I have instead of asking him to give me something I do not.

4. Made a searching and fearless moral inventory of ourselves.

This was maybe the hardest part of the process to go through. I had to go back through my life and ask questions of myself, some of which I had never previously wanted to ask. I had to talk about subjects that I would otherwise have gone to my grave without ever mentioning. In my early days of sobriety, I was constantly searching for the reasons why I had succumbed to alcohol. I wanted to blame other people, including close members of my family. Instead, I had to look hard at myself and learn my own character failings.

5. Admitted to God, to ourselves and to another human being the exact nature of our wrongs.
Confessing past sins to God was not hard, nor indeed confessing them to myself; talking about them to someone else was always going to be more difficult. I was advised to get a sponsor to help, so I turned to Johnny Murtagh. He had been on exactly the same journey and one alcoholic talking to another alcoholic can often be the best road to recovery. I think Lizzie slightly resented me seeking help from Johnny because she had tried for so long to save me and, through no fault of her own, had been unable to do so. I felt able to tell Johnny everything that needed telling and I got plenty off my chest. One of the issues that was haunting me concerned Lizzie. Part of me felt that I had married her simply because I knew that, as a hard drinker, I needed someone to look after me. Johnny told me that I had been a very sick lad at the time and that I should simply be grateful that Lizzie stuck by me.

6. Were entirely ready to have God remove all these defects of character.
I knew that I could be a nasty person. In my case, it most obviously came to the surface when I had not been drinking for a few days. I became irritable and snappy. The only thing on my mind was how long it was going to be before the next piss-up. I would turn into a time bomb waiting to explode. My life revolved around drinking, and that, in itself, was destroying my life. I had to face up to that, deal with it and move on.

7. Humbly asked God to remove our shortcomings.
When I was drinking, I would open a bottle when faced with a problem. Thanks to AA, I learnt to ask God for help through prayer.

8. Made a list of all persons we had harmed, and became willing to make amends to them all.

For some alcoholics this can be an arduous process. For me it was more straightforward. Although sometimes prone to terrible mood swings, I was generally a happy drunk. The bad side of me was seen only by those I loved most. I apologised to Lizzie, my mother and father for worrying them. However, I knew that I had also let down people outside my family, people I worked for. I sought to rectify that. I wrote letters to Teddy Grimthorpe, John Gosden and Barry Hills. I confessed to them that I was an alcoholic and that I was now doing my best to get better. I apologised for those occasions when I had been late to ride out and for failing to appreciate the kindness, support and generosity they had showed me. I heard nothing back from them there and then, but a few years later John approached me and mentioned the letter for the very first time. He said he had torn it up that morning and put it in the bin. He said those days were firmly in the past. That meant a lot.

9. Made direct amends to such people wherever possible, except when to do so would injure them or others.

This one is very similar to step number eight. I did try to make amends to those I had wronged, but in my case the person I had wronged the most, Lizzie, had long since known about my past indiscretions.

10. Continued to take personal inventory, and when we were wrong promptly admitted it.

Now that I am sober, I hate to upset others. There was an occasion not long ago when a young apprentice cut me up in a race. I was furious. When we were both back in the crowded weighing room I made a point of embarrassing and humiliating him in front of everyone else. Almost as soon as I had done so my actions began to gnaw away at me. What I had done festered inside me. I went over to him, apologised, and explained in a more reasoned manner why I had been so angry. There was a similar incident one day at Ascot, although on this occasion the person on the other end of my verbal assault was a steward who had been on a panel that had just given me a three-day suspension. Once again I felt terrible and so made a point of going back to see him, apologising, and asking if he would accept that apology, which he did.

11. Sought through prayer and meditation to improve our conscious contact with God as we understood God, praying only for knowledge of God's will for us and the power to carry that out.

At the end of every day I thank God for getting me through it. I say the serenity prayer and thank God for all the good things he has brought me. I make a conscious effort not to ask for a single thing for myself.

12. Having had a spiritual awakening as the result of these steps, we tried to carry this message to other addicts, and to practise these principles in all our affairs.

For me, this is perhaps the most important step of all. My spiritual awakening came around ten months into my second stint with Alcoholics Anonymous. I was sat at the back of a room that must have had 20 people in it when reality hit me. I just said to myself, 'I'm an alcoholic. Big deal.' I saw that I have a disease, but it's a disease that I can control and keep suppressed. People you see in wheelchairs are almost certain to be in that wheelchair for the rest of their lives. They are not lucky enough to have it within them to conquer their illness. I realised that I could conquer mine and, on top of that, I could help other alcoholics win their fights as well.

In fact, I believe it is true to say that I can only stay sober by helping other alcoholics to do likewise. I do this through regular AA meetings. I do my best to attend at least one a week, generally in Hungerford, Andover or Marlborough, but I will often go to meetings much further from home. If I feel that I need to go to a meeting, I know that I have gone too long without one. The meetings help me enormously and I hope I can help others. If I go to a local group, there might be stable lads in there who had no idea that I am an alcoholic. My wish is that if they see that a successful jockey can fall victim to the disease but beat it, so can they. Having gone through what I've gone through and come out the other side a better person, I know that they can do it as well. And when they do, I know from my own experience that it will be worth it.

I am a lucky man. I am an alcoholic who for seven years has not touched alcohol. That in itself represents a massive victory, but it has not been a lone triumph. Everything else in my life has improved as well. Most importantly of all, I am now the father of two children. Lizzie gave birth to Harvey in 2008 and Phoebe two years later. We are the parents of two wonderful little people who have brought us the sort of joy that neither of us had ever previously known.

Lizzie and I had been married for six years and a couple for 13 years before Harvey came along. He was a long time coming, but he was well worth the wait. He was also born at exactly the right time – a time when I was sober and able to appreciate him to the full. That said, we had been trying for a child ever since we got married. Despite all our efforts, nothing happened. At first I thought I was the problem. I lie in a hot bath almost every day and I decided that the hot water had affected my ability to father a child. My mother, who has been given three grandchildren – David, Philip and Alexandra – by my sister Sandra, was even more anxious than Lizzie and me. She was firmly of the opinion that a husband and wife needed children to cement their union. Whenever we saw each other I would reassure her that we were still trying. I longed to be able to give her some good news, and she did her best to help change our luck by going on a pilgrimage to the lake island of Lough Derg in County Donegal, where she fasted for three days.

It transpired that our difficulties arose from Lizzie's follicle-stimulating hormone (FSH) levels not being where they should have been. She bravely embarked on two years of tests, initially going down the intrauterine insemination (IUI) route but without any success.

After those attempts failed, the excellent Shaun Fountain at Odstock Hospital began giving Lizzie in vitro fertilisation (IVF) treatment, as a result of which she became pregnant.

Lizzie was overjoyed. I would not allow myself to feel the same. That angered Lizzie. She thought I was being weird, but I was exceptionally nervous. Inside me there was a sense of impending doom. I was expecting something to go horribly wrong. My apprehension was eased slightly when Lizzie sailed through the 20-week scan, but it was only when I saw her give birth to a completely healthy baby boy that I finally allowed myself to be happy.

I cried like a baby. The relief was overwhelming, as was my gratitude. Part of me believed that this was way more than I deserved. The overwhelming feeling, though, was that I now knew why I had been put on earth.

But there was more to come. Both of us were keen to give Harvey a brother or sister so Lizzie quickly resumed IVF treatment. Initially it yielded nothing so we halted the process. Soon after that we were in Barbados for the birthday party of Lizzie's sister, Claire, who has lived on the island for years. Lizzie was miserable all week long. She behaved like an antichrist from start to finish and her mood did not improve when she started to feel poorly during Claire's party. She had serious stomach pains, which Claire and Lizzie's other sister Fanny decided were just due to wind. The pains got worse and worse. A local doctor prescribed tablets for a urine infection. Lizzie was not suffering from a urine infection. It later transpired that she had suffered a miscarriage.

On the one hand, we were devastated. On the other, we had been given an unexpected lifeline as the miscarriage did at least show that Lizzie could now become pregnant naturally. In no time at all she was pregnant again, and early in 2010 we gave Harvey a baby sister. We had always liked the name Phoebe so we gave our daughter that as her first name, but we added as a second name Jacqueline, after the filly on which I had already won the Indian 1,000 Guineas, 2,000 Guineas

Cap Juluca completes a fine front-running success in the 1995 Cambridgeshire.

In the unsaddling enclosure after the Cambridgeshire. I had produced one of my best front-running rides and Cap Juluca had excelled under top weight.

Khalid Abdullah and his racing manager Teddy Grimthorpe. Thanks to them, I had seven great years as the Prince's retained rider.

Sergeyev gives me my first winner at Royal Ascot in the 1995 Jersey Stakes. Two days later I completed a memorable royal meeting double when landing the King's Stand Stakes on Piccolo. My Royal Ascot tally now stands at 26 winners. I would like to make it even more.

Above: Unsaddling Passage Of Time after her win in York's Musidora Stakes. We put on brave faces, but deep down I was very disappointed she did not win more easily.

Left: A mini me. Franny Norton joins me in the Abdullah colours at Ascot in 2003.

With Johnny Murtagh, a great jockey and a great friend. He helped me through my darkest days.

Below: A Hannon first and second at Windsor. Who says you can't get a laugh out of Ryan Moore?

Cockney Lad gives
me my biggest ever
jumps success when
taking the 1997 Irish
Champion Hurdle
from Theatreworld.
I was weighing in at
about 9st 10lb that
day – as you can see
from my face!

Oasis Dream is too good for Aussie superstar Choisir in the 2003 July Cup. I have ridden some fast horses but Oasis Dream was undoubtedly the fastest.

On the back of an old friend: Youmzain, pictured here with me in Dubai, could frustrate and delight in equal measure.

Dr M.A. M. Ramaswamy. Based in Madras, he is one of the biggest owners in the world with over a thousand horses in training. He's also a fantastic person and we became the best of friends.

Jacqueline after winning the Indian Derby, her fourth consecutive Classic, in February 2010, just five days after our daughter, Phoebe Jacqueline, was born. The best horse I ever rode in India had previously won the 1,000 Guineas, 2,000 Guineas and Oaks.

A rare visit to Hamilton during the closing stages of my 2010 championship battle with Paul Hanagan. There was enormous pressure on both of us but I enjoyed every minute of it. I finished second to a worthy champion jockey.

and Oaks. Just a few days after Phoebe Jacqueline Hughes was born, Jacqueline won the Indian Derby.

The children have changed my life. I remain a fiercely competitive sportsman and Lizzie knows that when allocating my time, racing must always come first. Thanks to my job we enjoy an excellent standard of living, and Lizzie understands that I must therefore always give my job the commitment it deserves. Even so, no time is more precious to me than the time I get with my family. Thanks to Harvey and Phoebe, the bad days are never quite so bad. If things go wrong on the racecourse, I can still drive home with a smile on my face because I know I will soon see my children.

Fate has been kind to me. Harvey and Phoebe came along at precisely the right time in my life. I thank God that my children have never seen me drunk. I will do everything in my power to make sure they never do. Lizzie has given me the two most precious things anyone could ever have given me. I owe her everything for that, as I do for sticking by me through times when nobody would have criticised her for running in the opposite direction.

I am an alcoholic, but an alcoholic who does not drink. For so many years alcohol controlled me. It came close to destroying my life, but, after years of misery, hurt and anguish, the hold it had over me is no more. To get here has been arduous but incredibly worthwhile. For those first few months as a sober man, the loneliness was terrifying. The first thing in the mind of any recovering alcoholic is that they will never drink again. I went through that stage and it scared me. For the first time since turning 16 I was faced with having to square up to the problems that life brings. In the past, I blocked them out by getting pissed. Now I deal with them and move on. The compulsion to drink has also totally gone, but shunning alcohol has done nothing to detract from the pleasure I derive from my existence. I am anything but miserable and have reached the stage where I can be in the company of people who merrily go from one drink to the next. As long as I can say my goodbyes before things get sloppy, I'm fine.

Thanks to Alcoholics Anonymous, I have learnt that I can only change myself, not other people, but that I can actively help others by telling them my story and offering support. Being of use to alcoholics helps me greatly, as does the realisation that, while I have responsibilities, I am not in control of my life. God is, and because he is, I can approach big races feeling zero pressure. If I am meant to win, I will win. If I'm not, I won't. Since signing up to sobriety I have enjoyed being a jockey more than ever before, and with Lizzie, Harvey and Phoebe at home, every day is a good one. Life has never been better.

12

AN AMICABLE ENDING

As retained rider to Prince Khalid Abdullah, I was a man with many bosses. Prince Khalid might have paid my wages but he was far from the only person I needed to keep on side. My employer sent horses to a significant number of trainers in Britain. By 2004 my contract gave me access to all of them, regardless of whether the animals were based with Sir Michael Stoute, Henry Cecil, John Gosden, Barry Hills, Roger Charlton or Amanda Perrett. Keeping all of them happy all of the time was never going to be easy, and with some it was harder than with others. That difficulty, combined with a period in which our horses were generally not talented enough to win the biggest races, left the ground on which I was standing increasingly shaky.

In my final four years working for the Prince, we won only two Group 1 races together. As a percentage return it was not good enough, but I firmly believe that the large breeding operations have cycles of success. The events of 2003 and the multiple top-flight victories of Oasis Dream and Nebraska Tornado had set a precedent we could not maintain. When a football team starts losing game after game, the manager's role is called into question. When a retained rider's mounts fail to fire in the most important races, an obvious solution is to assess the worth of the jockey. To the credit of the Prince and his racing manager, Teddy Grimthorpe, I was shown tremendous loyalty over a long period of time. Rare indeed is it for a jockey to hold a contracted position with a trainer or owner for seven years. Even rarer is it for the partnership to end with neither side holding a grudge or the slightest animosity towards the other. We showed that it could be done, so much so that even after we parted company I continued to ride some of the Prince's best horses.

Sadly, there were not many top horses for me to ride in 2004. Oasis Dream had been retired and Three Valleys, our runaway Royal Ascot winner at two, proved a major disappointment at three. What was available to me in Britain hardly set the pulse racing, and any hopes of developing my association with Andre Fabre were dashed when he shocked the racing world by appointing American superstar Gary Stevens as his stable jockey.

Nevertheless, my standout moment of the year – and very probably the most unusual big-race win of my career – came in France on a French-trained horse. A fall at Leicester in late April left me with a punctured lung and severe bruising. I was out of action for just over two weeks and missed both Newmarket's Guineas and also American Post's second outing of the season. Criquette Head had wanted to get him going long before the Classics so I'd enjoyed an earlier than usual trip to Paris for the Prix Omnium II, a Listed race at Saint-Cloud on the final day of March. It would have triggered a shock of seismic proportions had the colt not won easily, and he did, later mirroring the style of that performance with Christophe Soumillon back in the saddle in the Prix de Fontainebleau.

The Fontainebleau was staged over the course and distance of the Poule d'Essai des Poulains, France's 2,000 Guineas, for which the nation's racing nuts considered American Post to be a proverbial shoo-in. Such were the strength of his claims and the loftiness of his reputation that only six rivals were declared against him and none of them was rated highly enough to prevent him being sent off the 4-11 favourite. His starting price proved to be extremely deceptive.

We won but should not have done. We really ought not to have finished second, either. Third was what we deserved, but first is what we got following the weirdest race I have experienced. American Post was not at his best. From a long way out I was unhappy with the way he was striding. He was not covering the ground in the way he normally did, due, in my opinion, to the very fast ground that prevailed that afternoon. Once we turned for home I was one of the first riders forced to bring his mount under pressure. A horse who generally did everything so easily was labouring down the straight. Having finally overhauled Frankie Dettori on Byron, we were overtaken by Aidan O'Brien's Antonius Pius, on which Jamie Spencer had been sat motionless throughout. After Antonius Pius dashed past on our inside so too did Gary Stevens on Diamond Green. We were booked for third and a sense of deflation was setting in when, suddenly, unexpectedly and astonishingly, Antonius Pius veered violently right with just 50 yards to run. So erratic was his manoeuvre that he completely lost his balance and momentum, dropping back from first to fifth and almost bringing down the luckless Diamond Green in the process. Amid all the mayhem, American Post galloped past them both and crossed the line half a length in front of Diamond Green. Jamie Spencer, who was already enduring a torrid time in what would be his only year as Ballydoyle stable jockey, returned after finishing fifth with a bemused expression on his face. So did I.

I can't imagine that a set of connections have ever been so disappointed after winning a Classic. We had not deserved to win the race and were sure our horse had run a fair degree below the level we thought him capable of reaching. However, a gift horse is not to be looked in the mouth so we accepted our prizes, smiled for the photos and began thinking about Epsom.

Going into the Poulains, the plan had been to head next to the Derby. This was the race I had always cherished above all others. Much of my childhood had been spent watching videos of Lester

Piggott conquering Epsom's undulations and camber when winning the world's most important Flat race no fewer than nine times. My dream had been to win it just once. The dream remained the same. I had seldom gone to Epsom with a realistic expectation of making the dream come true, but American Post had a genuine chance. He was a Classic winner, albeit a fortunate Classic winner, and a study of his pedigree left us thinking that moving from a mile to the Derby's mile and a half would be in his favour. His sire, Bering, had been a high-class contemporary of the great Dancing Brave and excelled over 12 furlongs. His dam, Wells Fargo, was an unraced half-sister to two of the Prince's classy middle-distance mares, High And Low and Corradini. Everything about his breeding filled us with confidence. If he was not to win the Derby, the reason would not be stamina.

On the first Saturday of June, American Post failed to win the Derby. The reason was stamina.

For so far it had been a case of so good. He pulled a little harder than was ideal, but that was to be expected of a horse racing over 50 per cent further than he had ever gone before and therefore travelling at a pace somewhat steadier than he was used to. Descending the hill to Tattenham Corner, everything was as I wanted it to be. We were cruising. He negotiated the trickiest turn in racing without becoming in the least bit unbalanced. We straightened for home in fourth place. I had still not moved a muscle. As we cruised to the two-furlong pole, a little over two lengths down on the Kieren Fallon-ridden North Light, I remember thinking to myself, 'If you don't go too soon you'll win the Derby.' I sat and waited until the point came where it was right to make a move. As soon as I did, the Derby drifted from us. As we raced into the closing stages of the race I longed to win most, American Post's legs went to jelly. It was like driving a car that had run out of fuel. Even at the time it felt as though everything was unfolding in slow motion. As we retreated into sixth place, North Light stayed on stoutly to score.

I came away not gutted but strangely pleased with myself. I knew I had done everything as it should have been done. Some jockeys panic when faced with the possibility of winning the Derby. They get flustered and become more of a hindrance than a help. They get carried away and throw away their precious chance, but I had not done that. I had remained cool, composed and in control. My horse had not won the Derby but his defeat had been through no fault of his rider.

American Post ran once more, back down to a mile in the Prix du Moulin, but his time had passed and he beat only one horse home. One year earlier I had won the Moulin on Nebraska Tornado, but one year earlier I had also lost the previous afternoon's Haydock Sprint Cup on Oasis Dream. This time I won that race, in vintage Hughesie fashion, on Roger Charlton's Tante Rose.

Through her first and second seasons she had been trained by Barry Hills and owned by Wafic Said. In April 2004 she was purchased by Bjorn Nielsen, who immediately told Roger that he considered his new acquisition to be a perfect vehicle for Richard Hughes. I had not been available to ride her in her two opening runs of the year – both of which she had won – but I was around for her third and most important start.

Bjorn believed that Tante Rose was best produced on the line, and my instructions were to do just that. I carried them out to the letter. I buried her in the middle of the pack before showing her daylight approaching Haydock's final furlong. With Somnus, my nemesis from 12 months earlier, the horse to aim at, I galvanised the filly and fired her at him, grabbing him and passing him in the very last stride. To win that way was massively satisfying. It was a deadly feeling, and to win for Roger, whose support for me has been unending, was particularly sweet, especially as he had gone three weeks without a winner.

I had not long before gone three weeks without a winner myself, and, worse still, three weeks without a ride. In the middle of summer a slipped disc left me on the sidelines for an uncomfortably painful period. Frustratingly, I believe it was an injury that could have been avoided had I been driving a diff rent car at the time. Both Jimmy Fortune and myself had identical two-door sports cars and both of us ended up with the same injury. The car was great to drive but a nightmare to enter and exit. You had to get down very low when getting into or out of it and I think that the effects of doing that caused the back problems that both Jimmy and myself developed.

The day things clicked for me, so to speak, was at Newmarket. I was pulling up a horse after a race one evening meeting when I heard a sharp cracking noise. I didn't actually feel anything was wrong until I bent down in the shower to pick up a bottle of shampoo and found myself unable to straighten up. I had to lie flat on the floor that night and thereafter was required to undergo all sorts of physiotherapy.

Ten days in the Dubai sunshine proved highly beneficial and I came back as good as new in the middle of August. Fortunately, I did not miss anything of note during my absence. Sadly for both the Prince and myself, there would not be a great deal of note for me to ride or miss for the remainder of our time together.

Nothing much happened in 2005. The best I could manage for the Prince was wins in four Group 3 races, three of them on the same horse, the John Gosden-trained Day Flight, who mopped up the John Porter Stakes, Ormonde Stakes and St Simon Stakes. The other Group 3 success came on Notable Guest, who sprang an upset when turning over 4-6 favourite David Junior in Haydock's Rose of Lancaster Stakes. This was a day when I pleased the horse's trainer, Sir Michael Stoute. He was not quite such a fan of me the following year.

The cracks had already started to appear. A year as unproductive as 2005 left no one satisfied. The tide needed to start turning, but the ammunition needed to make that happen was not immediately obvious. Home Affairs was a horse I hoped could take us into some of the summer's key events. In his three-year-old campaign he had shown himself smart but not yet the finished article, never more so than when managing to take fourth in the Group 1 Prix Jean Prat. That effort was all the more praiseworthy because the bit came out of his mouth after 100 yards, meaning I only had the reins to steer him. He had potential, and I had my fingers crossed he could realise it.

His start to the 2006 campaign augured well. In a Listed race at Windsor we made all to win by two and a half lengths. From there it was on to Epsom and Derby day for the Group 3 Diomed Stakes. It was one of those races in which everything that possibly could go wrong did go wrong. To make matters worse for me, it happened on the biggest day in the Flat racing year in front of an enormous audience – and nobody in that audience was as annoyed as Home Affairs' trainer.

Sir Michael and I now have an excellent relationship. He is a master of his profession and a pleasure to ride for. But during my time as the Prince's rider I got the impression that there were many instances when he would have preferred to be legging up somebody else. When I first took the job I was told explicitly that I would not have the Stoute horses inserted into my contract. Even when I later did receive permission to ride them, I always felt that Sir Michael would have much rather been using Kieren Fallon, who, for most of my time in the job, was his number one jockey. That in itself put extra pressure on me. It made me feel uncomfortable and slightly awkward. It was as though I was in a kind of no-man's land. To sense that you are not wanted is the worst possible feeling for a jockey. It makes you try too hard, and when you try too hard you make mistakes. Which brings us back to the Diomed Stakes.

From the very start of the race I got myself trapped with nowhere to go. Home Affairs would often waste energy by racing too freely, which is one of the reasons why I'd let him bowl along at Windsor. On reflection, I should have let him do his own thing at Epsom, but instead I chose to try and settle him against the rail. As we made our way down the straight the horse was travelling with supreme ease with any amount in hand on those around him. He had so much to give but nowhere to give it. I was stuck against the fence and had no means of escaping because Fallon, on the William Jarvis-trained Momtic, had loomed up on my outer and locked me in. I frantically searched for a non-existent gap but Fallon had no intention of helping me out. In a desperate state, I pulled back and switched around horses. Running into the final 100 yards we were only in sixth. Such was the speed with which Home Affairs ate up the ground once released, we charged into a close and closing third that would have become a cheeky first had we been granted a few more strides.

Sir Michael said nothing. He did not need to. Teddy tried to use diplomatic language when approached by the press but even he was struggling. 'It was one of those things,' he said, adding, 'You saw what happened. It's history now, thank God.'

While God would have been forgiving, Sir Michael was not, at least not for a while. I continued to ride his Abdullah-owned horses for the rest of the season but we only combined for a single victory when Spanish Moon took a maiden at Newmarket's final meeting of the season in late October. After that I became a persona non grata. Sir Michael stopped using me completely and in 2007 the Prince's horses in his care were ridden by others. That Sir Michael was allowed to force his wish through annoyed me. I had hoped the Prince would stand firm and defend his jockey.

That said, for much of 2006 I did not think I would be the Prince's jockey in 2007. It was perhaps only because of one end-of-season success that I was given a final year. And, bizarrely, it was a win that came for a trainer who had not wanted me when I started working for the Prince and who then did not want me when my time was up.

Henry Cecil, then still some way off becoming Sir Henry, had been going through a desperate spell. In fact his time in the doldrums had lasted far too long to be described as a spell. Not since Beat Hollow won the Grand Prix de Paris in June 2000 had he trained a Group 1 winner. Henry, a man once accustomed to saddling more than 100 winners in a season, had seen only 12 of his horses win in 2005 having had a not much more enjoyable 21, 25 and 30 winners in the preceding three campaigns. His fortunes had slipped dramatically with the passing of many of the great owner-breeders on which his success had been built. To his credit, Prince Khalid always remained faithful to Henry and continued to supply him with prime bloodstock, of which the homebred Passage Of Time was a fine example.

I had not ridden the daughter of Dansili in her first two races so my initial racecourse experience of her came in the Listed Montrose Stakes at Newmarket on the same October card that Spanish Moon broke his duck. She was a superb example of why Henry remains the finest trainer of fillies the sport has known. After she won on Newmarket's July Course in August 2006, he saw that she was starting to go in her coat. He backed off, gave her time and pinpointed the slightly obscure Montrose Stakes. By doing so, he brought a relatively fresh filly to the Rowley Mile, on which she could not have been more striking. On soft ground that many fillies would have detested, she dazzled, powering to a five-length victory. Her asset was stamina, and I told Henry that she would have continued galloping up Newmarket High Street had I wanted her to. She was plainly in outstanding form, such good form that it seemed silly not to search for another chance for her to shine. At that stage of the year there are few options, but Henry found the Criterium de Saint-Cloud, a mile-and-a-quarter Group 1 contest at Saint-Cloud in mid-November. It was too attractive an option to resist.

I went into the race with the impression that I was on the rockiest of roads. I had not been told that I was being reappointed for 2007 and my expectation was that the job would not be mine the following year. I decided I had nothing to lose.

In the paddock, Henry gave me his usual instructions. He would almost invariably tell a jockey to let a horse flow. He did the same here. But asking a jockey to let a horse flow can be pretty pointless as a jockey does not ride a race in isolation. You have to react to what other jockeys are doing. Henry tends not to see things that way. When watching one of his own horses he can be oblivious to everything else that is happening in a race. Sometimes I had to forget about what he said and think on my feet. That was the case at Saint-Cloud.

I rode one of the most daring races of my career. Running into the final furlong, Passage Of Time was in third place and finishing better than anything but with little room to manoeuvre. I could have played safe and pulled her out around horses. That, however, might not have

163

got us to the front in time so I went for a tiny gap between Kieren Fallon on Soldier Of Fortune and Kevin Darley on Empire Day. It was a brave move and a risky move but it proved to be an inspired race-winning move.

I was genuinely delighted to have helped Henry to his first Group 1 triumph in six years. The victory was met with none of the enthusiastic and affectionate applause he regularly receives in Britain but only because, as is so often the case at a French racecourse, there was barely a spectator in sight. Even without his public, he was clearly over the moon. Henry would not mind me saying that he is not the best of losers – his competitive streak is what motivates him – but he is never happier than when celebrating a winner. I don't think many wins have delighted him as much as this one. Also thrilled was Prince Khalid. Not only could he celebrate a welcome Group 1 winner, he could also celebrate being crowned France's leading owner. The prize money earned by Passage Of Time at Saint-Cloud secured him the championship. Winning the race secured me one more year as his jockey.

In my heart of hearts I knew I was on borrowed time. Getting a seventh contract to ride for Prince Khalid had come as an unexpected bonus. I had clung on to the job with my fingertips, and was pleased to have done so, but I no longer viewed my role as one with a long-term future. I simply planned to enjoy it for as long as I could.

Numerically, 2007 was a solid year, one that I ended with 139 winners on the board, at that stage the most of my career. Once again, though, we did not have the right horses to win the right races. Prince Khalid had nothing good enough to run in either of the Newmarket Guineas, nor the Derby. Our flagship was always likely to be the filly who had put the icing on an ordinary cake the previous year. Yet on the day that mattered most, Passage Of Time was unable to deliver.

Her reappearance had been satisfactory but no more than that. Henry had targeted the Musidora Stakes from the moment she won in

France and he duly got her to York for what was expected to be an easy victory en route to the Oaks. What we got was indeed a victory but it was not one that left any of us seeing the filly as a certainty for Epsom. She ultimately had to dig quite deep to hold off Sweet Lilly and had only a neck in hand at the line. There were extenuating circumstances – she had been suffering from a well-publicised throat abscess and had also just come into season – but those excuses were not enough to leave me brimming with confidence in the build-up to the Classic. Not entirely surprisingly, she failed to fire at Epsom, where she ran terribly to finish eighth. For Henry there was splendid consolation as he also trained the winner, Light Shift. For Prince Khalid, there was no consolation.

A drip-drip effect seemed to follow me around over the next few months. Teddy Grimthorpe took me to one side one day and said that the boss was concerned that his horses always seemed to start slowly. He asked me to do all I could to make sure they were not left behind at the start, but I explained to him that I did not train the horses. If they were not educated to jump quickly, I could not make them do so. There were also horses in big races that I intentionally rode close to the rail in third and fourth. On occasion they looked a little unlucky in running, and Teddy, no doubt following direction from the Prince, pointed that out to me. However, these were horses that I knew were not capable of winning. By taking them the shortest way from start to finish I was merely doing all I could to get them into the best possible position.

If conversations like those were a signal that the end was drawing nigh, so too was the St Leger, in which I partnered Raincoat for John Gosden.

Raincoat had chased home the subsequent Derby winner, Authorized, in the Dante Stakes, after which he failed to build on the promise of his York run, managing only 11th in the Prix du Jockey Club and third in Goodwood's Gordon Stakes. Even despite those blips, John fancied him for the season's final Classic. I did not and reckoned the horse was Group 3 class at best. Even I was wrong, for when Raincoat was last seen in public he was only third in a maiden hurdle at Worcester. He ran just a fraction better than that at Doncaster, where I sat three wide and received no sort of response when I asked for some forward momentum early in the straight. John won the race with Lucarno but he still found the time to make it very clear to me that he had not been satisfied with my ride. He also made it clear to the press, telling journalists, 'It was disappointing that Richard could not get cover. Raincoat was always racing three wide with the choke out. He is much better than that.'

John had always been one of my most enthusiastic supporters. Without his backing, I realised it would be almost impossible to continue in the job. Within weeks, the job was no longer mine.

Matters came to a head in the days leading up to the Monmouth Park Breeders' Cup. Passage Of Time had bounced back to something close to her best, finishing third under me in the Prix de l'Opera on Arc Sunday. She was now earmarked for the Breeders' Cup Filly & Mare Turf, in which she had a favourite's chance. I saw no reason why I would not be riding her but began to get a little suspicious when Prince Khalid's Juddmonte office failed to get in touch regarding travel plans to America. A couple of weeks before the race I really started to smell a rat when I heard that Passage Of Time had been given a serious piece of work in which I had not been asked to ride.

I asked Henry what was going on. He apologised and said that I would not be partnering her at the Breeders' Cup because the Prince wanted to use an American jockey. I was furious and wasted little time before ringing Teddy. I told him what Henry had told me and made clear my anger. Teddy then painted a very different picture of what had occurred in recent days. 'I'm sorry, Richard,' he said, 'but it's the trainer who does not want you.' Teddy insisted that he had not been involved in the decision. He said that Henry had telephoned the Prince and asked that an American jockey be used on Passage Of Time.

I believed Teddy when he said he was sorry for what had happened and I accepted the news as a fait accompli. Henry did not want me on the filly. Had I kicked up a fuss and demanded to ride her, I would almost certainly have got nowhere. Even if I had been successful, I would have been on a hiding to nothing. Had she been beaten in America – which, under Ramón Dominguez, she was – I would have been blamed.

And that, pretty much, was that. I had another conversation with Teddy in which I made clear, very politely, that if I was not allowed to ride the Prince's best horses there was no point continuing as his retained jockey. I would have been little more than a work rider. I consulted Johnny Murtagh, who told me that all I could do was accept the inevitable. In the old days I would have got drunk and tried to put the matter out of my mind. Thanks to the lessons I had learnt at Alcoholics Anonymous, and heeding the words of the serenity prayer, I concluded that there was no merit in getting upset over something that I could not change. So, as Johnny had advised, I decided to take myself out of a situation in which I was not happy. My partnership with Prince Khalid had run its course. Teddy and I agreed that we should announce that Prince Khalid and I were separating by mutual consent. We genuinely were. There was no fallout, no bitter exchanges, no recriminations. It was, quite simply, time to move on.

There's an interesting postscript to this period in my career: I like to think that my family have had a bearing on some of the success that the Prince has enjoyed in the last few years.

For around ten years Dad went through the most wretched time. His horses were persistently under the weather. Horses that should have been winning, or at least coming close to winning, were running way below their capabilities. Try as he might, Dad found it impossible to put a finger on why. Then, with the help of Professor Tom Buckley at the Irish Equine Centre, he obtained a reason and a route to happier times. Professor Buckley discovered that Dad's stable was riddled with aspergillus, a fungus that does any number of unpleasant things to horses. It has the potential to give them the equine equivalent of asthma, it makes them more susceptible to internal bleeding and it decreases their immunity levels, thereby ensuring that they take longer to recover from viral infections. In short, it adversely affects their performance on the racecourse.

The fungus, which takes hold inside stables very often in hay, had been rife at Dad's yard. It had also become an unwelcome resident at Warren Place, Henry Cecil's famous Newmarket stables. Dad, who has become something of an expert in aspergillus, became convinced that Henry's horses were suffering at the hands of the fungus. He had been watching how they were running, largely because I was riding some of them, and he was sure that it was one of the reasons for the downturn in Cecil's fortunes. Dad spoke to Teddy and convinced him it would be a good idea for Henry to bring over Professor Buckley. Henry must have been persuaded that Dad was right because the Irish Equine Centre team was called into Warren Place. Aspergillus was detected and the necessary disinfection process was carried out. The rest, as they say, is history.

Henry has never spoken to Dad about this, but I'm sure he must be grateful. There could be any number of reasons behind his amazing comeback, but I think a few words of advice from Dessie Hughes might have had something to do with it.

And so, after seven years, I was no longer retained rider to Prince Khalid Abdullah. To have worked for him for so long made me the envy of many weighing-room colleagues, and justifiably so. Thanks to the Prince, I significantly boosted my number of major victories and enjoyed the luxury of riding some wonderful horses, whose sons, daughters, brothers and sisters I also got the pleasure of sitting on. However, I would not be telling the truth if I said I felt any closer to the Prince at the end of those seven years than I had when we first joined forces. I do not know whether I was intentionally hidden from him, but there were certainly days when I would have appreciated the chance to speak with him face to face, or even just on the phone. To have been able to explain why I had ridden a particular horse in a particular way would have made me feel more wanted, and of more use to him. In that sense, I always envied Frankie Dettori and his association with Sheikh Mohammed. Frankie was soon more than just a retained rider. He became a vital cog in the wheel, a man whose opinions were taken on board. Frankie became part of the team. At no point in my seven years as Prince Khalid's rider did I feel part of his team. I was an employee. I was a very handsomely rewarded employee, an employee who was treated fairly and kindly, but I was still no more than an employee.

There was never any realistic hope of changing that, and in no way did it diminish the respect in which I held the Prince. As I said, ours was the most dignified of partings. Teddy Grimthorpe was a friend and supporter from 2001 to 2007 and he has remained so ever since. Indeed, in the last couple of years I have become reaccustomed to wearing the Prince's silks. Trainers like Sir Michael, Sir Henry, John Gosden and Roger Charlton now all have their own stable jockeys so the chance of riding their Abdullah-owned horses are slim, but in 2010 and 2011 I was often booked when one of the trainers' riders was not available.

Last year was particularly satisfying as I was the man selected by Sir Michael to partner the high-class Sea Moon in the Great Voltigeur Stakes. That only came about because my very good friend Ryan Moore was injured, and I do think that Ryan's excellent relationship with Sir Michael has been in some way attributable to the more positive way in which Sir Michael now views me. I believe there were times during my years in the Prince's employment when not everyone who was close to Sir Michael spoke flatteringly about me to him. With Ryan now firmly ensconced as his stable jockey, that has changed. It was therefore with delight that I guided Sea Moon to such an easy win at York, and I was equally pleased when I was offered the mount on the colt in the St Leger. Sadly, due to my commitments to Richard Hannon, I was unable to take up the offer.

Sea Moon did not win, so nothing was lost, but there was plenty lost for me when Harbinger pulverised his opposition in the 2010 King George VI and Queen Elizabeth Stakes. Sir Michael ran both

Harbinger and that season's Derby winner, Workforce. Ryan, perfectly understandably, selected Workforce. Sir Michael rang me while I was on a golfing holiday in Scotland and said that he had talked about jockeys with Harry Herbert, manager of the Highclere syndicate that owned Harbinger, and they had decided I was the rider they wanted for Harbinger. I desperately wanted to say yes and I thought hard for 24 hours but Mick Channon had asked me to partner Youmzain and I felt I needed to show Mick some of the loyalty he had always shown me. It was the hardest decision I have ever had to make, but even after Harbinger stormed 11 lengths clear up the Ascot home straight I never regretted my decision. I had done the right thing. Had I not ridden Youmzain, the guilt would have been overwhelming.

When the chances arise, I hope that I will still receive phone calls from Sir Michael, Sir Henry, John Gosden and Roger Charlton, plus, of course, Teddy Grimthorpe. I no longer get to join forces with them as much as I used to, which is a shame, but my parting from the Prince did reopen an avenue that had been closed the moment I signed my first contract in 2001. When I took my first penny from him I agreed that I would no longer take rides over hurdles. Now I was free to rekindle one of my life's great passions. This particular cloud had a sparkling silver lining.

13

PLAYING AT BEING A JUMP JOCKEY

I was bred to be a jump jockey, but my breeder wanted me to ride on the Flat.

Dessie Hughes is synonymous with National Hunt racing in Ireland but he only switched to riding over fences and hurdles when his rising weight made it impossible for him to continue on the Flat. Like father like son. I started my career on the Flat and Dad made it abundantly clear that he wanted my career to stay there. He did not want me to be a jump jockey and nor did I. Growing up, my greatest ambition was to follow in the footsteps of Lester Piggott and to make a mark in Flat racing's biggest events. Lester, however, had also been known to dabble in jump racing. Sporadically, and with some success, I have done the same.

There seemed an inevitability about me making occasional forays into the world of National Hunt. It is in my blood, a passion that will not die. There have been times when it has been impossible for me to indulge that passion, but its flame has never been extinguished.

As a child I grew up watching Dad win a Champion Hurdle on Monksfield and a Cheltenham Gold Cup on Davy Lad. They are special memories. Sandra and I were never allowed to go with him to the Festival, which probably heightened my impression of Cheltenham as a heavenly, mystical place. I would go so far as to say that I am envious of Dad and his Festival achievements. For all that I have enjoyed amazing days at Royal Ascot and Glorious Goodwood, and in some of the most important Flat races across Britain, Ireland, France and beyond, nothing is bigger to those who love racing than the Cheltenham Festival. And if you are Irish, Cheltenham's place in your heart is magnified.

But for all that, I never wavered from feeling that the Flat was where I wanted to build my career. It was where the faster horses, the classier horses and, in truth, the better horses competed. It was a more lucrative sport and, crucially to Dad as a parent, it was a safer sport, a sport in which a career could last far longer than that of someone riding on a daily basis over jumps. Yet even though I wanted to be a Flat jockey and Dad wanted me to be a Flat jockey, he still wanted me to have some early experiences of riding over jumps. I think he thought that by giving me a taste of jumping, my appreciation of the Flat would be strengthened. To a degree he was proved right, but those early trips over hurdles also served to whet my appetite, especially as they came towards the end of my time based in Ireland, a time when my prospects on the Flat were looking increasingly bleak.

It was Dad who trained my first winner over jumps, a mare called Amari Queen, who ran out a two-length winner of the Brannockstown Handicap Hurdle at Punchestown on the final day of 1993. Amari Queen raced in the colours of Michael Ward-Thomas, who four years later became a Cheltenham Festival-winning owner-breeder when his Martha's Son, trained by the great Captain Tim Forster, won the Queen Mother Champion Chase. In time I would also get the chance to ride at Cheltenham, but my next jumps winner was at the somewhat more lowly Tralee, where I took a maiden hurdle in March 1994 on Conclave. That gelding would later switch to fences, but I would not.

Dad was happy enough that I dipped into riding over hurdles now and again. He would not have been happy had I told him of any plans to try my hand over fences. At the time of writing I have still to ride in a steeplechase race, although it remains something I would love to do. Until now I have been sufficiently sensible – if that is the right word – to stick to hurdles.

Quite simply, your chance of suffering a fall increases when you start negotiating fences. It is much easier to see a stride on a chaser, but a chaser who falls will almost certainly be travelling more slowly than a horse jumping hurdles. As a result, the prospect of your mount landing on top of you is much greater. I have always believed that horses jump well for me, and I think Dad would say the same, but even the very best jump jockeys will fall in, on average, one out of every nine rides. Someone who weighs less than nine stone is not physically capable of taking hard falls on such a regular basis. I had to conclude that riding over hurdles was risky enough.

But even riding over hurdles was never going to be a regular activity. When I moved to Britain and began living with Norman Williamson, I saw what jumping had done to his body and those of the other jumps lads I was getting to know. I would see Norman come home in bits. That was depressing, and so was watching him walking down the stairs like an old man. I didn't want that for me. I have been relatively lucky in avoiding serious injuries. In what is now a long career, I have broken a leg, punctured a lung and cracked ribs, but over nearly a quarter of a century that is more than acceptable. I did not want to heighten the risk of adding to that tally, but nor did I want to put jumping to bed. I decided that occasional rides over hurdles were a risk worth taking, not least because they allowed me to keep fit during those winters when I was not permanently based abroad.

I continued to take the odd ride here and there after relocating to Britain. In my first two British winters I rode in six British jumps races and 20 in Ireland, where Dad used me when he could, including at the 1994 Leopardstown Christmas Festival, where I rode him a winner on consecutive days. Approaching the end of the 1996 Flat season I decided to take jumping a little more seriously and announced that I would ride full time over hurdles that winter. I had not arranged any long stint abroad and I could not muster much enthusiasm for a winter spent shoving poor horses around the all-weather tracks. I decided that a few months riding over hurdles would keep me busy, keep me fit and keep me happy.

I had good reason to be pleased on the first day of my new season when I won a handicap hurdle on Alasad, one of the lower lights in Noel Meade's powerful jumps squad. Noel had been a strong supporter of mine when I was riding on the Flat in Ireland and he began to be the same over jumps. When I was in action in Ireland that winter, it would invariably be for either Dad or Noel, who liked me as a person and also liked the way I rode. Unsurprisingly, therefore, he also liked the way Paul Carberry rode, because Paul copied my style.

These days people marvel at the way Paul slices through a field, super stylish and incredibly cool. That, though, is now. When he first arrived on the scene, he was horrendous. Paul would be the first to admit that initially he was extremely sloppy and untidy. Then he started to watch me – very probably, I would say, because Noel told him to. Paul and I are a similar height and build, so I was the perfect person for him to mould himself on. We became good friends and, as a friend, I can confirm that Paul is as mad as everyone says. You never know what he is going to do next. He is not a mouthy person and tends to prefer doing the wrong thing to saying the wrong thing. I remember riding with him in a race at Leopardstown, where we took a hurdle alongside each other. Paul's horse made a mistake and he started to fall out the side door towards me. Being a generous soul, I pushed him back into the saddle. 'Thanks, Yoss,' he said, using a nickname of mine after the character Yosser Hughes in the 1980s TV serial *Boys from the Blackstuff*. It wasn't so much what he said as the nonchalant, carefree way that he said it. I honestly don't think he would have cared had he hit the deck. The term 'laid back' does not do Carberry justice.

Although we were mates, Paul and I were also vying for the same rides on Noel's top horses. Two of them ran in the 1997 Irish Champion

Hurdle. I was booked to partner Cockney Lad and Paul had his name put alongside Dardjini. Both of us thought the other was on the better horse. I had ridden Cockney Lad into second in the Grade 1 Hatton's Grace Hurdle at Fairyhouse in December, after which he was a beaten favourite under Paul at Leopardstown's Christmas meeting. Dardjini, bred by the Aga Khan but better as a jumper than a Flat horse, had won a Grade 3 contest in my hands at Fairyhouse before we were turned over when 4-9 favourite to win a conditions contest at Thurles. I still thought Dardjini was the one to be on. Paul thought Cockney Lad was the one to be on. Noel didn't care what we thought.

When Noel came into the weighing room to collect our saddles, he was greeted by his two jockeys sporting the colours the other was supposed to be wearing. 'Get those bloody colours off and the right ones back on,' he said, showing much less of a sense of humour than usual. Not long after that he was all smiles, as was I, although taking the penultimate flight it seemed that Paul was on the right one. Dardjini was cantering. But Dardjini, we came to learn, was a bridle horse: he went like a dream on the bridle but found little off it. He went in pursuit of Charlie Swan on Theatreworld going to the final flight while I chased them both on Cockney Lad. As Paul had moved away from me, I shouted across to him, 'I bet you're glad you're on the right one now!' He was, but not for long. Theatreworld blundered at the final flight, which would have presented a great opportunity to Dardjini had he not got it wrong as well. Now they had both presented a great opportunity to me, and I took it, getting after Cockney Lad for all he was worth, passing first Dardjini and then, 20 yards from the line, Theatreland.

Winning an Irish Champion Hurdle was a marvellous feeling, but at that point I still felt that I had not achieved over jumps what I wanted to achieve. I wanted a Cheltenham Festival winner. I would not get one, but I got very close and had a lot of fun trying.

There is only one Cheltenham. There is also only one Taunton, where I rode my first winner over jumps in Britain. And there is very definitely only one Martin Pipe, for whom I rode that first winner on a December day in 1996.

I had already become good friends with Pipe's new favourite jockey, Tony McCoy, when I was asked by Martin if I would ride one of his in a selling hurdle at Taunton. The prospect of a long drive to the West Country only to ride in a seller was hardly enticing, but the prospect of forging an association with Martin was extremely attractive. Tony was going down to school for Martin on the way to Taunton and Martin asked me if I would come along as well. Tony had warned me that Martin was a little on the eccentric side but also a genius, and he was right in both descriptions. He said that he was a bit weird but that he loved the guy, and that I should do whatever he said without questioning it.

On that morning we schooled 26 horses between us, one of which was Theme Arena, the tiny filly I was riding in the Taunton seller. Trainers occasionally do school a horse on the day of the race, but that tends to be only horses with jumping issues. Theme Arena had never run over hurdles before, so I did not view being asked to give her a final late pop over hurdles as a particularly encouraging sign. Martin showed me two small baby hurdles and asked me to take her over them, which I did. She jumped them beautifully, so when I trotted her back to Martin I was left perplexed when he told me to get off her. I asked him if he was sure that was all he wanted me to do. Instead of directly answering the question, he asked me, 'How did she jump?' I told him she had been brilliant, to which he said, quick as a flash, 'Yes, I know. I just wanted you to know that before the race.'

Martin had gone to the trouble of bringing me into his stable purely so that I would have no doubts about the jumping abilities of a petite hurdling newcomer. The exercise had been carried out so that I would go into the race full of confidence in the filly. His plan worked. In the paddock, Martin told me to try and jump off in front and go as fast as possible from start to finish. I carried out his instructions and discovered what so many other jockeys, trainers and punters had long since realised: Martin Pipe's horses never stopped galloping. He had revolutionised the sport by making his horses fitter than anyone else's, and, even at the level of a lowly Somerset seller, Theme Arena was an example of that.

Martin Pipe did not only call on my services for sellers. Tony McCoy now had first pick of the vast majority of the Pipe string but Martin was still good enough to use me whenever he could. And on one of those occasions he was responsible for giving me a major thrill at the greatest meeting of all, the Cheltenham Festival.

I can clearly remember my first visit to that incredible racecourse. It was different to what I had expected, but still wonderful. I knew Cheltenham primarily from the pictures that Mam and Dad had put up around the house, and from watching the BBC's television coverage as a young lad. When I first went, the winner's enclosure and weighing room had all been changed from the days when those pictures at home were taken. It was an even bigger and an even more breathtaking place than I had imagined. And it was so very beautiful. The sight of Cleeve Hill guarding the racecourse filled the eyes and swelled the heart. Watching races there was more exciting and intense than anywhere else, and the reception given to winners, particularly during the Festival, was so genuine, loud and stirring that the hairs on the back of my neck stood to attention. I adored it. Then, when I first got the chance to ride there, I was reminded why I so loved jumping.

When you ride a horse over obstacles you feel part of a team in a way that never happens on the Flat. It is horsemanship raised to a new level. The feel of riding over a jump is incomparable. The speed, the exhilaration and the sense of balance are intoxicating. I found Flat racing easy. I let the horse find its own rhythm and then worked off instinct. Jump racing required more connection between man and beast. And at Cheltenham, man and beast had to work as one more so than anywhere else.

Dad had given me my first Festival mount, Final Run, who finished 14th in the 1995 County Hurdle one year before managing a more respectable sixth in what is now the Pertemps Final. The 1997 Festival promised much more, and began in earnest with a ride in the biggest hurdle of the year, the Champion Hurdle, aboard Dad's Guest Performance. Unfortunately, Guest Performance needed more help than I or any other jockey could possibly have given him. He finished where his 100-1 odds suggested he would finish, in last place.

The Festival's second and third days were always likely to give me my best chance of a winner. That proved to be the case. I was no stranger to winning at Cheltenham having landed a novice hurdle at one of the track's December meetings on Daraydan. Martin trained the former classy Flat stayer for his biggest owner, David Johnson, and they were good enough to let me get back on the horse for the Royal & SunAlliance Novices' Hurdle, then the Wednesday opener. David is a very keen punter and tends to place a fair bit more than your average £20 merchant so I knew there was a lot at stake when I was told that he had backed Daraydan each-way. David's support played a part in what should have been an outsider being backed into 16-1. Approaching the final flight he must have thought himself in with a chance of collecting not only on the place part of his bet but also the win half. Three of us jumped the flight in unison, but I felt I was ever so slightly in front of Mighty Moss and the future triple Champion Hurdle winner Istabraq. Not for long, though. Up the hill Istabraq and Mighty Moss both began to edge away from me, and despite rallying close home, my lad had to settle for an extremely honourable third.

Later the same afternoon I rode a future Festival winner – that day under Andrew Thornton, not me – when helping French Holly into sixth in the Champion Bumper. He was trained by Ferdy Murphy, as was the horse who one day later provided me with my most embarrassing moment as a jump jockey.

Paddy's Return should have won the Stayers' Hurdle but did not, very largely down to me and the tactics I adopted. The previous year's

Triumph Hurdle winner was stepping up to three miles for the first time but was doing so without the help of usual jockey Richard Dunwoody, who preferred the claims of Jimmy Fitzgerald's Trainglot. Paddy's Return had won the Triumph Hurdle thanks to his stamina and a power-packed finish that propelled him up the fearsome Cheltenham hill. Ferdy wanted me to ride him the same way, so I set out with the intention of dropping him in and bringing him with a late run.

The early stages went as I had hoped they would, but only to a degree. I settled him into last place, which is what I had wanted to do, but he was not showing his hurdles any respect and was nudging flight after flight. I decided he needed a bit of a wake-up call so I looped him around some of the other backmarkers, my thinking being that this would rev him up a little. I had revved him up a lot.

Going down the back straight for the second time he jumped his way on to the heels of the leaders. Another big leap at the ninth of 12 hurdles took him into the lead. I was praying that someone would take over in front, and one hurdle later someone did, David Bridgwater on the 9-2 favourite Escartefigue. David, however, did not just go on. He set about ripping the rest of the field apart. All of a sudden he was galloping away from the rest of us. I had to decide what to do. Should I go in pursuit and follow him or should I play a waiting game in the hope that Escartefigue ran out of puff and came back to us?

I went for the first option, and in doing so made a terrible mistake. Escartefigue's move took its toll much sooner than I had expected. Having got Paddy's Return into top gear running down the hill, I had reeled in the leader by the second-last flight. Now I was in front and my only option was to carry on kicking and hope that the pack would not catch me. It was a faint hope. The run between the final two hurdles on Cheltenham's New Course is both long and uphill. Out on his own with no other horses to help him, Paddy's Return ran into a metaphorical hole. Karshi and Anzum collared us at the final flight, which my horse walked through. He had died in my arms. There was no more he could give, and he finished third in a race he ought to have won.

Ferdy was not happy, and nor was the owner Paddy O'Donnell. They pointed the finger at me, and I had to take their criticism on the chin because they were right. Had I ridden Paddy's Return in the usual Hughesie style I would have enjoyed Cheltenham Festival success for the first time. I had only myself to blame. What didn't help was that everyone else blamed me as well. Norman Williamson, Charlie Swan and Paul Carberry slag me off about it to this day. Even Dad has been known to join the attack!

That was an off day, but, without trying to sound cocky, it misrepresented my capabilities as a jump jockey. I believe that had I wanted to I could have got to the top of the jumping game. Others thought so too, including one of Ireland's top jumps trainers, Mouse Morris, who once offered me the chance to ride all his horses. I was unable to accept his offer but I did ride the horse that he sent to the 1998 Festival as the Irish banker.

His Song possessed exceptional claims. I had been on his back when he won a Grade 3 novice hurdle at Leopardstown's Christmas meeting, and again when he stepped out of novice company to beat everything but Istabraq in the Irish Champion Hurdle. He had made Istabraq dig deep and on that form had to be the one to beat back against his own kind in the Festival's traditional curtain-raiser, the Supreme Novices' Hurdle.

The pressure of riding Ireland's banker was immense and, unusually for me, I felt it. More than I ever had before, I saw myself as a Flat jockey playing at being a jump jockey. I got it into my head that if anything went wrong, I would get the blame. I did not want to be branded as the Flat jockey who messed up. That said, I do not feel that I did mess up. Mouse told me to play safe and line up on the outside. I did not. I rode him with balls. I positioned him on the inside and gave him the perfect ride. Running down the hill towards the third-last flight we were cantering. I was already imagining what our victory reception was going to be like. But then, when I began to push him, I had to think again. French Ballerina and Graham Bradley were not stopping in front and we were not catching her. On good ground that was quicker than His Song wanted, he was unable to find the turn of foot needed to reel in the leader. A sinking feeling came over me on the run to the last hurdle as French Ballerina quickened further away. Riding up the hill with no hope of winning was a dejecting, deflating experience. The fact that the winner was trained in Ireland was no consolation whatsoever.

It was a turning point for me. I felt that a jump jockey had beaten a Flat jockey. Since then, part of me has always believed that I would now be out of place riding at the Festival. It is jump racing's flagship fixture so should it not be for jump jockeys to enjoy? Would I be an interloper, an outsider seeking to muscle in on their special four days, if I ever again tried to take rides at the Festival? I'm sure that if Paul Nicholls or Willie Mullins ever rang me asking if I could ride an odds-on favourite in the Champion Hurdle I would bite their hand off. But if I did, I would still be a Flat jockey pretending to be something else. And even if such an opportunity did come along, I doubt it could ever top my most memorable Cheltenham moment, a moment in which I had no direct involvement but one that left me as happy and emotional as I have ever been on a racecourse.

The horse at the centre of it all was Hardy Eustace. He came along just as Dad was climbing out of that horrible slump in fortunes, after Professor Tom Buckley and his team at the Irish Equine Centre discovered aspergillus in the yard, which started to turn things around. Hardy Eustace seemed to represent Dad's revival, but his was not a story without enormous sadness that far exceeded any disappointments we might have known on the racecourse.

When Hardy Eustace won for the first of three times at the Festival, his jockey was Kieran Kelly. By the time he won for the second time, Kieran was no longer with us. Kieran, a fine rider and a lovely fellow, established a place on the racing map by winning the 2003 Royal & SunAlliance Novices' Hurdle on Hardy. He had needed confidence going into Cheltenham and the victory gave him that confidence. I don't think that Kieran had believed in himself or in his talent until he proved himself by winning a Grade 1 race on jumping's showpiece stage. Five months later he was dead, after a fall from one of Dad's horses, Balmy Native, in a handicap chase at Kilbeggan. Balmy Native was a horse that Kieran knew well. As Dad was his boss, he had ridden him in numerous races – 20 in all – and had won on him twice. His fall, five fences from home, was the sort of tragic accident that can always happen in our sport. Kieran, just 25 years old, suffered head injuries from which he could not recover.

Dad, understandably, was devastated and felt inevitable pangs of guilt, even though he had done nothing wrong and nobody blamed him for what had happened. Five of us flew across to the funeral on Richard Hannon's plane. It was a distressing occasion, a permanent full stop on a life cut cruelly short.

Hardy Eustace, however, was still an active racehorse with, in theory, his best days in front of him. Part of me had yearned to ride him when Kieran was Dad's jockey. My job with Prince Khalid Abdullah prevented it happening, but even if it had not, I am sure Dad would have turned me down as Kieran was his rider and Dad has always been fiercely loyal. After Kieran died, I can honestly say that the thought of taking over on Hardy never crossed my mind. Conor O'Dwyer was the first person to ring with an enquiry about the mount, and he was the one who got the ride. He proved the perfect replacement for Kieran.

Going into the 2004 Festival, Hardy had been having a fair season but no more than that. He had finished second back at Cheltenham in the Cleeve Hurdle, and in his final Cheltenham prep race finished second in an uncompetitive Grade 2 event at Gowran Park. A few days before the start of Festival week, Dad was still not sure which race to run him in. He had left him in the Champion Hurdle, but his form during the season did not merit running in it and bookmakers made him a 50-1 outsider. More attractive to me was the Coral Cup, a handicap in which he could have carried 11 stone – equivalent to a mark of 150, about 20 pounds shy of what you would expect an average Champion

Hurdle winner to be rated. I told Dad he surely had to run the horse in the handicap. Dad did not agree. He was very much swinging towards the Champion. I pointed out to Dad that any winner at Cheltenham is special, but Dad was convinced that Hardy Eustace could take out the Champion. The horse had been flying at home in blinkers. He was not necessarily the fastest or classiest horse, but neither was Monksfield. You really have to stay two and a half miles to win the Champion and we knew that Hardy did that. 'I've got to let him take his chance,' said Dad. It was a reckless, foolish and completely brilliant decision.

When at Cheltenham, I love watching races from the stands, and I found myself an ideal space among the masses for the Champion. I borrowed a pair of binoculars and fixed them on Hardy as he set off in front. As the race continued, the binoculars became redundant because I couldn't keep them still. I fixed my gaze on the big screen instead and saw that Hardy was not stopping. Every time a horse got close to him, he pulled away. He was utterly relentless. Even when the previous year's winner, Rooster Booster, came at him on the final bend, Hardy found another gear and drew clear to win by five lengths.

Just thinking about it now almost makes me want to cry. I have never been so emotional after any race. Dad had nearly been driven mad during his time in the wilderness. For far too many years he and Mam had only been able to maintain any sort of positivity by watching me winning Flat races. Dad knew he had not become a bad trainer, and Mam, my sister Sandra and I knew it as well. As ever, he was a real steady Eddie after the race, but the rest of us were ecstatic, more jubilant than we had ever been before. We could not have been more proud. A thoroughly fine man had been given the reward he deserved.

And then he did it again the following year. I remember being stood in the stands with Dad and Noel Meade, whose Harchibald was strongly fancied to run a big race under Paul Carberry. As in 2004, Conor sent Hardy straight into the lead, from where he expertly dictated a moderate pace, which he gradually wound up from the top of the hill. Jumping the final flight, he was locked in a titanic battle with Harchibald and Brave Inca. With 100 yards to run, the writing was on the wall. Brave Inca had been shaken off but Paul was sitting motionless on Harchibald, just waiting to complete one of the cockiest, cheekiest wins in Champion Hurdle history. 'Well done Noel,' said Dad, resigned to second place. The resignation did not last long, for when Paul got serious on Harchibald, the horse found absolutely nothing. He had loads of talent but he was not a grinder and he either could not or would not go past Hardy. Dad, a Champion Hurdle winner as a jockey, had now trained a dual winner of the race.

It was a memorable time for us all. Just a few days later I had the final drink of my life. Since Hardy's second Champion Hurdle I have been sober and Dad's training career has soared to new heights. Hardy Eustace, a jumper I never rode over jumps, gave me by far the best jumps experience I have ever had.

When my job with Prince Khalid ended, so did the ban on me riding over jumps. As one door closed another was opening, and I wanted to go through it. I wanted to enjoy another fling with racing over hurdles.

It turned out to be a very brief, albeit enjoyable, dalliance. Over the next two seasons I rode in a total of just 18 hurdle races, 11 of them in Ireland and seven in Britain, where in December 2007 I posted my only winner of the stint, on Dad's Lyceum in an Ascot novice hurdle. There were no notable near misses but I did come close to riding in two of the winter's most prestigious events.

In 2008 I was offered the mount on the previous year's Champion Hurdle winner, Sublimity, in a Fighting Fifth Hurdle that was due to be staged seven days late at Wetherby following an abandonment at its usual venue, Newcastle. Regular pilot Philip Carberry was unavailable and I was keen to take the ride but was unavailable to do so due to other commitments. I had also wanted to take a ride at Newbury on the day the Fighting Fifth was originally supposed to be held. The problem was the horse was due to run in the Hennessy Gold Cup, one of the great staying chases. The horse's trainer asked me if I could be at Newbury, and

I could, and I wanted to ride him, and I knew that it would be a dream fulfilled, and yet I knew that it was not going to happen. I felt I had to consult Dad, knowing full well what his answer was going to be before I asked the question. He told me I would be mad to ride him. He reckoned the horse had no chance of winning (Dad turned out to be right), and that even if he had I would be risking a heavy fall. His considered view was that I would need my head testing if I agreed to the offer. I didn't.

It did not take long for someone else to take umbrage at my jumping jaunts. I was leading a huge field in an Irish handicap hurdle when my mount fell, sending me crashing to the ground and into the path of over a hundred hooves. Luckily I had a soft fall, but that had no impact on the opinion of Richard Hannon, who watched the race at home and was horrified by what he had seen. When I had ridden over hurdles in the years before the Abdullah job, Richard had been one of the trainers who had supplied me with mounts. Now, though, I was Richard's stable jockey and his operation was considerably bigger. Richard called Lizzie that night and told her to tell me that if I carried on riding over hurdles I would have to find a new trainer. He meant it, and I totally understood where he was coming from. At the time, Richard would have had around 150 two-year-olds being prepared for the new Flat season. He needed my help, but I was putting myself at risk. In his eyes I was being selfish, and I could not really challenge that view. There and then I closed that chapter of my life.

And as I close this chapter of the book, I look back on my jumping days with a smile on my face. I emerged from them in one piece having achieved a fair amount, if not everything I had wanted. I still have to ride over fences – watch this space – and a Cheltenham Festival winner has eluded me. Maybe one will come my way, but maybe it is best that one does not. As I said, a Flat jockey at Cheltenham is a jockey muscling in on an event that really belongs to others, to people more deserving of the unparalleled buzz it provides. Those who risk their lives and limbs on a daily basis should be the ones who get to enjoy the Festival.

And how they deserve it. I like jump jockeys, respect them and admire them. They are a breed apart, sportsmen and women of the very highest order. I love the atmosphere you find in a Flat weighing room, but to be inside a jumps weighing room is different. A sense of incomparable camaraderie unites its members. I doubt you would experience that feeling anywhere else. Sit inside a weighing room at Cheltenham, Aintree, Plumpton or Punchestown and you will see lads laughing and joking. But there is another layer to their behaviour. When Flat riders come into the weighing room, we change our colours, tie our caps and head out for the next ride. Jump jockeys have more respect for what they are about to do. Without being in the least bit scared they embrace a fear factor. There is always the unspoken understanding that when ten riders go out for a race, one might not come back.

When I think of a jumps weighing room, I picture men with cuts to their lips, bloody noses, and arms in slings. More than anything, I smell the unmistakable odour of Deep Heat. Part of me longs to be back with them. Part of me knows they are a class apart.

14

THE BOSS

Richard Hannon could hardly have been more different to Prince Khalid Abdullah. For seven years, my boss had been someone with whom I had next to no direct contact. As Prince Khalid's retained rider I was committed to up to seven of his trainers at any one time, but I had also always ridden regularly for Richard when that suited us. With my services now freed up, it made sense for both parties that our association became fixed. It has been a dream union, so much so that I cannot ever imagine riding as stable jockey to anyone other than Richard Hannon. In time, it is almost certain that I will be stable jockey to another Richard Hannon, a younger version of the one who now holds the trainer's licence, but I don't believe for a second that things will significantly change.

It is true that Richard and I are bound together by more than just horses, but that has little bearing on the way he treats me. I may be the husband of one of his daughters and the father of two of his grandchildren, but when on the gallops, in the office or at the racecourse, I am his jockey. I would not want it any other way, nor would I want to work for anyone else for as long as Richard is happy running his championship-winning stable.

It was Richard who first offered me my ticket out of Ireland. It was Richard who, way back in the summer of 1994, told me that he would support me with rides and opportunities if I moved to Britain. Since then he has been a constant supporter, through bad times as well as good. When I have made mistakes in my personal life, he has forgiven me; even when things were at their worst I never once felt anything other than a loved and valued member of his family. It takes a special man to treat me in the way that Richard has treated me, and that deep decency extends not just to matters at home but also at work. Richard was a tremendously successful trainer long before I came along, but I would like to feel that I have at least made some contribution towards the success that made him champion in both 2010 and 2011. During my seven years riding for Juddmonte, Richard trained four Group 1 winners, of which I partnered two. In the following four years he saw his star soaring and trained ten Group 1 winners, of which I was on eight. When working together we have become a potent force.

Even before I parted with the Prince, Richard showed enormous loyalty towards me, never more so than before the 2007 Coronation Stakes, in which we were due to run Indian Ink, with whom we had combined to land the previous autumn's Cheveley Park Stakes at Newmarket. Back on the Rowley Mile for the 1,000 Guineas, the filly was only able to manage fifth. She was at her best in the mud – as she had emphasised when taking the Cheveley Park and also a valuable Ascot sales race – but the Guineas took place on conditions that were every bit as quick as the official good-to-firm description. The Rowley Mile is a track that I feel has deteriorated since I came to Britain and the ridges that run down the racecourse are now more pronounced than they once were. It can be a horrible place if your horse meets the ridges wrong, and on fast ground the problems become magnified. Indian Ink did not enjoy the experience so I minded her with an eye to the future. I thought I had done the right thing, and so did Richard, but it seemed that someone close to Indian Ink's owner, Raymond Tooth, did not. When we opened a midweek copy of the *Racing Post* we saw that Seb Sanders had been jocked up for the ride. Richard was incensed and rang Raymond to find out why he did not want to use his stable jockey. Raymond replied that he had no idea what Richard was talking about. As Richard and, it turns out, Raymond had always wanted, I rode Indian Ink at Royal Ascot, where on testing ground she strolled home for a six-length win.

That year's Royal Ascot also showed me a lot about Richard as a person. We had been enduring a desperate time. For us, as for so many yards, Royal Ascot is the most important meeting of the year. We always plan for it months in advance. The owners adore having runners over the five days and winning at Royal Ascot is undeniably more enjoyable than winning anywhere else. It therefore follows that when things go badly at the royal meeting, the let-down can be enormous. That year things were going particularly badly. Come the Coronation Stakes, the fourth-day highlight, we were still without a winner having seen a lot of horses from whom we had expected big things flop. In the minutes leading up to the Coronation I was feeling depressed, and when Richard came into the weighing room to collect my saddle I asked him what on earth we were going to do. 'What are you worrying about?' he responded. 'We're here now. We might as well enjoy it.'

In those few words, Richard summed up one of the reasons why he has been among the best of his profession for so long. His constitution for taking disappointment and defeat is unbelievable. Any racing stable, no matter how brilliant their horses, will always endure times when little goes right. The trainer, as head of the stable, needs to send out the right signals to his staff and his owners. Richard is as good at doing this as anyone I have met. He is as magnificent in defeat as he is in victory.

Richard is also not the person that almost everyone seems to think he is. For a start, he is incredibly shy, bordering on soft, as you sometimes see from his emotional reaction to important wins. As such, he hates confrontation and will do anything he can to avoid it. If something has bugged him at the races, he will invariably say nothing until safely on the way home. And when he is at home and relaxing he enjoys watching a bit of TV with a cup of tea – which brings me to another popular conception about Richard Hannon.

He is not a big drinker. It bugs me when people describe him as someone who always has a champagne glass in his hand. Nothing could be further from the truth. Richard will happily go from one week to the next without having a single drink. When he is having dinner at home you will not find a glass of wine to the right of his plate. It's just not him. Richard's philosophy is simply that when he is out for a few drinks he will have a few drinks. When he goes racing he enjoys himself and makes sure that his owners do as well. That is one of the reasons why people love having horses with us. When owners come to the yard, Richard will always open a few bottles, but once the owners go home, Richard stops drinking. When I was drinking we often had some great craic together, but I was the one you saw running down to the cellar for another bottle.

It's not just me he treats so well. Richard is a star boss. You would need to do something pretty horrific to hear him shouting around the yard. Admittedly he is prone to a spot of grumpiness, but Richard has lived long enough, seen enough and put up with enough to be allowed a few grumpy mornings. You tend to find that if Richard has a cigarette in his hand he is in a good mood – and when he has a cigarette in his hand it often means he is heading off to the races later that day. Richard does not like being cooped up in the house too much. He lives for being in the yard or at the racecourse. But even when he is feeling a little grouchy, he is never a tyrant towards the stable staff. The yards at Herridge and East Everleigh are free of tension. If someone turns up for work late, he is late. He or she doesn't have £20 docked from their wages. Richard appreciates that anyone can sleep in or not hear their alarm. Crucially, because he is so easy-going with the staff, they respect him, work hard for him and want to please him. The last thing anyone tries to do is take advantage of his kindness.

In terms of his approach to training, Richard believes in his own ability and keeps things simple. People think that we gallop the brains out of our horses, but in fact exactly the opposite is true. Our horses are never overworked. Having ridden for numerous leading trainers, I think I can say with some confidence that Richard Hannon's horses gallop less than anybody else's. However, where they also differ is that they are given fast canters every day. It is this that makes them so fit. The groundwork is laid down through the depths of the winter so that come the middle of March they are ready to start working hard in advance of the new season. Some trainers take a very softly-softly approach with their juveniles before galloping them hard. Richard does it the other way around. The two-year-olds canter quickly on a daily basis and might only have a couple of pieces of proper work before they make their debuts. The intensity of the process can give them sore shins, but that happens to almost every horse at some stage of their lives and they emerge from the experience stronger, hardier and more durable athletes. Initially it can be arduous, especially for the slower babies. You spot the ones who just physically can't keep up with the rest and they are dropped back to third lot. However, at the same time the cream rises to the top, and when you spot a juvenile sailing to the peak of the gallop on the bridle while an older horse is being pushed along, you make a note of his name.

Key to Richard's strategy is that when he does find a two-year-old of way above-average ability he is never afraid to run him or her, regardless of how early in the season it is. Many trainers will spy a smart colt and put him away for the autumn. Richard runs horses that others would not. If one of ours comes to hand early, he runs. Moreover, some of them win races exactly because they are bigger and stronger than the horses they are racing against. Come their three-year-old season, the other horses might progress faster and overtake them. We give horses the chance to give of their best when it is the right time for them to give it. That is why I think we clean up in so many of the major two-year-old races.

Another reason behind our recent domination of two-year-old events is Richard's magic eye at the sales. With the help of his old friend

Peter Doyle, he annually comes home from Tattersalls, Doncaster and Goffs with outstanding prospects for the following year. If he sees a yearling walking by him that he likes, he will set out his stall to buy the horse, even before he has seen the pedigree. There are certain stallions that he does not admire, but generally he is very open-minded. Understandably, when a yearling looks likely to make serious money, Richard becomes more cautious and makes a closer inspection of the animal's breeding. What he likes to see is that the bloodlines on the top and bottom of the page show consistency. By that I mean that if a yearling's sire was a sprinter, Richard will look for plenty of speed throughout the sire line. He hates to see a yearling whose sire was a sprinter by a stayer out of a miler. To Richard, that does not bode well.

Some people say that he buys cheap horses and gets lucky but that is absolute rubbish. There is no luck involved whatsoever. Every horse that Richard buys at auction is available for anybody else to purchase. The fact that they do not means that either he is better at it than they are or they are worse. Not everybody realises this either: Richard spends a considerable seven-figure sum each September and October buying yearlings using his own money. He is rarely sent orders. He buys the animals that he likes and then sets about selling them on to owners. Such is his track record, owners now come to him, queuing up to take advantage of his expertise. Should any remain without immediate takers, Richard does not fret as he is an expert salesman. He could flog sand to Arabs. Once a horse is sold, Richard will correctly identify it every time he sees it. He will be able to tell you the yearling's sire, dam, where he bought it, how much he paid for it and who he sold it to. And once a horse does get a new owner, Richard keeps him or her regularly updated on its progress, whether the owner is a long-standing client, like Julie Wood, or a newcomer to the business.

Every one of Richard's owners is important to him, but it would be fair to say that one stands out in particular. He takes huge pride from being one of the Queen's trainers. Richard is not what you would expect a royal trainer to be. He was not born into money and bought a yard that contained just 12 horses when taking over from his father in 1970. He is a grafter who speaks without the slightest hint of a plum in his voice. He is a man who climbed the racing ladder without any fancy patrons until the Queen first sent him horses. Indeed, it was only in the autumn of 2011 that Sheikh Hamdan joined the yard, giving Richard his first link-up with the Maktoum family since the mid-1990s, when he briefly trained the odd horse for Mana Al Maktoum, for whom he won the 1995 Jubilee Handicap with a smart miler called Desert Green.

Having the Queen as one of his owners means a massive amount to him and he gets a huge buzz out of the days when she comes to see her horses. After the inspections have taken place, Her Majesty is shown into Richard's sitting room, which is in itself an honour as most other owners, even Sir Alex Ferguson, get entertained in the kitchen. Richard's wife, Jo, will have bought some nice smoked salmon and the Queen will enjoy either a coffee or a gin with Dubonnet. Also in the room will generally be the Queen's racing adviser, John Warren, his wife Carolyn, Richard junior, Ryan Moore and myself, both of us in our best jodhpurs. We might spend as much as an hour together and Richard will be at his brilliant best, completely relaxed, completely natural and thoroughly entertaining.

Like Richard, I find it a privilege to be able to work for the Queen. She is a lovely lady to be around and an extremely easy one to ride for. She sees her horses as her little babies and just wants you to do your best on them. I remember Richard once passed his mobile to me and said one of the owners wanted a word. It was the Queen. I nearly died. A little less nerve-racking was the 2008 Chesham Stakes, in which we gave the Queen a Royal Ascot winner with her then two-year-old Free Agent. From early in the spring the plan had been to give the colt one run in a maiden, win it, and then go on to the Chesham and win that as well. The plan was executed to perfection, and anyone who saw the television pictures of the Queen's reaction will know just what winning the race meant to her.

Having the Queen as one of his owners is, I believe, one of the reasons why Richard has been reluctant to retire and hand over to Richard junior. He has nothing to prove and he knows it. He is very much prepared to pass on the licence, but he has it in the back of his mind that when he buys yearlings and sells them on to owners, it is then his duty to train them. It is for that reason that I think Richard will announce his retirement in the middle of a season.

When he does, the two yards will carry on as usual. I am convinced that Richard junior will make a fantastic trainer in his own right. He is more like his dad than you could ever believe and is also a genuinely nice, unpretentious guy. Importantly, he keeps good company, and in the last few years has developed an impressive number of his own clients. In tandem with Peter Doyle's son, Ross, he also buys many of the yearlings himself, and he buys too many good ones, including Canford Cliffs and Paco Boy, for him to have a bad eye. Richard junior also has at his side a real asset in the form of his wife Jemima, a fine event rider and for a short while my apprentice when she was training for a charity race at Newbury, where she discovered the joy of riding with a shorter stirrup length.

Richard junior does like to have a good time, as he showed when his dad invested in some quad bikes. Richard junior, Sylvester Kirk and I were out on them one morning when Richard junior got a bit carried away and seemed to convince himself that he was the new Evel Knievel. He was having a right old time, messing around and spinning in circles, when the guv'nor approached in his Jeep. Richard junior was oblivious to this, and noticed all too late, by which point his father was stood by him with a face like thunder. Richard junior got off the quad bike, looked at it and kicked the tyre before saying that he thought there was something wrong with it. 'The only thing wrong with it is the pillock who was riding it,' said Richard. Sylvester and I watched events unfold in hysterics.

Both Richards are top men, as are the people around them. Two key members of staff, and two men I regularly consult, are Tony Gorman and Steve Knight, the excellent head lads at Herridge and East Everleigh respectively. I rely on both. Richard's phone never stops ringing and he is constantly talking to owners. I try, where possible, not to bombard him with any more questions, so I speak regularly with Tony and Steve. If I need to know something about one of the horses I will often turn to them first.

Given the quality of the people working for Richard, the two yards are great places to spend time, and at the heart of it all is not just Richard but also his wife. Jo Hannon is in fact the backbone of the entire operation. There is always someone unconnected to the family walking into and out of her kitchen but she never complains and instead welcomes everyone with open arms and an oven full of sausages. She is also hugely proud of her husband and makes a daily check in the *Racing Post* to see exactly where he stands in the trainers' championship.

The other members of the family are less connected to the yard but are all smashing people, not least Mrs Lizzie Hughes, who also pops in to see her mum and dad whenever she can. Lizzie and Richard's twin brother Henry works in property, but he does begin to take a close interest in the yard about ten days before Royal Ascot, which he looks forward to as much as Christmas. He is a great help to both Richards during the meeting and when things aren't going so well he is very much like his father, in that he is able to see the bigger picture. He knows that there is much more to life than racing, and he tells us so.

Fanny, though married to Sylvester, remains part of her father's team and goes through all his sales catalogues, marking out which lots she thinks he should look at. She has a great eye for a horse, not just on the page but also in the flesh. Dad bought a yearling at Goffs a while back that he asked Fanny to inspect. She told him she didn't like the horse, which Dad was understandably not thrilled to hear. A year later he rang me to say that Fanny had been spot on.

Richard's other two daughters, Julie and Claire, do not have an involvement in racing but I am very fond of them both. Julie is a hairdresser and does her best to make my locks look as presentable as possible. During the height of summer she will often come to Herridge and give me a trim between lots. Also regularly seen at Herridge is Julie's son Ollie, who enjoys getting his hands dirty with us during the school holidays.

As individuals, the Hannons are smashing people. Combined, they make for an amazing family and one that never ceases to surprise me. There are few things I enjoy more than when we all get together for one of Jo's gorgeous Sunday lunches. Quite how she manages it I don't know, but Jo somehow prepares enough to feed Richard, Lizzie, Harvey, Phoebe and myself, Richard junior, Jemima and their recently born daughter Eliza, Henry, Julie, her husband Andrew Garrod, Ollie and his little sister Grace – a good pal of Harvey's – and Fanny, Sylvester and their children James (my godson) and Harry. Even if I try to get some time away from the Hannon clan by going to my favourite haunt, Barbados, it's a Hannon occasion again as we see plenty of Claire, her husband Martin Ince and their children Georgie, Joseph and Hannah.

You might think me soppy for wanting to mention them all, but the Hannons mean more to me than I can say. I am an Irishman living in Britain and I now have two families, one in each country, both of which I adore.

It is not just within Richard Hannon's family and stable that I have been lucky enough to meet some smashing people. As a jockey you spend most days of the year with the same guys. Weighing rooms become like second homes. You spend hours inside them every week and it's important that you get on with its other members. For the most part, I have done. I have made friendships that will last for the rest of my life. Trying to think of jockeys I have not clicked with is difficult. There are a few, past and present, that I don't like, and they know who they are. Being a jockey is about give and take. Some want to take while giving nothing back. That annoys me.

Much more common have been the lads that I've bonded with brilliantly. There are some great characters in the weighing room and I absolutely include in that number one of my very best friends, Ryan Moore. I know full well that Ryan is not everyone's cup of tea. To outsiders he can seem sulky and rude. He is well aware of that and I have tried to encourage him to give of himself a bit more and to let the media and the public see the person that we see. Believe it or not, he is great fun to be around and enjoys a laugh as much as the rest of us.

What everyone can agree on is that he is an outstanding jockey. Seeing Ryan riding sharper and better than me was one of the motivating factors I used in the early weeks of coming off alcohol. He has remained at the top of his game ever since. Crucial to Ryan's effectiveness is that he is not afraid to lose. He knows how each horse should be ridden and he is not afraid of the consequences should things go wrong.

Like Ryan, Pat Dobbs is another member of the wider Hannon riding family whom I like, respect and admire. Away from the racecourse he is a true friend and a regular golfing buddy. At work I find him an enormous help. When faced with choosing between two of Richard's horses I don't always make the decision myself. Dobbsy knows them just as well as I do and I give a lot of weight to his views. Richard values him greatly, and I wish other trainers would value him just as much because he is an underrated jockey who deserves to get more chances in the big races.

Any discussion of my riding mates would be incomplete without mention of Martin Dwyer, or Livewire as his friends know him. With his Scouse wit, he never fails to brighten the day. He loves a joke and a prank but he can take one as well. In fact, when I was in my heavy drinking days I put the poor sod through more than he deserved. I remember – although I only just remember – one particular Ebor meeting when hotel rooms in York were even harder to come by than usual. Martin eventually found a place with one spare room, not in York but in the nearby town of Harrogate. Unfortunately, the only room that was available was the honeymoon suite and, perfectly understandably, the hotel staff assumed that Martin and I were a cosy gay couple. That impression was reinforced when we ordered room service breakfast one morning and the guy who brought it up found us lying next to each other in a four-poster bed wearing nothing but boxer shorts.

Apparently, I went particularly nuts during that trip. There was one especially difficult night that I have completely forgotten about but Martin remembers all too clearly. He had gone back to get some sleep in our four-poster but I was keen to carry on getting hammered in the bar. At 3 am Martin was woken by a phone call: it was the night porter, asking him if he could retrieve his 'friend' from the bar. When Martin came down he found me lying sound asleep on a pool table while a cleaner vacuumed the carpet around me. Martin found it impossible to wake me and had to heave me on to his shoulders and give me a fireman's lift back to the room. To show how far gone I was, I didn't stir for a second when Martin got his timing wrong carrying me into the lift and its doors closed hard on my head.

Poor old Livewire suffered when I stayed with him in Yorkshire hotels. He was again the victim during a St Leger meeting when we were booked into the Moat House hotel in Doncaster. Martin had said his goodnights first – always a dangerous thing to do – and when he tried to leave his room the following morning he found that he couldn't open the door. The reason for that was that Jimmy Fortune and I had decided that it would be a hoot to barricade Martin into his room. We dragged every bit of furniture we could find and pushed it all up against his door. There were chairs, tables, and I think very possibly a wardrobe and snooker table as well. Martin did not instantly see the funny side of his entrapment. He very much failed to see it when one of the hotel's less intelligent members of staff somehow didn't notice the stacked furniture and pushed a copy of the *Racing Post* underneath the room's door.

Readers should not, however, feel too sorry for Martin as he has been the culprit every bit as much as the sufferer, although often with me at his side. I fear that Martin and I knocked a year off Pat Eddery's riding career. We re-christened Pat 'Granddad' and took more pleasure than we should have done from winding him up. Pat was famous among other jockeys for fleeing the weighing room quicker than anybody else. After his final race Pat would be leaving the shower before you could get into it. Martin and I decided that, in his advancing years, Pat would benefit from taking things more slowly. To help him with that, we would cut off the ends of his socks so that when Pat put them on they came up to his knees. To add a little variety we would often tie knots in the arms of his shirts. The sight of a furious Pat spending half an hour undoing one of these knots while everybody was saying goodbye is one that both Martin and I hold dearly.

I must also make room here for another of my best mates, Jimmy Fortune. A fantastic rider, Jimmy can also be great craic, as I remember from one riding stint in India that we spent together. Back in the day when you were able to exceed ten miles per hour in Mumbai, Jimmy was driving another great friend, Niall McCullagh, Kieren Fallon and myself down the city's Marine Drive. Jimmy had somehow got hold of a taxi and he was speeding down the road at 60 miles per hour. Jimmy's driving seldom fails to terrify so the rest of us had donned our riding helmets, which probably left us looking a bit odd to pedestrians. This had us in stitches. We were left wetting ourselves when Jimmy changed gear and managed to pull the gearstick out of its socket. We were belting down one of Mumbai's tourist highways at the time, with Jimmy, bemused and confused, staring at this gearstick in his hand. How we survived that one remains a mystery to this day.

I remember that as a great Indian trip. There have, however, been many others. I have made countless friends in Ireland and Britain, but I have also met people in India who have come to mean an awful lot to me. They have become an important part of my life. So, too, has that incredible country.

15

MUMBAI MADNESS

You can never be prepared for India. People who have visited the country tell you what to expect. They warn you that it will be like nothing you have ever seen, but it is more than that: India is like nothing you have ever imagined. It is bewildering, intoxicating, infuriating and heartbreaking. India is, as the adverts say, incredible, and Mumbai is India at its most extreme.

I was barely more than a boy when I first went to Mumbai in early 1991, a young apprentice jockey just turned 18. I had spent the previous winter in Australia. India was nothing like Australia. India was nothing like anywhere else.

Johnny Murtagh was my travelling companion, as he had been when I made my debut in Australia. 'Travelling companion', however, makes my station in life sound far grander than was really the case. We did not go there as equals. In some ways I was merely coming along for the ride. Johnny had accepted a job riding in Mumbai during the core part of the city's racing season, which runs from December to March and therefore fits in perfectly with the off season back home. I was offered a ticket out there by Iqbal Nathani, the same owner to whom Johnny had signed, and gladly agreed, but I was fully aware that Johnny, then far more high profile than me, was the jockey Nathani really wanted. I was the equivalent of an extra little present in the Christmas stocking.

Go to Mumbai now and your breath will be taken away for a multitude of reasons. It was an astonishing city in 1991. Many of the skyscrapers that now soar into the clouds were then not even in the design stage, but Mumbai was nonetheless very much the heaving mass of people and business that it is today. The first thing that struck you was the heat, certainly if you had arrived from an Irish winter. Then you were bowled over not just by the sheer number of people but the sheer number of everything. As you walked out of the airport terminal and headed for whoever was awaiting your arrival, you were immediately approached by one person after another, all making gestures but few saying anything you understood. What they wanted was your money, and these people continue to provide the opening welcome to Mumbai. They might offer to lift your suitcase into the back of a car, but essentially they are begging. And they are not alone. The beggars were everywhere and still are today. Children on street corners hold out their hands, trying to catch the eyes of the drivers and passengers of the cars that crawl towards them. I have come to learn that many of these poor kids are merely tools of the criminal underworld, but if I see what I reckon is a genuine beggar I'll give him or her 100 rupees. It means a lot to them, and I would be lying if I said it did not make me feel better about myself.

I just described the speed of the cars as a crawl, and in large parts of Mumbai that's entirely accurate. Unsurprisingly in a city that has continued to develop rapidly, the traffic situation has only got worse. If you lack confidence driving in Britain or Ireland, go nowhere near a steering wheel in Mumbai. Driving there can be a terrifying experience. During busy times – which is most times – cars, lorries, motorcycles and bikes fill the streets. Anarchy rules. Traffic signals tend only to be obeyed when a policeman is in sight. White lines might as well not exist. If a road divided into three lanes can physically accommodate five cars then it's an odds-on shot that five cars will duly use up every available inch. They fight for space and they fight to be heard. The sound of Mumbai is the car horn. Everybody uses them. If the person in front of you is half a second late in pulling off, you beep him. If someone edges in towards your vehicle, you beep him. If you see your next-door neighbour's second cousin's best friend's sister-in-law, you beep her as well. You just beep. It drives you insane, until you become almost immune to it. Almost, but never totally. It's hard to become completely accustomed to, or at ease with, a driving environment in which many cars are not fitted with wing mirrors. There is no real need for them. For a start, they take up too much space. More importantly, nobody uses them.

The longer I have spent getting to know Mumbai, the more it has changed while always staying the same. Its soul has never altered but, like Dubai, it has modernised in parts at an incredible rate. Twenty years ago you struggled to find anything other than local products. When I first arrived in India you could not buy a can of Coke. Now it's everywhere. It is there because Mumbai has developed into one of the world's biggest centres of commerce. Some of the world's richest people live there, and if you are rich in Mumbai you are very rich indeed. Vast apartment blocks are often inhabited by a single man or family. But as the rich have got richer, the poor have got poorer. Mumbai is the city of the slums. One ramshackle hut is built to the side of, and sometimes on top of, another ramshackle hut. You wonder how on earth its inhabitants survive from one day to the next. This is poverty in its purest form, but its victims often do not see themselves as such. Mumbai might seem mad to outsiders, but to most of those who call it home it is all they have ever known.

Amid all the mayhem and confusion there is a racecourse. Mahalaxmi, a galloping right-handed track, measures almost a mile and a half in circumference. It is not the world's best racecourse but I have ridden at many that are far worse. The going is invariably rock hard but it is perfectly flat and without ridges so horses, even those with leg issues, allow themselves to stretch out. Mahalaxmi is India's premier racing venue, home to all the nation's Classics, and the centre of a vibrant racing community. Trainers have their yards based around the perimeter of the racecourse and horses are exercised on the track in full view of anyone who wants to watch. Everything happens within the confines of the community, and like any racing community, be it in Newmarket, Lambourn, the Curragh or Chantilly, it becomes its own little society.

In Mumbai you have to learn quickly, and I did. It took me very little time to realise that a jockey needed to be careful. You constantly had to have your wits about you. There were people you could trust and people you could not. The racing mattered in itself but it was primarily a vehicle for betting, even in the eyes of many owners and trainers. People were suspicious. Because on that first visit I had gone to work for a renowned gambler in Nathani, they presumed that I was his man and his alone. I suffered because of that. I was riding out every morning, but on the two afternoons each week when racing took place I was largely just a spectator. Thankfully for me, there was Ivor.

If there is a lovelier man in the world than Ivor Fernandes he would be hard to find. Ivor began his life at Mahalaxmi as the racecourse commentator before embarking on a training career in 1983. He is a gentle, kind man, and he saw in me a young foreigner who was new to Mumbai and frustrated. Ivor approached me and asked if I would ride for him, and I readily agreed. We clicked immediately and have gone on to become great friends. Whenever I have returned to India I have ridden for Ivor, but he has done more than just supply me with rides. On those occasions when I have been in trouble with the local stewards and called into disciplinary hearings, he has advised me, prepared submissions for me, and then represented me. He is a fine trainer, but he would be an equally potent barrister.

Ivor also knows how to ready a horse to peak on the day that matters. Together we became adept at pulling off some monster gambles, including one with a two-year-old newcomer.

At home, punters know nothing about unraced horses except for the bare facts laid out in the racecard. You might hear of gallops reports, but apart from that you're in the dark. Not so in India. Everything that happens in the mornings is watched and noted. All horses have an official number that must be shown on a cloth whenever they work, a policy that allows official gallops watchers to record the times of each and every piece of work that takes place. As a result, punters can have an informed view on a horse's ability when it makes its debut. To get around this, we worked our two-year-old in the deep sand track that runs around the racecourse. His times were, unsurprisingly, ordinary, but he was not, and he pulled off a sizeable coup first time out.

Another early triumph for us came with a horse called Wings Of Freedom. To evade prying eyes, we galloped him in the dark for six weeks. He had plummeted in the weights and ended up on a very attractive handicap mark. We had no doubt that he could win off his new rating and by bringing him out before daylight nobody but his connections knew that he was in flying form. One problem was that my presence on the back of a runner tended to make it a shorter price than would otherwise have been the case, so to ensure we got the best possible odds we ran him in a race that was barred to foreign jockeys. One of Ivor's apprentices, heavily tutored by me, took the mount, and steered Wings Of Freedom to an easy and extremely rewarding win.

On both occasions we beat the system, a system that is riddled with paranoia, intrigue and suspicion from top to bottom. The amount of money bet in India is barely believable and those who find themselves on the losing side of a bet always think the worst. In India you cannot be unlucky. If you are, everyone assumes you have deliberately lost. Foreign jockeys often socialise together, but if people see us they think we're planning how to fix races. They doubt everyone.

If a favourite gets beat and a punter complains, the stewards hold an inquiry. They question every ride. If you go to the rail they want to know why you didn't go to the outside, and vice versa. Every time you ride a favourite, the stipendiary steward will come into the paddock to listen to the trainer giving your instructions. If you don't ride to those instructions you're in trouble. Some days you leave the weighing room crapping yourself, and God forbid if you drop your stick. If you do, they'll accuse you of throwing the race. Every time you go out to ride you feel you have to prove your innocence by winning. It's harder for the young Indian riders as they are seldom brave enough to use their instinct. In the valuable events, they panic. They get so terrified of being blocked in they run wide off the final bend and I nip up their inner. That's how I win most of the big races – and I have been lucky to win plenty of them.

For more than two decades I have been returning to Mumbai. Some years I have headed elsewhere, including South Africa and Japan, but India has become much my most regular winter base. I have ridden for some of the top owners and trainers, including Pesi Shroff, who for years was India's outstanding jockey and has now become the dominant trainer. His horses cost more than anyone else's, they boast finer pedigrees than anyone else's, and they look better than anyone else's. The playing field is not level. Competing against him can be extremely difficult so I was fortunate to be on his side during the Classic campaign of Jacqueline, a filly who rewrote Indian racing's record books and remains by far the best horse I have ridden there.

It was partly out of respect for Pesi that I wanted to partner her in the 1,000 Guineas, held in the December of the 2009/10 season. Jacqueline raced in the colours of two of Mumbai's most respected racing figures, Vijay Shirke and Khushroo Dhunjibhoy, but she went into the Guineas as Pesi's second string. I was flown to India especially to be her jockey, which hardened my view that she must be fancied. She proved me right, showing a super turn of foot to come from almost last to first. Seven days later she completed a Classic double by beating the colts in the 2,000 Guineas, and then in early January a double became a treble when she stepped up from a mile to a mile and a half and sauntered home in the Oaks.

I like to think I looked a little like Lester that day. I went into the race oozing with confidence and settled the filly in last place. We were still out the back as we turned into the two-furlong home straight, but at no point was I ever anxious. As usual, the other jockeys fanned out across the track, leaving me with room to manoeuvre by the inside rail. When I let her go, Jacqueline went forward on the bridle. The owners told me they suffered multiple heart attacks due to the way I rode her, but Pesi praised me as the easy races were helping him to keep his champion at the level he wanted for longer. I also think the manner of the victory increased the aura around her. It was good for Jacqueline the brand.

We had to run her in the Derby. The race would have been devalued without her. She was much the best filly in training and her defeat of the colts in the Guineas suggested that she might well be the best of both sexes. We went to the race expecting to win, only for doubts to develop following a dramatic turn of events on the day of the race.

On Derby morning, Pesi was approached by a man who told him in Hindi, 'Your filly is going out of the race.' The mystery man repeated his prediction and then disappeared, leaving Pesi unsure if he had been confronted by a criminal or a madman. The encounter stayed in his mind and resurfaced in the minutes leading up to the off when it became apparent that Jacqueline was drifting badly in the betting. Pesi became agitated. He asked me how the most popular horse in India, a filly who had amassed a huge public following and was being backed by 70 per cent of punters, could be so weak in the market. I told him I had no idea why, but I was nervous. When this happens in India everyone begins looking at the jockey. I knew that if Jacqueline lost, the finger would be pointing at me.

Jacqueline was not as impressive as she had been in her three previous Classic wins but she did enough and completed a famous four-timer. She was the heroine of Indian racing. If she had raced in Europe she would have won a Group 3 but probably nothing more. In India, however, she was outstanding. She gave me some wonderful times, so much so that when our second child Phoebe was born a few days before the Derby we gave her Jacqueline as a middle name.

I have been lucky to win more Indian Classics since Jacqueline was retired. In all, I've landed 11, the most recent on Pronto Pronto in the 2011 2,000 Guineas. They might lack the equine talent of European

Classics but they are nevertheless great races to win. My most recent Indian employer, the owner Rakesh Wadhawan, told me that winning Mumbai's major races was his priority. His line to me was that he wanted a house full of trophies. He got them.

Wadhawan, like many of Mumbai's leading owners, is a prominent businessman. He has a police escort everywhere he goes, gets driven around in a bullet-proof car, and has machine guns placed all around his house. He is used to getting what he wants and, over time, he decided he wanted to win some money off the bookmakers. To help him land one punt, we began to work one of his two-year-olds in the dark. If people had known what times he had clocked he would have been a 6-4 shot, but instead he opened up at 7-1. We told the boss he would not get beat but I begged him not to back him until I had left the paddock. He followed the advice and ended up winning what must have been the guts of £1 million.

To a large extent, that is what Indian racing is about. There are always gambles that need to be landed. As a jockey, you are constantly seeking to prove yourself, not merely to demonstrate that you are a talented jockey but that you are a clean, honest jockey. Punters tend not to look favourably on anyone who has ridden a losing bet. The abuse you receive when riding back to the unsaddling enclosure can be frightening, even if you were on a rank outsider. At Bangalore racecourse, the management have had to build a large metal fence on the walkway from the paddock to the track, simply to ensure that jockeys are not attacked. It can even be dangerous in the weighing room, as the jockeys at Bangalore discovered when a riot broke out following defeats for a series of odds-on shots. During the riot's ugliest moments, a television was pulled off a wall and hurled through a weighing-room window. As far as I know, that has never yet happened at Wolverhampton.

That sort of atmosphere can make Mumbai a tense, stressful place to ride. It has never really been anything other than that, but I keep going back. Or, rather, I kept going back. I enjoyed riding morning trackwork, I enjoyed being around the horses at evening stables, and I enjoyed sitting in the racecourse breakfast garden eating melba toast spread with chilli sauce. I sometimes even derived a weird sense of amusement from being verbally abused by a crazy punter. More than anything, I enjoyed the quality of life. Lizzie and the children came out with me, which gave us the chance to enjoy some valuable time together. We stayed in a nice apartment, a lovely lady called Anita worked as our maid, and her husband Kamruddin drove me wherever I needed to go, as he had for many years.

Sadly, I cannot envisage me ever riding in India again. My latest stint in Mumbai, from December 2011 to February 2012, was a nightmare, one that I have no desire to repeat.

The problems stemmed from the fact that the horses I was riding were largely no good. Wadhawan had opted not to reinvest in top-quality new stock, which left us with second-rate performers. However, given the success we had enjoyed the previous season, punters expected us to continue our winning streak. My mounts were backed in to much shorter odds than they should have been. When they failed to oblige, punters started gossiping, complaining and making wild accusations. The stewards heard, and in Mumbai the stewards listen closely to what punters are telling them.

Early in the year I began to feel that I was a marked man. In January I became involved in a little scrimmaging and was accused of elbowing another jockey. It was a ridiculous charge but one that earned me a six-week suspension. Ivor came to my rescue. He prepared a detailed case in my defence and used my own DVD player to give a second-by-second account that proved I was innocent. Inside the appeal hearing it was faintly embarrassing. When we brought in the DVD player and showed them the still-by-still shots, the panel was left flabbergasted. They asked me about this amazing piece of technology I had brought before them. I explained that it was the machine my son used when he wanted to watch one of his Mickey Mouse cartoons.

They had no choice but to rescind the suspension, in no small part because a ban would have ruled me out of the Indian Derby, in which I was due to ride for owner-breeder Cyrus Poonawalla, for many years the most powerful man in Indian racing. Instead of a suspension, I received a tiny fine. I still felt like they were out to get me, and that they wanted me to leave. They managed it. In late February I was found guilty of not following the instructions my trainer had given. The rule in itself is plain stupid as jockeys have to act on instinct and cannot blindly follow a script. I had legitimate reasons for riding the race in the way I did, but they dismissed those reasons, and did so again at an appeal, leaving me with a six-week suspension to serve. There was a silly rumour doing the rounds that I had orchestrated a gamble on the horse who won the race. In any advanced racing nation, officials and regulators are not so naive as to act on gossip and innuendo. That is not my perception of India.

As a result of the way I was treated, I do not imagine that I will want to ride in India again. Even more significantly, I would be surprised if other leading European jockeys do not think twice about plying their trade in the country. I have always tried to plug and promote Indian racing. Efforts like that, however, will forever be in vain until India's racing authorities get their heads out of the sand and bring the sport in line with the rest of the world. At the moment, India is a racing nation where regulation is based on rumour. And that makes it look ridiculous.

It saddens me that my riding career in India could be over. With Lizzie and the children I got to live a proper family life there. But in India I have a wider family as well, a family that includes Kamruddin, Anita, their son Ketan, Ivor Fernandes, the Chenoy family, Paddy and Sharmila Padmanabhan, Dr M. A. M. Ramaswamy and so many other friends. Mumbai is a city that people tend to either love or hate. I love it. If you're not riding winners it can be a miserable place, but when things are going your way, when the sun's beating down on the back of your neck and you're surrounded by people whose company you adore, Mumbai can be wonderful.

For a long time it was my home from home. I will not allow those who ruined my last season there to destroy all the happy memories that Mumbai and its people have given me.

16

CANFORD, PACO AND SOME OTHER FAVOURITES

I love horses. Always have and always will. It might seem an odd, unnecessary thing for a jockey to say but I think it's a point worth making.

The vast majority of jockeys, I'm sure, feel like me. But not all of them. There are definitely jockeys out there who do not like horses and, worse still, who do not even respect horses. I won't name them, but they know who they are. It bugs the hell out of me that they can make a living out of the sport. They view thoroughbreds as nothing more than the tools of the trade. I hate that expression, and I hate the fact that people I ride with can demean horses to such a level. Perhaps it's because I was brought up with horses, and that my very first memories are inextricably linked to horses, that I feel about them the way I do.

It is a jockey's duty to look after the animals he rides. Our safety and future are in their hands, but it works both ways. Now and again you see a horse go down in the starting stalls. By that I mean they panic and try to flee from underneath the front or back of the gate. A horse that does that is in obvious danger of becoming wedged and breaking a leg. Sometimes I see a jockey in that situation let go of the reins and try to get out of the way. Essentially, what he is saying is that as long as he is okay, sod the poor horse. Jockeys like that should not be riding in races. The horse has not set out to hurt the jockey. The horse has just panicked. He needs to be helped, not abandoned. The jockey ought to get out of the sport and do something else.

For all that I adore horses, I try not to get too emotionally attached to the ones I am riding. A jockey has to be professional about his business without ever being heartless or unsympathetic. Sometimes, however, it is impossible not to form bonds, and there have been horses who came to mean an awful lot to me.

I was particularly close to a staying handicapper trained by Charlie Egerton called Paradise Navy. Between 1995 and 1998 I rode him 24 times, and in 16 of those races we finished fourth four times, third seven times, second twice and first on three occasions. He was exactly the sort of horse I get the biggest buzz from riding. You had to put him to sleep in the early stages and then make steady headway until you had arrived on the heels of the leaders without being noticed. The last race I won on him, a two-mile handicap at Nottingham in May 1998, was especially memorable as he won without me putting him under any pressure whatsoever. The form book describes the manner of victory as 'hard held', which pretty much sums it up. It also helped that he was owned by a racing club with thousands of members, many of whom would often turn up at the races to cheer him on.

Another good friend was Mr Aviator. Like Paradise Navy, Mr Aviator was no superstar and he was never going to win Group 1 races but he did have a real day in the sun when bagging the 2008 Royal Hunt Cup at Royal Ascot. He carried 9st 5lb, not an inconsiderable weight, and gave me everything he had and then a bit more. Through the final quarter mile he was locked in a fierce battle with the eventual second and third, Docofthebay and Royal Power. He could not have been more courageous. He just refused to throw in the towel. In the end, it was his will to win that won us the race.

Far too cruelly, his will to win was snubbed out at Lingfield only five months later. He had started to make headway at the top of the all-weather home straight when he broke down desperately badly. Sometimes you know straight away when there is no way back for a horse. This was one of those moments. The green screens went up around him and I held on to him while the racecourse vet pulled the trigger. I cried my eyes out. I was in bits. Racehorses die on racecourses, but, however often it happens, it never gets any easier, especially when you have developed a relationship with the horse.

When a horse is in that situation it is of paramount importance that he or she is treated quickly, professionally and with dignity. On the vast majority of occasions that is what happens, but on Arc day in 2011 I was involved in a horrible incident in which that was not the case.

I was riding Dever Dream for an excellent trainer, William Haggas, in the Prix de la Forêt. Early in the straight she faltered and broke down. As with Mr Aviator, it was clear that she would need to be put out of her misery, but the process was carried out abysmally by the Longchamp officials. It took them 20 minutes to euthanise the poor filly, which in my opinion was disgusting. Initially she was not injected with enough substance, and then the very cheap, flimsy sheet they put up around her began to make a terrible rattling noise. Terrified, the stricken horse reared up and almost fell over. Having been cared for superbly throughout her life, she was made to suffer needlessly in her final moments. I hope what happened caused them to reflect on how they handle similar incidents in the future.

I endured a disappointing moment of a different and far less serious nature on Arc day four years earlier when narrowly denied what would have been a fantastic win in the Prix de l'Arc de Triomphe. The horse I was partnering was another of those I've enjoyed riding most, Youmzain. Many people who watched the 2007 Arc felt Dylan Thomas was sure to be disqualified after beating Youmzain by a head.

The French stewards are notoriously strict - far too strict, really - and although Kieren Fallon, Dylan Thomas's jockey, did no harm to me, he appeared to cause what I and others considered to be serious interference to one of the leading fancies, Zambezi Sun, when shifting right and crossing him a furlong and a half out. By doing so, he arguably cost Zambezi Sun any chance of winning and, based on the French rule book, could easily have been demoted to one place behind Zambezi Sun, who passed the winning post in eighth.

I felt confident that Youmzain would be promoted to first place. I think he might well have been, but for the evidence given in the stewards' inquiry by Zambezi Sun's jockey, Stephane Pasquier, who, in my opinion, painted a very different picture of what happened on the racecourse to the one that the television pictures showed. Pasquier, for whatever reason, conveyed the impression that his mount's prospects had not been seriously damaged and that he therefore had no legitimate complaint. He turned out to be more a witness for the defence than the prosecution. It was, to say the least, frustrating.

As, very often, was Youmzain. How else do you describe a horse who finished second in the Arc three years in a row? In that sense he was undeniably frustrating, but he was also undeniably one of the most talented middle-distance horses to have raced in recent years. The summer after we finished second to Dylan Thomas there was compensation of sorts when we returned to Paris and landed the Grand Prix de Saint-Cloud. Next time out we finished third in the King George, a far from poor run that left me looking forward to another tilt at the Arc.

On this occasion he went to Longchamp without me after the owner, Jaber Abdullah, informed Mick that he wanted Richard Hills to ride. At first glance, it seemed a strange decision. Richard barely ever rode for Mick, and if I was to be replaced, nobody would have guessed that Richard would be the one doing the replacing. Jaber, however, was not always the easiest owner to satisfy, which was a factor; but a bigger one is that Sheikh Hamdan, Richard's boss, let Jaber know that his jockey did not have a ride in the race and so, as an act of courtesy and deference, Jaber informed Mick that Youmzain would have a new rider for his second tilt at the Arc.

Youmzain also had a different rider for his third tilt. This time, and with some irony given what had happened in 2007, Jaber selected Kieren Fallon, who guided the horse into the same runner-up position as myself and Richard.

Then, for Youmzain's fourth Arc assault in 2010, and the final race of his career, I was back in the plate. I had been reinstated for the Grand Prix de Saint-Cloud, which we failed to win by a matter of inches, but come the autumn he was not the same horse and managed only tenth. That was actually an extremely rare below-par effort from a grand horse who was very consistent. His downfall was that he needed races to pan out the way he liked. He loved passing dead wood. Get him in a contest where a furious gallop was guaranteed and he would thrive because he got a huge kick out of passing horses that were coming back to him. That's why he was so effective in the Arc. In a fast-run race around Longchamp's mile and a half, the inferior runners begin dropping away down the false straight. Once he had passed them, Youmzain would gather a head of steam, and although he would gallop with his head to one side he would still gallop forwards.

He was, in so many ways, a fun horse to ride. It was impossible not to like him. I do, however, think that we never ran him in the race for which he was made. Had he been trained for the Gold Cup, Youmzain would have won it. He would have tanked along most of the way before picking off those in front of him. I am confident that even the mighty Yeats would have had trouble holding off Youmzain. Unfortunately, Jaber did not fancy the idea of running his best horse in long-distance events so we never got the chance to put my theory into practice.

Even though I only won two races on Youmzain – the 2006 Great Voltigeur Stakes was the first – he very much earned a place among my list of favourite horses. However, right at the top of that list have to be the two outstanding milers who over the course of four years provided me with a constant stream of big-race victories. No account of my career would be complete without fulsome mention of the excellent Paco Boy and the sublime Canford Cliffs, the finest horse I have ever had the pleasure of riding.

Paco Boy was not as good as Canford Cliffs but he was better than any other miler I have ridden. He was small and not exactly perfectly formed, but what there was of him was all athlete. He was willing and very able and over the course of four seasons proved to be one of the smartest horses ever trained by Richard Hannon.

It was not Richard who bought him. The credit for bringing Paco Boy to the yard belongs not to Hannon senior but Hannon junior, who secured the 30,000gns purchase at a Doncaster breeze-up sale in April 2007. As a yearling nobody had wanted him, and he went through the Goffs ring without meeting his reserve. A few months later he did find a taker in Richard junior, but on pedigree, as a Desert Style half-brother to a handful of just ordinary winners, he was certainly no obvious superstar on paper. The guv'nor was very much getting the same impression when the then two-year-old Paco Boy began to be tested up the gallop. After he worked one Sunday morning, a far from impressed Senior asked Junior why he had bought a juvenile who was either slow or backward, or possibly both.

Although relegated to third lot for three months, he was persevered with, and as summer turned to autumn there were signs that he was starting to come good. Even so, when Paco Boy made his racecourse debut in a September maiden on Kempton's all-weather track, I was certainly not desperate to ride him. Brian Meehan had offered me the mount on a sure-to-be odds-on favourite called Lodi, so I asked Richard if I could have permission to temporarily jump ship. With permission granted, I helped Lodi to what was ultimately a hard-fought neck victory. A further two lengths back in third, noted staying on nicely under Ryan Moore, was Paco Boy.

The *Racing Post* race analysis remarked that 'he should be better for the experience' but I doubted that he would be good enough to win next time out at Newbury, where I preferred the claims of a stablemate who had been working nicely at home but who turned out to be useless. Ryan remained on Paco, and Paco did him proud, storming to a two-and-a-half-length win. This win was followed by another, at Newmarket's final meeting of the year, at which an initially ordinary racehorse was made to look anything but by beating a three-year-old rival into second in a six-furlong conditions event.

The runner-up that day was Wid, a decent John Dunlop-trained filly who had finished second in a Listed sprint two weeks earlier. Richard Hills had expected her to go one place better and was surprised that a two-year-old had been capable of stopping her. Impressed, he suggested to Sheikh Hamdan that he should buy Paco Boy. An inquiry was made, and a potential deal got as far as the medical examination. There it stopped. Paco was failed by the vets.

I am glad that the vets came to the conclusion they did. Had they not done, I would have missed out on three smashing seasons with a smashing horse, albeit not a horse who was always the easiest to ride. He proved particularly tricky at the start of his three-year-old campaign in 2008 when, following a winter's break, he became extremely keen at home. Back on the racecourse for an early reappearance in a Lingfield Polytrack Listed race, he was almost unmanageable. Through the event's early stages he stubbornly locked his jaw and proved incredibly difficult to pull off the rail. I dropped right out the back, mainly in an attempt to educate him. We both learnt a lot from what was ultimately an impressive win. He became an easier horse to handle and I realised just how useful a horse I was riding.

We barely had to work any harder to win the Greenham Stakes next time out, but I didn't see him as an ideal candidate for a Classic on the Rowley Mile so I suggested to Richard that we should target the French 2,000 Guineas instead. Things did not really work out for us at Longchamp, but the rest of the season was largely perfect with Paco picking up Group 2s at Goodwood and Newbury. He then finished third back at Longchamp in the Prix du Moulin before running away with his first Group 1 prize, the Prix de la Forêt, at the same venue. Not for the first time, I deserted the horse that day, choosing instead to ride at Newmarket, where I had plenty of good rides for Richard, including in two hugely valuable sales races, plus the ante-post favourite for the Cambridgeshire and the Aga Khan's Darjina, an 11-10 hotpot in the Group 1 Sun Chariot Stakes. None of them won. I have made many better decisions.

While missing out on the Forêt was disappointing, I still had plenty to look forward to with Paco Boy as a four-year-old. During the early weeks of the season I was not the only one talking about him. It did not go unnoticed that all five of his wins at three had come over seven furlongs. In his two attempts over a mile he had been beaten, firstly in the French Guineas and then when third in the Moulin. Some punters and pundits were therefore surprised by our plan to concentrate on the top mile races. We had absolutely no doubt that Paco's stamina stretched to an eighth furlong. He had only been beaten a length and a half by Goldikova in the Moulin and had not been defeated by the distance but by an outstanding mare, one who would continue to deny him over the following two years.

Winning the Group 2 Sandown Mile on his reappearance did nothing to silence the doubters. They suggested that the steadily run race, won in a relatively slow time, had represented little more than a walk in the park and that winning it did not conclusively prove his effectiveness over the distance. Leading the attack, although in a very polite and friendly way, was professional punter Matt Williams, then also one of the *Racing Post*'s leading tipsters. I became increasingly annoyed by the constant knocking of the horse. The way I saw it, had he been trained by Aidan O'Brien or Sir Michael Stoute, nobody would have questioned the programme we had planned.

When I felt close to bursting with frustration, I did something I had not done before and have not done since: I wrote a letter to the *Racing Post*. (I do now admittedly have a weekly column in the paper so I have the chance to get things off my chest on a regular basis.) In it I wrote:

I confess to having the utmost respect for Matt Williams as a racing journalist, but I must say I am somewhat baffled as to his comments regarding Paco Boy following the colt's success in the Group 2 Sandown Mile.

Matt describes Paco Boy as 'a seven-furlong specialist', and, despite the fact that the mile at Sandown is as stiff as any in Britain, I would agree that seven is arguably his ideal trip.

But with no Group 1 race in Europe over seven furlongs until the Prix de la Forêt at Longchamp in October, what does Matt expect us to do – have him kicking his heels at home until the autumn? Paco Boy has a bunch of sporting owners, who would rather have a crack at the top mile races through the summer. We'll head for the Lockinge – surely it is better to have tried and failed than never to have tried at all.

If you owned Paco Boy, Matt, what would you do – run him with his Group 1 penalty in the Group 2s, the Hungerford and Challenge Stakes, and not take on the best until Longchamp? That faint-hearted attitude has never been acceptable at Richard Hannon's stable.

Richard Hughes, Marlborough, Wiltshire

I was a man on a mission. I was desperate for Paco to prove a point by winning the Lockinge. Instead, all the race did was add fuel to the case against him. Sent off 11-8 favourite to win at Newbury, he pulled hard through the first couple of furlongs but was still seemingly full of running going into the final furlong, at which point I asked him to quicken. He did quicken, but he did not quicken for long and instead weakened into a bitterly deflating fourth.

At face value, there seemed an obvious explanation for his defeat. The *Racing Post* analysis said that Paco Boy had 'ultimately failed to get home' and highlighted my easing of the horse through the final 100 yards as evidence to support that view. However, I had eased him only because we were safely clear of the fifth and, just as importantly,

I felt something was not quite right. I was correct. When we got him home we found he had been suffering from a poisoned foot. In the circumstances, he'd done well to finish fourth.

Despite holding a genuine excuse for being beaten at Newbury, there were still plenty of people who seemed to be enjoying with a little too much relish their knocking of the horse. Undeterred and in no way disheartened, we pressed on to Royal Ascot, where we planned to stay over a mile for the Group 1 Queen Anne Stakes. If Paco was going to win he was really going to have to stay.

Gladiatorus, the favourite and, at the time, the world's highest-rated horse, was a confirmed front-runner. At Ascot he took front-running to a whole new level, setting off like the proverbial scalded cat under his Dubai jockey Ahmed Ajtebi. It seemed inconceivable that any horse could maintain that speed, so I sat well off the pace and waited to make my move. With two furlongs still to run, Gladiatorus was a spent force. Richard Hills took over on Aqlaam, closely tracked by Johnny Murtagh on Cesare, who made his bid for glory just a few strides later. All the time I was waiting, watching and ready. Racing towards the furlong pole, I was faced with a question: do I sit and showboat or do I make an early attack and prove conclusively that Paco Boy sees out a mile? I plumped for the latter and sent Paco into the lead with a stiff uphill furlong still to cover.

That final furlong was one of the proudest of my career. Having gone to the front, Paco thundered towards the winning post and pulled a length and a half clear of Cesare. In a race run at a scalding gallop over one of the toughest miles in Flat racing, Paco Boy had scored in style. I was thrilled for Richard Hannon and thrilled for the Calvera Partnership that owned the horse. But more than anything, I was thrilled for the horse.

Richard, who had been getting almost as irked as me, expressed our feelings perfectly in the winner's enclosure, saying, 'If he didn't stay today, he stayed better than the rest.' He most definitely did stay that day, and he stayed all the other days he raced over a mile. What we learnt over the coming year and a half was that while there was the odd horse better than Paco Boy, there was none braver. He would pull out more and more for you, giving so much of himself that it reached the stage where it felt as though you were riding an old man.

When he returned to Newbury the following May for a second crack at the Lockinge, there was no poison in his feet and he sauntered to the cheekiest of triumphs. Richard, who had grown extremely fond of the little horse, broke down in tears when the press started asking him questions. His reaction said plenty about him and about how much the horse he was talking about meant to him and the whole yard.

Paco was not quite able to win again after Newbury, but not for the want of trying. Nor was there any shame in his subsequent runs, in three of which he had the misfortune of coming up against Goldikova. At Royal Ascot, when attempting to defend his Queen Anne crown, he came close to taking her scalp. He was not quite able to manage it. The following year we were represented by the horse who could and did. That horse was Canford Cliffs.

The first time I had anything to do with Canford Cliffs was when Richard Hannon told me one morning to 'get on the Tagula'. After I got off the Tagula I told Richard that I had just ridden a swinging canter on the best horse he had ever trained. Nothing that happened afterwards came close to making me change my mind.

At the time, he was far from the finished article. He was still growing and was by no means the most comfortable horse to be on. Most thoroughbreds have fine big necks. In his early days Canford Cliffs did not. When you rode him at the walk it felt as though you were going downhill even when you were not. However, while he might not have been perfect in his slower paces, he was sensational when he started to go through the gears. From that very first canter I was certain we had something special. His early pieces of fast work had to be seen to be believed. But I had not just seen them, I had experienced them. I believed in them, and in him.

As with so many of his most exciting juveniles, for Canford's introduction in 2009 Richard selected Newbury. I can't ever recall being so excited about the debut of any two-year-old. Not every horse translates gallops promise to the racecourse but I could not conceive of this horse being beaten. I don't normally like giving tips but I told a few close friends that if they fancied an ante-post bet for Royal Ascot they should have whatever they could afford on Canford Cliffs for the Coventry Stakes. Richard was surprisingly nervy at Newbury, fearful, I suppose, of the bubble being burst. I tried to allay his fears. I also told Lizzie, who came racing that afternoon, that we would win by ten lengths. I was wrong: we only won by nine. I was not disappointed. He did everything that I hoped he would do. He settled beautifully – something that would not be a given in the future – he displayed a potent cruising speed, and when I asked him to quicken he responded instantly. It was a debut that had the wow factor written all over it.

It was also a debut that got us both thinking and worrying. Canford Cliffs had announced himself to the world in no uncertain terms. It rapidly dawned on us that he would suddenly have soared to the top of many shopping lists. Our fear was that Sheikh Mohammed's Godolphin operation would seek to steal him from out of our hands. We decided we had to do something about it.

At the time, Canford was owned solely by Robin Heffer, a lovely man who worked in the meat business. Robin had acquired his star horse slightly by chance. We had bought two sons of Tagula at the previous autumn's yearling sales. Canford had cost 50,000gns at Doncaster; the other, Suited And Booted, cost 48,000gns at Tattersalls. The two horses were offered to a syndicate, whose manager flicked a coin and ended up with Suited And Booted, who turned out to be by no means a bad horse but still only fetched 8,500gns when resold three years later. Canford, who remained in need of an owner after the coin toss, was eventually sold to Robin.

Although a wealthy man, Robin would have found it hard to say no if Godolphin had come along waving an open cheque book. We considered it vital to do all we could to ensure that Canford stayed with us. The thought of him disappearing one morning in a horsebox was terrifying. Richard junior, who had picked out Canford at Doncaster, was charged with finding someone who could buy 50 per cent of the horse. That way, Robin, who shared the colt with his five children, would retain half of Canford while also banking a handsome sum of money. Crucially, though, we had to find the right person, a person who we felt would be keen to continue racing the horse with us. It was decided that the right person could be Paul Roy.

We valued Canford at £600,000 and, with Robin's agreement, let Paul know that he could purchase a half-share for £300,000. Paul was no stranger to owning top racehorses having seen Sixties Icon win a St Leger in the colours of his wife Susan. The likes of Dutch Art and Fleeting Spirit had also won the couple Group 1 races, so Paul had a taste for success, as you would expect of a man who was also chairman of the sport's governing body, the British Horseracing Authority.

Not long after Paul was offered half of Canford, I got a phone call from his racing manager, Jane Allison, asking me to get in touch with her boss. I was riding at Lingfield that day, so in between races rang Paul's mobile. I told Paul I judged Canford Cliffs to be potentially the best horse I had ever ridden. Nothing I said in any way inflated my view of the horse. I meant every word and anticipated that the flattering assessment would be enough to seal the deal.

It wasn't. I must have been phoned at least six times by Paul that day. He seemed completely unable to make up his mind. He kept asking me the same questions over and over again, constantly seeking reassurance that buying into Canford Cliffs was the right thing to do. In the end, my patience snapped. It had to be his decision and I told him so, but added, 'All I can tell you is that he will win the Coventry by a street.' At long last, Paul needed no more convincing. He stumped up the money and bought the half-share.

As Canford completed his Royal Ascot preparation, I had no doubts that Paul had done the right thing. In one particularly memorable piece of work, Canford was asked to go alongside Paco Boy, who was being prepped to run on the same afternoon in the Queen Anne Stakes. Canford made Paco look ordinary. Paco might never have been the most enthusiastic horse on the home gallops, but for Canford to have run all over a Group 1-winning stablemate two years his elder was still massively impressive.

What he then did in the Coventry was even more impressive. Indeed it was awesome. I said to Lizzie on the way to Ascot that I would be disappointed if Canford didn't win by six lengths. My enthusiasm was only heightened when Paco posted a famous victory in the afternoon's opening race. Less than two hours later I was taking Canford down to post for the Coventry. In those few minutes I became ever more certain that this horse was not going to get beaten. He floated to post. The animal who had been so uncomfortable to ride in the early weeks had turned into an armchair conveyance.

Once the stalls opened he was not quite so perfect, although only in the sense that he wanted to do everything faster than me. My intention had been to drop him in before pressing the go button approaching the final furlong. Canford had other ideas. He burst out of the stalls and made my plan to get cover immediately impossible. Television pictures do not really show it, but he took a strong hold and resolutely refused to settle. At no point through the first two-thirds of the race was I in full control. Only the smallest handful of horses could possibly have maintained their effort to the line, but he not only did that, he quickened after I had taken a peek for possible dangers two furlongs from home. When I gave him a couple of educational smacks he edged left – something he would do again more than once – but despite going slightly sideways he was nevertheless still going forward at an amazing speed. I was riding an aeroplane, an equine Concorde who passed the post a six-length winner of one of the year's most demanding two-year-old tests.

I had never sat on a horse who could over-race for so long and still win. I described Canford to the waiting press as a freak. The bookmakers made him as short as 6-1 favourite for the following year's 2,000 Guineas, although Richard suggested that had he been trained by Aidan O'Brien he would have been priced up at 4-6. Robin, who had never clapped eyes on Paul Roy until that day, was ecstatic. I was equally elated, and soon even more so as I completed a wonderful Royal Ascot treble on the Jane Chapple-Hyam-trained Judgethemoment in the marathon Ascot Stakes. I had enjoyed the best day of my racing life.

Canford's unbeaten record was lost on his third start in the Prix Morny, but to the man on his back it did not feel as though I was riding the same horse. At Ascot he had oozed class, but in Deauville he was much more workmanlike. When I sought a change of gear from him, very little was given in response. We had to settle for third, a neck and a short neck behind the winner, Arcano, and runner-up, Special Duty. Future events made the form look extremely respectable as Special Duty went on to win the Group 1 Cheveley Park Stakes and, as a three-year-old, both the 1,000 Guineas and French 1,000 Guineas, although both times after being promoted from second in stewards' inquiries. At the time, though, we were gutted. On reflection, the ground might have been too quick for Canford in France – it was certainly quicker than the official description of good – but it was also noticeable that he began to edge left when I put him under pressure, just as he had done at Ascot. We concluded that it would be wise to ease off him and put him away for the rest of the season. The 2,000 Guineas remained our aim.

Through the early weeks of the spring of 2010, the aim began to look a little less realistic than we had hoped. As a juvenile he'd worked the house down. He no longer did. It was not that he was working badly, but the amazing zip that used to be present was missing. Given how highly we regarded him, we were inclined to mind him, to forgive him and to put any doubts to one side, but the doubts came to the surface when he was beaten on his seasonal reappearance in Newbury's Greenham Stakes. I opted to let him roll, as he had at Ascot. Only four rivals took him on, two of which were Arcano and another of our top three-year-olds, Dick Turpin. For much of the race Canford looked likely to see them off with plenty to spare. However, when I asked him to win his race he went quite violently left, moving from the centre of the track to the far rail in very few strides. It was another warning sign. He ran on at the one pace but it was not enough to stop Dick Turpin getting up in the final strides.

Dick Turpin again had his measure in the 2,000 Guineas, and so did the 33-1 winner Makfi. Canford finished third, his performance solidifying in my mind how I viewed the horse. He did not run a bad race, far from it, but he did not run the best race he was capable of running. From what turned out to be a nightmare draw towards the far side of the track, I struggled to get cover. He took a fierce hold, the strongest hold he had ever taken. To make matters worse, the early pace was just ordinary, but that should, in theory, have suited a colt with such an explosive turn of foot. When I asked him to deliver it, he declined. This time he shifted right. He had shirked it.

I knew what was wrong. The fire was no longer in his belly. We had mollycoddled him all winter and had then been too easy on him in the spring. He had become accustomed to having a relatively easy life and had developed a taste for it. That mentality had always been within him and it was now plainly manifesting itself. When he came off a straight line at Newbury and Newmarket, he was looking for a way out of having to work. There was no reason to give him the benefit of the doubt. The evidence was too obvious and plentiful. I remained convinced that Canford had every bit as much ability as ever. I now severely questioned his enthusiasm and resolution.

Something had to be done, and in the build-up to the Irish 2,000 Guineas I did it. Canford Cliffs needed to be put in his place and informed who was boss. He had to be taught that while he might be living in a five-star equine hotel, he had to pay for his keep. One work morning I took him to the bottom of the gallop. Then I steered him round in circles and taught him a few home truths. The air-cushioned whips we use do not hurt horses, but I still used mine enough to make my point clear. This might sound cruel, but it was not. Canford Cliffs was bred to be a racehorse. He had a job to do. By issuing a few smacks I was sparing him what would otherwise have been many more smacks in future races. I was being cruel to be kind, and my actions had the desired effect. He accepted straight away that the party was over. When he went up the gallop he was like the Canford of old. As I pulled him up at the top of the gallop, I looked at Richard and said, 'Boss, we have him back.' Richard looked at me and he looked at the horse. He knew.

Canford Cliffs hardly ever had to be smacked again. The days of downing tools were over. I knew he would demolish the opposition in the Irish 2,000 Guineas at the Curragh and I was not proved wrong. Both Makfi and Dick Turpin were missing, so we had a favourite's chance on paper, but to some the biggest doubt hanging over us was the distance. We started to hear the questions regarding staying a mile that we had heard so often with Paco Boy. Paco had silenced his critics, and so did Canford. This was the simplest of Classic wins. Never travelling anything other than strongly, he was ruthless when asserting at the furlong pole and thereafter drew clear for a breathtaking triumph. Not a single stroke of the whip was needed. I had promised Richard that we had our horse back and he was indeed back with a vengeance. It was satisfying for all of us, and perhaps for me most of all given that I was winning a 2,000 Guineas within walking distance of the family home. I was a Classic winner in my home country. It felt sweet.

Just over three weeks later we took the obvious route and contested the St James's Palace Stakes. This represented a stiffer assignment than the Irish 2,000 Guineas as both Makfi and Dick Turpin were in the line-up, but I was sure that, though they had beaten Canford at Newmarket, they would not be capable of besting the revitalised Canford at Ascot. All went as I had planned until I saw something flying through the air while turning for home. It was one of Canford's shoes. That was a worry, but what did not concern me was that we still had five lengths to make up on the leaders. I was certain that my colt had the acceleration to wipe out the deficit. Halfway down the straight I put my theory to the test. For a few strides we hit a flat spot but a couple of reminders did the trick. Dick Turpin was the horse to pass and we nailed him 75 yards from the finish. In the end it was more than a shade cosy.

In the weeks after Ascot he improved. His homework became ever more thrilling and from an already high level he got better and better, as he showed to stunning effect in a racecourse gallop at Kempton. The Sussex Stakes was the plan and, despite being squared up against the previous year's winner, Rip Van Winkle, we were hot favourite to win. This was Canford's first outing against older horses, and Rip Van Winkle was a genuinely top-class older horse, but I was not in the least bit frightened. Perhaps the most unnerving aspect of the contest was that Aidan O'Brien saddled three of the seven runners. Rip Van Winkle was being joined by a Dewhurst Stakes winner in Beethoven and a decent pacemaker in Encompassing. It was inevitable that both Beethoven and Encompassing would be deployed to help Rip Van Winkle and, if possible, to hinder us.

I thought it best to let them do their own thing and let Canford do his. I intentionally missed the kick and held him back in the stalls. The first furlong of Goodwood's mile is downhill and the last thing I wanted was for Canford to start freewheeling along the descent. That would have been sure to cause a fight between us for control. Up front, Encompassing set off like his backside was on fire. To his credit, he lasted until just past the two-furlong pole, at which point Ryan Moore fired Rip Van Winkle into the lead. The O'Brien plan was obvious. They had set out to run the finish out of Canford Cliffs, and now, by making a long run for home, Ryan was trying to draw the string out of my boy's turn of foot. It was a futile mission.

As we got close to the furlong pole, Rip Van Winkle was still at least two lengths clear. I was not concerned, but then, just as I began to gather up Canford, he lost his footing and slipped. Valuable momentum had been lost. I had learnt that the best way to use Canford was to always get his revs up before asking him for everything. To do that was now going to be difficult. Time was not on our side.

From the stands Rip Van Winkle must have seemed by far the most likely winner, but the people in the stands could not have known the amount of horse I still had under me. In an impossibly small number of strides, and with only minimal pressure required, Canford reeled in Rip Van Winkle. With 50 yards to run I was able to start pulling back on the reins. It looked cheeky, cocky even, but adrenalin and euphoria were washing over me and I wanted to show off my horse. He had been magnificent.

A trio of Group 1 victories had been completed in mesmerising fashion. To Richard, his team and myself, Canford Cliffs was priceless, but to others he most definitely had a price. It was once again inevitable that suitors would come calling. We knew that Paul Roy was prepared to listen to offers, and in the weeks following the Sussex two offers of note came his way. One was from Coolmore. They had tried to beat him with Rip Van Winkle, and on the basis that if you can't beat them you buy them, they tried to buy Canford. The other offer came from a less obvious source, Sheikh Fahad Al Thani, a young member of Qatar's royal family. Sheikh Fahad had started to take a real interest in British racing. Through his racing adviser, David Redvers, he was beginning to make some choice purchases, and in Canford Cliffs he saw a horse he could race at the highest level before standing him as his first major stallion.

Paul was keen to carry out the negotiations on behalf of Robin and himself. Coolmore offered £4 million for Canford Cliffs. So too did Sheikh Fahad. Paul went with Coolmore, who were, of course, welcomed into the Canford camp with open arms. John Magnier is an incredible man who has created a racing and bloodstock business greater than any in the industry's history. The agreement that was reached allowed for Canford to race in the colours of Robin and his family until the end of his four-year-old season, at which point he would stand in Ireland at Coolmore's main Tipperary stud. Paul Roy walked away from his joint ownership of Canford Cliffs with an extra £2 million to his name – not a bad return on a £300,000 outlay.

After the Coventry Stakes, Paul promised me that if Canford Cliffs won a Group 1 race he would make me a member of Sunningdale Golf Club. I am still not a member. Now seems a good time to remind him of that!

Plans to end Canford's three-year-old season in the Queen Elizabeth II Stakes came to nothing. He scoped ever so slightly badly on the morning of declarations. Given how valuable a commodity he had become he was too good to risk.

We also knew that we had 2011 and his four-year-old campaign to look forward to. It began where his first two seasons had begun, at Newbury. The Lockinge Stakes had become like a home from home for me and we were back in it once again, this time not with Paco Boy but Canford Cliffs. There were other factors that made me feel a sense of deja-vu. Also facing the starter was Canford's regular rival, Dick Turpin. He was clear second favourite, and justifiably so. Given that he ran for the same stable as Canford, Dick Turpin was always in the shadow of another horse, but he was very smart in his own right. After he had finished second in the St James's Palace Stakes, I had ridden him to a Group 1 success in the Prix Jean-Prat at Chantilly, and he was heading to Newbury a fitter horse than Canford having made a winning seasonal reappearance at Sandown.

Even so, there was never any danger that I was going to jump ship. I was confident that a rusty and burly Canford Cliffs would still be good enough to bag the Lockinge. We knew we would not be seeing the horse at his best but we also knew that he was a better horse at four than he had been at three. We don't weigh our horses at home, but when you sat on him he felt bigger, wider and stronger. In his work he had been taking too much of a pull, but a trip to Newbury for a racecourse gallop two weeks before the Lockinge removed the excess fizz and freshness.

We expected him to win and were more than satisfied with a comfortable defeat of the talented Italian raider Worthadd. Dick

Turpin could only finish fourth, but he would have other days in the sun and subsequently added a second Group 1 and a third Group 2 to his cv. With Canford, the only possible races we could have on our minds were Group 1s, and the next race on his itinerary was obvious. We would have to have another go at the great Goldikova.

By now, Goldikova was something of a turf legend. The previous November she had become the only horse in history to win the same Breeders' Cup race three years in a row when taking the Mile at Churchill Downs. She was a record-breaker on a wider level, too, having smashed the European best by winning 13 Group 1 prizes. She was also our nemesis, having beaten Paco Boy more times than I cared to remember. I knew Goldikova's backside all too well.

I planned to see plenty of her rear end in the Queen Anne Stakes. In a perfect world, I wanted to sit right on her tail before shocking her with one blistering turn of foot. I felt that was achievable. In the days after Newbury it was as though a light had been turned on inside Canford. He had been a little lethargic in the Lockinge but that was now a thing of the past. I was legged up at Ascot bullish in my belief that racegoers were about to see a sharper, fitter and faster horse than the one who had raced at Newbury.

The expectation that day was enormous. Royal Ascot has always been my favourite Flat meeting of the year, and the opening day of the 2011 fixture was serving up as mouthwatering an afternoon's action as anyone could remember. The first three races were all Group 1s: Goldikova versus Canford Cliffs, followed by the King's Stand Stakes, a five-furlong dash that was being contested by some of the world's best sprinters; after that there would be Frankel, the mesmerising, devastating winner of the 2,000 Guineas, in the St James's Palace Stakes. The Goldikova–Canford duel was up first. It was my job to get the party started in the best possible way.

After 100 yards I felt that only jockey error could prevent us from winning. The race began perfectly for me. I wanted to get in behind Goldikova, in one sense because that would help Canford settle but also because that would allow me to watch my main danger like a hawk. It did not help that Goldikova and I were drawn wide apart. When the stalls opened, she broke well and began tracking her pacemaker, Flash Dance. I started to move across towards her but Ryan Moore, who had been drawn much closer to her than me, had the position I wanted. When he saw me edging in his direction, he would have been entirely entitled to stay where he was. Instead he tugged Cityscape to the right and to a position on the outside of the field where he now had no cover. Ryan did me a huge favour. As I have said before in this book, he is a good guy and a great friend.

It was a case of so far, so good. Canford travelled beautifully, exactly as I had wanted him to. Goldikova was moving just as well. As we thundered past the two-furlong pole, her regular partner Olivier Peslier sent her past Flash Dance and into the lead. He did not, however, ask her for maximum effort. He waited in front. He intentionally delayed making his challenge. He knew that I could not kick until he kicked. Olivier was riding a super race, one that was aimed at getting the best out of Goldikova while disturbing Canford Cliffs. The fact that he put up three pounds overweight was more than made up for by his brilliant ride.

Passing the furlong marker, he went for everything. In the space of 200 metres, Canford Cliffs first had to quicken to get alongside Goldikova and then quicken again to shake her off. He did that. Goldikova quickened once. Canford quickened twice.

This was probably the first real battle my lad had ever been involved in, and to make his task even harder, he was probably up against the toughest mare in the world. He had won in spite of the way the race panned out, not because of it. Canford Cliffs was a brilliant racehorse but he was not a courageous racehorse. He was not a grafter or a grinder. He was class, and lots of it. That was him. You can make a horse fitter but you cannot make him braver, and we did not, but we discovered at Ascot that he was maybe a little braver than we had thought.

In the Ascot winner's enclosure I made a bold prediction. I told the press, 'I'm sure that no matter what horse you put in front of him, he

With Richard junior in America before the 2011 Breeders' Cup at Churchill Downs. We will hopefully enjoy plenty more Breeders' Cups together after he takes over from his father.

Paco Boy (nearest rail) becomes a Group 1 winner for the third time when seeing off Ouqba in the 2010 Lockinge Stakes at Newbury.

The boss, also my father-in-law, in typically emotional form after Paco Boy's Lockinge win. I wish every trainer enjoyed a winner as much.

The idyllic summer setting of Herridge Stables in Wiltshire, one of Richard Hannon's two yards. Why wouldn't I want to go to work each day?

Above: The big day in Barbados. Richard escorts Lizzie down the aisle as our families are joined by my best man Adrian Regan. I was minus crutches for the first time in five months.

Left: A proud family moment with Lizzie and my parents.

A chance to relax in the paddock with Her Majesty in the minutes leading up to the 2008 Chesham Stakes. We had laid down plans to win her the race with Free Agent in March, three months before he duly obliged.

The Queen's annual visit to Newbury racecourse. The Queen is one of the most knowledgeable and expert people on both racing and breeding matters. It's a privilege to ride for her.

Getting instructions from the boss at Goodwood. Usually it's – 'Go down slow and come back as FAST as you can.'

Phoebe, Harvey and two proud parents.

Canford Cliffs beats Goldikova in their eagerly awaited Royal Ascot showdown. The anticipation before the race was matched by the thrill afterwards. Canford was not only the best horse I've ridden but also the best mover – just look at the way he points his toe.

What a feeling! Celebrating in front of the Ascot grandstands. It doesn't get much better than this.

The boss and I after Canford Cliffs' Queen Anne win. Richard has just said to me, 'Were you trying to give me a heart attack?'

Clockwise from top left: Wedded bliss in Barbados; Harvey and me at Paultons Park (I'm enjoying the visit more than Harvey); Lizzie and me at Royal Ascot in 2011.

This is better than any winner.

would go by them.' I said that at about 2.45 p.m. Just over an hour later, Frankel followed up his 2,000 Guineas rout with a win in the St James's Palace. We had started the day with everyone talking about the showdown between Canford Cliffs and Goldikova. By the end of the day the race that was being universally craved was one between Canford Cliffs and Frankel. It was a race we wanted, and it was a race that was going to happen. We were both heading towards Glorious Goodwood.

It is a credit to the two horses' connections that they honed in on the Sussex Stakes despite knowing that the other horse was being trained for the same race. At no point did Coolmore or Robin Heffer ever try to persuade Richard that the Prix Jacques le Marois, another Group 1 mile staged a couple of weeks later, might be a more sensible target. Nor was there any wavering from the Frankel team. He was already priceless but they showed no signs of wrapping him up in cotton wool. For me, there was some irony in that I was taking on my old boss. Frankel was owned and bred by Prince Khalid Abdullah. Had I still been his retained jockey, I would have been the one on his back, just as I had been the one who rode his dam, Kind, in every one of her 13 races, winning on her six times, including in Listed events at Hamilton and Nottingham. She had been good, but her son was awesome and already being hailed as the world's best racehorse. I had been confident that we would beat Goldikova. I genuinely did not know if we could beat Frankel. Nobody knew.

In our favour was the fact that Frankel had been nowhere near as impressive at Ascot as he had been in the Guineas. At Newmarket he had led from start to finish, setting incredible fractions and maintaining them. Ascot had been a very different race. His trainer, the recently knighted Sir Henry Cecil, was aware that Frankel's career would be short-lived if he put as much into all his races as he had on the Rowley Mile. He had apparently told Tom Queally to ride a more conservative race, but Tom panicked when he saw that the pacemaker Rerouted still held a massive lead leaving the back straight. He fired up

Frankel, who upped his speed faster than any horse I have seen. I had finished second to Frankel in the Guineas on Dubawi Gold and I was riding him again in the St James's Palace. When Frankel quickened at Ascot, he took eight lengths out of the field. It wasn't that we let him go, it was simply that we couldn't keep up. Frankel's instant burst must have used up an enormous amount of energy. It was no surprise that he seemed all out to hold on at the finish.

In some ways, that should have boosted our confidence. It did not, because we all knew that Frankel was better than he had showed. As I have said before, Sir Henry is not the best at coping when his horses perform below their best and this was a victory that felt like a defeat. He made it very clear that he had not been happy with Tom's riding. Tom must have been hurt and his confidence shaken, but he has an old head on young shoulders and he got on with the job. I knew that Tom would not mess up in the Sussex and that Frankel would be devilishly hard to beat. I also knew that Canford Cliffs was the best horse I had ever ridden. What I did not know was whether that would be enough to stop Frankel.

This was always going to be the biggest race I had ever been involved in. I cannot ever recall the sport getting so excited about a Flat race. That did not bother me. Some people might get tense in advance of days like that. Not me. I love rising to the big occasion and I was loving the thought of taking on Frankel. But then, as we drew closer to the race, I began loving the prospect less and less. Doubts started surfacing in my mind, doubts that were triggered because of the way Canford was performing in training. During one key gallop at home I thought he neither worked well nor felt right.

'He looked good,' Richard said to me after I pulled up.

'Well, he didn't feel good,' was my honest answer.

Nothing seemed wrong with the horse, though.

Racecourse gallops had helped during his preparation for some of his other races so we chose to do the same again and sent him to Salisbury, along with Dubawi Gold and another classy performer,

Moriarty. The ground that morning at Salisbury was soft, which was not in Canford's favour. I was conscious not to leave the Sussex behind in a meaningless workout on testing ground, so I was far from hard on him. Even allowing for that, I was disappointed by the way he went. Worryingly, there was nothing electric about the feel he was giving me.

I succeeded in putting the anxiety to the back of my mind, attributing the Salisbury showing to the mud. Moreover, any horse was allowed the odd off day. I could not afford to be negative. I took an upbeat, positive mindset into the Sussex. I so dearly wanted Canford to win. I had invested so much emotionally into the horse and, for his sake more than anybody else's, I wanted him to beat Frankel.

It did not take long for me to realise that he was not going to win. Normally, Canford Cliffs moved beautifully to post. Not this time. Horses are creatures of habit. Whenever I asked Jacqueline to canter down to the stalls, she would stumble on her first step. When I asked her to canter in her final race, there was no stumble. At first, I thought it was a good sign. It was not. We were beaten for the first time.

I had Jacqueline in mind as I took Canford down to the Goodwood mile start. I was hoping for the best but fearing the worst. I was right to be concerned. At the five-furlong pole we were not going overly fast but we were still off the bridle. One furlong later, with half the race still to run, I knew I was beat. All that made Canford so special was missing. I had wanted to reach the two-pole on the bit, just as I had when we took Goldikova's scalp. That was not to be. I wasn't able to loom up on Frankel's girth and serve it up to him. Instead Canford flattened out and hung badly left, just as he had in the previous year's Greenham Stakes. Frankel had made all and beaten us into second by five lengths. I was devastated, utterly heartbroken.

What really upset me was that I knew what people would say, and they said it. I knew that Frankel had been sensational and that he would be lauded as the vastly superior horse. Pundits talked of the drubbing he had given to Canford Cliffs, but he had not taken on the real Canford Cliffs. We had gone to Goodwood hoping to learn something and had learnt nothing.

A few days later we discovered why Canford had run so badly. A scan revealed that he had injured his near-fore pastern. The explanation I had wanted was there. I was delighted, not because the horse was hurt but because we had concrete evidence that proved he should be forgiven his Goodwood display. Yet, although there was this consolation, there was also the horrible realisation that Canford would not get the chance to redeem himself. He had to be retired. It was the only sensible course of action to take.

Part of me still thinks that Canford Cliffs, at his very best, could have beaten Frankel. I know that I am in a very small minority in holding that view, but I am also in an even smaller minority in that I was the only person who ever got to experience the thrill of riding him in a race. And it was a thrill – a huge thrill. I spent over 20 years trying to find a racehorse as good as Canford Cliffs. Richard Hannon had spent twice as long. We both agreed that he was by far the best to have come our way. If I never ride one as good again, I will have no reason to complain.

I have been supremely fortunate to ride some tremendous thoroughbreds. Canford Cliffs had that rare, special something that none of the others possessed. It was a pleasure and a privilege to come along for the ride.

17

CHASING HANAGAN

It was only when the prospect of becoming champion jockey was dangled before me that I realised the title was something I wanted.

Growing up, I'd never thought twice about being champion, either in Ireland or Britain. All I'd really dreamed of in the early days was winning the Derby. When I was riding at home, there was never the slightest opportunity of challenging for the Irish championship. Without being stable jockey to one of the top yards, you had no chance. I never held such a position. When established and successful in Britain, the championship was still not something I craved. It was a crown that other people fought over. To win it required an awful lot of work – too much work, and over too long a period. Even if you won it, all you had to show for it was a trophy, an aching body and enormous bags under your eyes.

Briefly, and only briefly, in 2002, I changed my mind. My season was going so well by the midsummer period that I was within touching distance of the title leader, Kieren Fallon. Prince Khalid and Richard Hannon were supplying me with plenty of ammunition and I decided that chasing Kieren could be fun. It was, but it was also exhausting. But for a series of run-ins with racecourse stewards I might have got close; in the end, Kieren took the trophy with 18 winners to spare.

Eight years went by before I even contemplated putting in the effort that is needed for another assault on the championship. Some jockeys, even some talented jockeys, will ride fewer than nine winners in a whole season. In 2010 I rode nine winners at a single festival. Over the course of five days I broke the modern-day record for winners at Glorious Goodwood. I had a spectacular meeting. Lester Piggott, Johnny Murtagh and Kieren had all managed eight in a week at past Glorious Goodwoods but nobody had equalled or bettered nine since Sir Gordon Richards netted ten winners from 23 rides in 1947.

What happened at Goodwood did not take me by surprise. Goodwood is my favourite racecourse and one at which I have always done well. Royal Ascot is a wonderful meeting, unsurpassed for concentrated quality anywhere in the world, but the Glorious festival is a joy for so many different reasons. For a start, it is more relaxed. The pressure on trainers and jockeys is not as great because there are fewer races of huge significance. One of the lovely things about Goodwood is that over the five days there are plenty of maidens, nurseries and mid-level handicaps, which means there's always a chance that a small man can have a winner. There is also always a chance that Hannon and Hughes will have a few winners as the race programme, full of two-year-old contests, suits our stable. And the track itself suits me. A jockey riding over Goodwood's contours and undulations must have self-belief. You might not get a run on one horse, but you have to have the balls to ride the next race the same way. At Goodwood, if you try to make the gaps happen, they won't come. If you let them happen, they do come. It's all about confidence and sticking to your plan. I love it.

In fact, I love it so much that I sacrificed nearly two weeks of the season to make sure I got there. As I approached the middle of July I knew that I was already banned on the Saturday of Newbury's Weatherbys Super Sprint, a race that we have traditionally dominated. Goodwood was around the corner and, as bans committed in Britain start 14 days after the offence, I was conscious of receiving a suspension that could rule me out of some or all of the meeting. A silly one-day ban had already cost me two winners at Newmarket's July Festival. That had hurt, and I did not want a repeat of the pain during Goodwood. Also in my thought process was that I was sitting on 15 days of careless riding bans within the 'totting up' window. Under the system, a rider is not allowed more than 24 days of interference suspensions during any six-month period. Once you get past 24 days a hearing in London automatically follows, as, almost certainly, does a further lengthy ban. Essentially, you are punished twice for the same offence. A collection of trivial transgressions can result in a long and expensive spell away from the racecourse.

I decided to take out some insurance and sat out the vast chunk of two weeks. In effect, I was serving a self-imposed suspension, but I felt I had to in order to be sure of riding at Goodwood. I wanted to be there, and Richard needed me there. A mini sabbatical seemed a sacrifice worth making, and when I left Goodwood at the end of the meeting's fifth and final day I had no doubts that it had been a price worth paying. Had I not been at Goodwood, I would not have won the Sussex Stakes on Canford Cliffs, nor the festival's three showpiece races for two-year-olds on Zebedee, King Torus and Libranno. All four of those Group-race winners were trained by Richard Hannon, who was also responsible for my other five winning mounts.

Goodwood was also significant in a wider sense. Eucharist, my ninth and final winner of Glorious week, was also my 100th winner of the championship season, which runs from the opening turf meeting of the year at Doncaster in March to the last, at the same venue, in November. Paul Hanagan had been setting a fierce pace in the title race following an opening-day four-timer, but despite his excellent run of form he was only 11 winners in front of me. Ryan Moore, who had started the year as hot favourite to become champ for the fourth time in five years, was two winners adrift of me. Without actively trying to get into the mix, I found myself in contention. One leading bookmaker was quoting me at 6-1 to win the title. Paul was a hot odds-on favourite at 8-11, but his odds were drifting and mine were shortening. I also knew that he had noticed what had happened at Goodwood. He could see me coming. He was slightly rattled. And I liked that.

But it was still going to be hard. Paul was ruling the north that year. He had never mounted a championship challenge before, but he was more than good enough to be the sport's champion and he had momentum behind him. Richard Fahey, the excellent North Yorkshire trainer to whom Paul was riding as stable jockey, had been in flying form all season and there was no sign that his constant flow of winners was about to slow down. Also in his favour was that Paul was immensely popular, and understandably so. You would struggle to meet a nicer, more genuine guy than Paul Hanagan. Everybody loves him, and in the close-knit northern racing community that counted for a lot. Trainers who did not normally use him were booking him for fancied rides in an effort to win him, and the north, the title. There was a real feel-good factor about his bid. From a long way out, people, north and south, wanted Paul to win it.

If I was to get into a serious fight for the title, I had to keep up the pressure through August. It was early in the month when a single incident convinced me I had to go for it. Ryan suffered a wrist injury in a Monday-night fall at Windsor. He was 16 winners behind Paul at the time. That would not have been a big enough deficit to stop him but the injury meant he would be sidelined for a few weeks. That would be enough to stop him. Suddenly, Paul Hanagan was the only man to beat. I felt sure I could beat him. Tony Hind, my long-term friend and agent, rang and asked me if, with Ryan (another of his jockeys) out of action, I wanted to go for the title. Other people had been talking about me as a championship challenger for weeks. In my head, I had not been. Now I was. I told Tony that we should give it our best shot.

Over the coming weeks the battle quickly intensified. August yielded plenty of winners. I rode a treble at Lingfield, then a double at Ffos Las, then a double at Salisbury, then a double at Kempton, then a double at Newbury. The month was also dotted here and there with single winners at individual meetings. I even had a successful day on a card at which I drew a blank, as I captained the Irish team that won the Shergar Cup for the second consecutive year under my leadership. In 2011 we made it a treble. The Shergar Cup is an event that racing fans tend to either love or hate. No prizes for guessing on which side of the fence I sit.

As August ended, I was able to reflect on a successful month. Unfortunately for me, it had been even more successful for Paul. As September dawned, he was 16 clear. September, however, went more my way than his, and it was in September that a great friend, John Reddington, greatly increased my chances by handing over his helicopter for the rest of the season. Having the helicopter opened up many more options than had previously been available. Where before two meetings in a day were not possible, now they were. John said he wanted to try in any way he could to make me champion jockey, and by lending me the chopper he gave me exactly the help I needed. Through the final two months of the season I was using it four days a week, most often when there was an afternoon meeting followed by an evening fixture at Wolverhampton, of which there were plenty over those final few weeks.

Through September I was like a man possessed. On the first Saturday of the month I somehow managed to ride in the 3.50 pm race at Kempton before dashing off to Pewsey, about 20 miles south of Swindon, to attend the 5 pm wedding of Richard Hannon junior, for whom I was acting as an usher. I managed it, and over the days that followed I ate into Paul Hanagan's lead. At one point I rode nine winners in four days, and across the month as a whole I added a massive 33 wins to my tally. Plenty came at my usual haunts, such as Kempton, Salisbury and Goodwood, but there was also a victory in Hanagan land at Hamilton. That one was a significant shot in the arm. Tony Hind, or Boney as everyone calls him, was doing an amazing job getting me rides, even at far-flung racecourses that I seldom visited.

On this occasion he'd booked me for Fujin Dancer, a horse trained by Kevin Ryan – often a source of rides for Paul – in a lowly claimer. Paul was riding the 11-10 favourite for Richard Fahey. He looked all over the winner entering the final furlong, but I managed to grab him in the final strides. If I'm honest, I had gone to Hamilton partly because I knew that any winners for me there would be extra painful for Paul. Nicking a race from him close home had to leave him smarting. The fact that he squared the afternoon's honours by winning the final race was not enough to stop me leaving Scotland with a smile on my face.

When September ended there were only ten winners between us. Paul was on 161, I was on 151. I was increasing in confidence and enjoying the fight far more than I thought I would. I was often tired and getting little sleep but I was on a roll. I believed that things were going my way, and they were, until the second division of the Cleanwastesolutions Handicap at Wolverhampton on 2 October. I won the race by a neck on the Barney Curley-trained Aviso, but the price I paid for winning was hefty. The stewards gave me a six-day careless riding suspension. To make matters worse, I picked up another one-day whip ban in a later race. I was deemed to have hampered several horses on the bend, but I did not think what I had done merited such a severe punishment. I appealed the careless riding ban five days later but came away with not one of the days given back to me. Just one or two might have been all I needed.

On the day of the Aviso race, Coral had been quoting Paul at 8-11 and me at evens. After my failure in the appeal hearing, I was out to 9-2 and Paul cut to as short as 1-8. In total, I was faced with having to sit out eight days of racing before 22 October, including the valuable Champions Day fixture at Newmarket. Until that point I had also been hoping to miss the final two days of the campaign so that I could fly to America to partner Paco Boy in the Breeders' Cup Mile. I knew that plan might well have to be revised.

In the days leading up to the start of the suspension I did everything I could to close in on Paul. I remained hungry, and so did Boney. A fellow agent had rung him after the appeal's outcome was announced. He had said to Boney that I now had no chance. That had incensed Boney and spurred him on even more. He had already been working his guts out, but now, if it were humanly possible, he was working even harder. I rode a winner on 8 October, another on 9 October, a treble on the 13th and another single winner on the 14th. Painfully, during this period Paul exacted revenge on me for the Hamilton victory by driving south and riding winners at Goodwood and Windsor on consecutive days. The Goodwood winner was bad enough but the Windsor success left me completely heartbroken. I always cleaned up on Mondays at Windsor. To see Paul striking on my stomping ground killed me.

There had also been another reverse of sorts the day before Paul rode at Goodwood. What I found hard to bear was not so much that Paul won the final race of the afternoon at York but that he came away from it without a suspension. Paul seemed to get away with murder that year. He hardly ever got into trouble with the stewards, even following races that seemed sure to trigger a suspension. That York race was a case in point. He forced Richard Fahey's Tepmokea home on the line but in doing so carried the runner-up left. It was only slight interference but the margin of victory had been similarly tight. Friends of mine were convinced that Paul would get a couple of days, but he walked away a free man. I am sure that if I had been riding the same horse in the same race at the same course I would have been banned.

Races like that left a sour taste in my mouth. There were other occasions when I felt the same. More often than not, the Hanagan–Hughes race was the cleanest of clean fights. However, there were a few occasions when things got a little nasty, although never between the two of us. At no point did Paul put a foot wrong. He is completely honourable and decent. I have not a single bad word to say about him. Others, on the other hand, did not always behave so well.

I consider Richard Fahey a friend and I am sure he feels the same about me, but he is far closer to Paul and he was extremely keen for him to become champion jockey. There were times when I think he was a little too keen and I do think that he started to lose his composure towards the end. I think one reason for that is that I had won a valuable Ascot handicap for him on King George day in July. He knew that if I took the title by a single winner, he would have been partly responsible.

There were others who showed themselves in a poor light. A Midlands-based trainer told Boney that I should ride one of his horses in a handicap race. He said the horse would definitely win. The horse performed poorly. I rang Boney from the racecourse weighing room and told him that the animal had been as fat as a pig and badly in need of the run. I said that we should be wary in the event of the trainer wanting to book me for any other horses. He had told me earlier in the year that he had backed Hanagan for the title. He must have forgotten telling me but I remembered it clearly. I began to put two and two together. A few days later, he rang Boney again and asked if I could ride one for him later that week. Boney and I smelt a rat. Boney got me on another horse in the same race but intentionally did not put my name against the horse on the Weatherbys entry system. The Midlands-based trainer did not know this. On the morning of declarations, he rang Boney to say that the horse had gone lame. That came as no surprise. Fortunately, we had made alternative plans. We never had any intention of me riding his horse.

When my enforced layoff began, the gap between Paul and myself stood at nine. When I returned on October 22, with barely two weeks of the season remaining, it had risen, but only to 13. Ladbrokes, in what I considered to be a cheap publicity stunt, had already paid out on Paul winning the title. I wanted it to be a very expensive cheap publicity stunt.

In those last few days, Paul rode winners but I consistently rode more. On October 25 I bagged a Leicester treble, all of them for my great friend and ally, Mick Channon. On the 27th there were two winners, on the 28th a further two winners and on the 29th there were three, the first two at Newmarket, the third at Wolverhampton. The gap was down to six. The racing press were engrossed. We were stoking up the dying embers of the Flat season. Hanagan and Hughes had become compulsive viewing.

By now I had already decided that there was no way I could go to the Breeders' Cup. I had worked so hard - and other people had worked so hard for me - that it would have been wrong to effectively give up so close to the winning line. I pressed on and notched two wins at Lingfield on October 31. Paul only rode one winner at the same meeting. In effect, that gave me the advantage on the day, but there was far more to the day than that. Boney thinks it is the day that cost me the championship.

Lingfield staged a one-mile-five-furlong handicap that afternoon. Two days earlier, at 9.45am on the morning of declarations, my intended mount was withdrawn. Boney looked to see if there were any late options. Paul Hanagan was jocked up to partner Encircled for John Jenkins, a trainer for whom I regularly rode. I had ridden the horse in the past and, had I been available when John was looking for a jockey, I would almost certainly have been selected. Boney was torn. Part of him knew that to ring a trainer and suggest he replace Hanagan with Hughes seemed wrong. Yet he also knew that, if the roles had been reversed, Paul's agent, Richard Hale, might well have done the same. He decided to ring John Jenkins. John, perfectly understandably, said that swapping jockeys would not have been the right thing to do, but then, half an hour later, he rang back to say that his wife owned the horse and she was keen that I ride him. John said that he would replace Paul with me but only if Boney rang Richard Hale to explain what was going on.

Boney got in touch with Richard Hale and passed on the bad news. We do not know for sure who then rang who, but not long after the conversation between Boney and Richard, Joe Fanning, who had been due to ride Herostatus in the Lingfield race for his boss, Mark Johnston, got off the horse. Paul Hanagan took the mount instead. Herostatus won. Paul had never previously been widely used by Mark but over the coming week a number of rides that Joe would normally have taken for Mark were taken by Paul. One of those rides, on a three-year-old called Home Office in a Wolverhampton maiden on the season's penultimate day, gave Paul another winner. Almost certainly as a result of us nicking one of Paul's rides, Paul had forged a late link with Mark Johnston that had brought him two unexpected winners. At the end of the season, two was a seriously important number.

That penultimate day sticks in my memory for another reason. The final race on the Wolverhampton card was a maiden, as poor a race as you could find. Paul did not have a ride in it. I was on the hot favourite, Colour Scheme, an 11-10 shot trained by Manton's new tenant, Brian Meehan. Richard Fahey, a friend of Brian's, was not exactly thrilled that he had been given me the mount. He was desperate for Paul to win the title. He was Paul's employer, Paul's friend, and as a stalwart of northern racing, he knew how significant it would be for the region were Paul to take the title. Fahey rang Brian and asked, as one friend to another, if he would take me off Colour Scheme and use Hanagan instead. Brian told Fahey that although he was his mate, he was also my mate - and I lived a lot closer to him than Fahey.

Colour Scheme won easily by seven lengths, but that does not tell the whole story. I had spoken to one of the other riders before the race and asked him what tactics he was planning on using. The jockey in question said nothing and shrugged his shoulders. Early in the back straight, he rushed his mount up to my outside and attempted to ride me into the horse to my front. I could very easily have found myself blocked in at a crucial stage of the contest. I was wise to what was happening and extricated myself, but the incident came close to causing Stevie Donohoe on my inner to be unseated.

I was incensed. When we were all back in the weighing room, I told the jockey what I thought of him, making sure that everyone else in the room could hear. I said that if this was going to be a fair battle, that sort of behaviour could not take place. I said that I would not allow one of my friends to do that to Paul Hanagan and I expected to be treated in the same way in return. The other jockey insisted he was innocent but I did not believe him and I do not to this day. I do not, for sure, know why he did it, but what I am certain of is that Paul Hanagan would have known nothing about what went on and would never have sanctioned it.

It was not a nice way enter the final day of what had been a momentous season. Paul went into it leading by 191 winners to 189. The score did not change. I would have loved to draw level on that final day but I would not have wanted any more than that. I wanted to be champion jockey but I did not want Paul Hanagan not to be champion jockey. I had started working hard in August; Paul had been dedicating his life to the title since March. He deserved to win, and had I ridden two winners at Doncaster, I would have suggested to him that we both stop riding. I am positive he would have agreed.

I reflect on that fight with pride and pleasure. I am sure that without the Wolverhampton suspension I would have been 2010's champion jockey, but I have come to learn that there is no point getting upset about something that cannot be changed. In some ways it was an odd experience. I was locked into a pulsating duel with Paul Hanagan, and yet, with him riding largely in the north and me in the south, I barely ever saw him. He was, and is, a great champion and a real credit to the sport. I like to think that I would also have been a worthy champion, and maybe one day I will be. If I ever am, it will be in no small part down to the person who helped me so much in 2010. Tony Hind was superb. He could not have done more for me. He lived off four hours' sleep a night for four months. He was sat in front of his computer from 6 am to 1 am the following morning. We made and continue to make a fantastic team.

I lost, but I tried. There were some unpleasant, regrettable aspects to Hanagan versus Hughes, but it was good for both of us and good for the sport. It was my finest defeat.

18

THE WHIP WAR

Racing enjoyed a vintage year in 2011. There was the unbelievable Frankel on the Flat, Kauto Star the comeback king over jumps and, most importantly of all, Richard Hughes showed that jockeys can also be journalists by embarking on a weekly 2,000-word column for the *Racing Post*. To those of us who love racing, it was truly a fabulous year.

Yet to those outside the sport it must have seemed that there was only one racing story. The furore over the whip was the gift that racing gave to the world during a year that became needlessly acrimonious. Some of the responsibility for that lay at the hands of jockeys. Much of it, however, was due to the way racing's rulers turned what should have been a minor drama into a huge crisis.

Like any jockey, I have had my moments with racing officialdom. I have had my fair share of suspensions, generally for careless riding offences, but in a career that has spanned nearly a quarter of a century it would have been impossible to avoid such charges. Sometimes I have agreed with the decisions, sometimes I have not. What has never changed is how much I detest being suspended. Anybody who loves riding racehorses in races as much as I do could never be anything other than mortified at being told to watch and not participate. It annoys the hell out of me.

There have been times when I clearly saw that I was in the wrong, but that sometimes makes it even worse because on those occasions I have had only myself to blame. I have always tried – although not always succeeded – not to hold a grudge against the racecourse stewards themselves. They have a hard job to do, and they cannot possibly keep everyone happy. I can fully appreciate that theirs is a difficult task. More often than not they are directed towards their final decisions by professional stipendiary stewards, some of whom I respect greatly, others less so. Inconsistency is inevitable because stewards and their stipendiary assistants are not machines. They will often see the same incident in different ways. When inconsistency works against you it can be frustrating, but I accept that it goes with the territory.

What can be more upsetting is when you feel that you are a marked man. That does happen. There are periods when you seem to be called into an awful lot of stewards' inquiries, periods when you appear to be getting banned for things that have in the past gone unnoticed. There have definitely been stages in my career when it has felt as though the eyes of all stewards have been on me, and when that is the case it is almost impossible to escape without penalties. Racing is a contact sport. Sometimes rules are going to be broken. What happens to you when you break them can often hinge on little more than luck.

More often than not, when I ride on Monday nights at Windsor, luck is on my side. I love the place. It is my patch, the place where I am the governor. I have ridden 75 winners there in the last five years and I normally come home with a double every Monday evening. It's a fun place to work, a place where the atmosphere is full of people having a great time in a picturesque, relaxed, riverside setting. It is also the track where I show I'm not a one-trick pony. Everyone associates me with a certain style of riding, but at Windsor I show them that I can do more than bring a horse from off the pace. So many of my Windsor winners either make all the running or race very close to the lead. Around the figure of eight's many bends, that's the best way of getting your horse from start to finish in first place.

Windsor is my friend. I have had some fantastic nights there. But on 20 June 2011 I endured one of my worst when the racecourse stewards handed me a seven-day careless riding suspension that had wider implications for me than just the seven days. In a one-mile maiden I was on Puttingonthestyle, the 15-8 favourite, for Richard Hannon. Not long after passing the two-furlong pole I was found guilty of causing interference that led to both Michael Hills and Jimmy Fortune hitting the deck.

Here is how I reflected on the incident, and the stewards' response to it, in my *Racing Post* column:

> **I made a mistake and am being punished for it in the most draconian way. What could have been my first championship has been snatched from me. The thrill of riding at the Newmarket July Festival has gone and, most worryingly of all, every ride I take in the next three weeks could result in me being denied the chance to partner Canford Cliffs at Goodwood in what should be the most important race of my career. In case you hadn't guessed, I'm gutted.**
>
> **At Windsor on Monday night I received a seven-day ban for careless riding. I believe I was very unfortunate. The ground was soft and when it's like that at Windsor jockeys always move across to the far side down the home straight. In an ordinary maiden worth just over £2,000 to the winner, I was in front with Michael Hills to my left. As we crossed the intersection we began to steer from one side of the track to the other. I was only in a position to see the one horse next to me and therefore left enough space for one horse, but as Michael dropped away Kieren Fallon, who had been behind us, kicked up Michael's inner as he was entitled to do. I came in a bit – but not outrageously so – and Michael's horse, now going backwards, became tight for room and fell. Further back a stablemate of my mount was brought down.**

I nearly died when I pulled up and realised that two horses were riderless. I didn't mean to cause anyone to fall and Michael knew the same. I immediately apologised to him but he told me it wasn't my fault. He accepted it was half his mistake. Fallon said the same and agreed that he had just seen a gap and gone for it.

The stewards didn't agree. I was told afterwards that had there been no fallers I would have been given no more than a two-day ban or maybe even a caution. Instead I got seven days. Michael pointed out to the stewards that it wasn't my fault and that this was one of those things that happens in a race, but they took no notice. That's not unusual because during an inquiry the evidence of the person who suffered is never really considered. The stewards just go blindly by the rules and there are so many of them in the book that the officials get tied up in knots. As such, there's no point appealing. It would make no difference.

When I got home I realised that under the totting-up system I had reached a total of 21 days. There and then it felt like my whole world had fallen apart. The next time I receive a careless riding ban a referral to Shaftesbury Avenue will automatically be triggered. Once there the range of additional suspension is from ten to 28 days.

It's now going to be very hard for me to do my job because I know that the first mistake I make will result in a huge suspension. And so for that reason you won't see much of me for the next month. The stewards have banned me for a large chunk of the next three weeks, but even when I'm not suspended I won't be on a racecourse much. The more you get banned the more you become scared of being banned.

I'm therefore resigned to another long spell on the sidelines and, because of that, I won't be going for the championship. It would be impossible for me to win it, especially as when you come back from a totting-up ban there are still some days deferred. The stewards have knocked the jockeys' title on the head for me for the second year running – I might have won last year but for getting a six-day ban towards the end of the season. It's incredibly frustrating. I had just got to 50 winners and I'm sitting close up behind Paul Hanagan. I've only been in third gear so far this season and wasn't planning to go full welly until after Glorious Goodwood. I think I had a massive chance of being champion jockey. Now I don't.

So much of the present system is wrong, not least the totting-up rules. We are being punished twice for the same offence. I'm sure it wouldn't withstand the scrutiny of the European courts. The BHA says the referral rule stops jockeys from re-offending, but we are riding in a contact sport. Horses do not run straight all the time and, now and again, you are going to interfere with someone. For me that's even more likely. Last year I rode in 1,098 British races. In 600 of those races I finished in the first four and by being so closely involved at the end of so many races – in many of them on inexperienced two-year-olds – I am bound to transgress the careless riding rules more than most others in the weighing room.

A good jockey should want to be competitive. It's only the ones who don't care that spend all their time going around the outside. Instead of denying me the right to work, why don't they fine me £10,000 and put it towards prize money? Everyone would benefit from that.

If I keep re-offending maybe I do need to have a look at the way I ride, but I still don't think my punishment fits the crime. All I want to do is ride horses. I absolutely love it, but the stewards are taking my chance to do it away from me. I can't tell you how angry and upset what happened on Monday has left me. For me, it's a complete disaster.

I was genuinely devastated, and the pain did not ease. At the end of the year I still regarded it as by far the lowest point of my season. I had built up tons of momentum and was riding lots of winners, so much so that I was ready to launch a major assault on the jockeys' championship. However, with the totting-up rules at the front of my mind, I had no choice but to ease off considerably and become more selective about where and when I rode. I had the threat of a lengthy suspension hovering over my head for a long time, and when that cloud was finally lifted, my chance of catching Paul Hanagan was gone. But for that Windsor suspension I have no doubt that I would have been the champion jockey of 2011. It was my championship for the taking and it's a massive disappointment to me that I could not take it. I feel as though I was robbed of the title two years in succession.

And that was far from it so far as my 2011 campaign was concerned. I have never been a whip jockey, yet that year I was the jockey who found himself at the centre of the whip storm.

The stick became an issue following the Grand National, in which Jason Maguire struck the winner, Ballabriggs, 17 times on the two-furlong run from the final fence to the winning post. With the world watching, and a television audience of nine million people in Britain alone, Jason's transgression not only led to a suspension but also a media storm. The British Horseracing Authority responded by revealing that they had already embarked on an extensive review of the sport's whip rules the previous autumn.

In my first *Racing Post* column, on 30 April, I set out my views:

> I am prepared to bare my backside and be thrashed in public if it helps bring some sense to the whip debate. Let me explain why.
>
> Nothing riles me more than seeing a jockey who is not in the first four whipping a horse. On many occasions I've ridden past a young jockey and said 'put your stick down' or bollocked them on pulling up. It was drummed into me that the last rider who goes for his stick usually wins. That was the old school approach, but times are different now and jockeys do use their whip more than they used to.
>
> However, you can't stop jockeys using the whip, especially in the current climate where some punters lack faith in the sport.
>
> I do believe that you have to take a different approach to jumping, but on the Flat I would like to see Britain adopt the whip rules used in India, where I ride during the winter. In India, there is a fixed number

of times you can hit a horse – which I believe should be between eight and ten – and if you transgress that once you are handed a massive fine. It should be the same in Britain. If you commit the same offence again within a set number of rides you should get hit with an even bigger fine, and then for a third offence you should have your whip taken away for a month, which would effectively mean a jockey wouldn't get any rides for that period.

The punishments have to hurt and if we used the Indian system they would. I'm certain that jockeys would no longer be prepared to take a ban in order to win a big race. The whip rules would stop being transgressed there and then.

People also seem to be forgetting that jockeys love horses. They also forget that we now use air-cushioned whips that don't hurt horses. Slap your hand with the whip and you'll see what I mean. What horses react to is the noise of the whip, particularly the first couple of times it's used in a race.

If it helps, I will happily stand in the Newmarket paddock, pull my pants down and have my arse beaten with the whip for half an hour. I can't say fairer than that.

Nobody took up my offer, but the whip wasn't a major issue over the coming months, save for one high-profile race in which Frankie Dettori, riding Rewilding in the Prince of Wales's Stakes at Royal Ascot, received a lengthy suspension for using his whip 24 times in the final two furlongs. Rewilding won the race but Frankie would say, with hindsight, that he regretted his actions. His use of the stick, like Jason Maguire's in the Grand National, looked horrible and presented racing's opponents with an open goal. The stewards were right to dish out meaty punishments to Frankie and Jason, but one of the reasons why the offences made the headlines was that trangressions such as theirs had become few and far between.

Long gone, thankfully, are the days when the Cheltenham Festival was marred by jockeys flailing tired horses on gruelling ground. Jockeys no longer consider such behaviour defensible, and have not done for many years. Moreover, as I pointed out in my column, the air-cushioned whips we now use are designed to ensure that horses are not hurt when smacked.

There was, therefore, consternation in the weighing room when the BHA stunned us with the findings of their whip review. The review, part of which was based on a study of public opinion, resulted in drastic changes to the landscape in which we operated.

The previous guidelines had suggested that a Flat jockey who hit his mount 16 times during a whole race, or 13 times in the final two furlongs, was likely to be suspended. Jump jockeys were told they would be in breach of the rules if they hit their horse ten times after the final obstacle or 16 times over the course of a race. Those pages in the rules book were shredded. Under the new rules, we were informed that a Flat jockey could only use his whip a maximum of seven times and a jump jockey eight times. In a further significant change, jockeys would not be permitted to deliver reminders more than five times inside the final furlong on the Flat or after the final obstacle over jumps. Anyone who contravened the rules would receive a minimum ban of five days and also forfeit their riding fee and any prize money earned in the race.

The number of times a jockey could use the whip had been roughly halved and the penalties linked to the rules had been raised to near draconian levels. Also concerning us was the fact that the changes had been unveiled on 27 September and would come into effect as quickly as 10 October, just five days before the sport's new flagship afternoon, British Champions Day at Ascot.

This is how I reacted in my *Racing Post* column on 1 October:

> **It won't come as a surprise to learn that there has been plenty of talk in the weighing room about racing's new whip rules.**
>
> **It is clearly helpful that the rules are now going to be clear in black and white with no grey areas. However, I don't think we have arrived at the perfect solution.**
>
> **I personally do not believe that the old whip rules were being**

abused. As such, I would have much preferred to keep the old rules but massively beefed up the penalties so that the punishments for offenders were even more severe than they will be from October 10.

The changes that are coming are extremely drastic, so much so that I think the proposed system should first have been tried and tested over a specified period. I am of little doubt that the first month is going to be extremely difficult for jockeys and I think it's inevitable that there are going to be many people finding themselves in trouble. Jockeys will have to learn to ride differently, but even when they have, the new rules will be broken far more regularly than the old rules ever were.

People will say that jockeys will know how many times they can hit a horse but it's not as simple as being able to count to five or seven, which I think most of us can manage. Jockeys ride on instinct. When I watch racing on TV I wince when I see lads about to go for some gaps, but when I'm riding the following day I'll go for gaps that are just as tight. That's because we operate on instinct.

There was less than two weeks between the announcement of the rules and their implementation. It became increasingly obvious to us that they would not work, as I hinted at in my column a week later, just two days before the new rules came into effect:

> For jockeys – and not just for jockeys – everything changes when British racing's new whip rules come into force on Monday.
>
> Some of the stories in the Racing Post this week have suggested that there is frustration and anger within the weighing room and I can confirm that to be the case. There is nothing we can do about it and we will just have to do the very best we can but we find ourselves in a far from perfect situation.
>
> As has been reported, the BHA's regulation director Jamie Stier spoke to Flat jockeys at Newmarket last week and made it very clear that we are lucky to be able to use the whip at all. He also said the problem was one of public perception, but we wanted to know

which members of the public perceive there to be a problem? I don't imagine that many people out in the real world spend hours agonising over jockeys' use of the whip and they certainly don't seem to mind in Ireland, France or America, where jockeys are shown on At The Races every night using the stick far more than we do.

All jockeys recognise that the BHA is under pressure on this subject, but I'm not sure that what is going to happen from Monday onwards is going to help. There are going to be many more jockeys being suspended and I don't see how that is going to be anything but bad for public perception. What will also be bad for the public's view of the sport is that the top jockeys will now ride at less meetings because they will be frightened of picking up silly suspensions that could rule them out of the top fixtures. That has to be bad for the sport.

As I said last week, I don't think there was anything wrong with the old rules, just the penalties that went with them. The breaking of the rules in a couple of the year's biggest races has left us all tarred with the same brush. And it has left us far from happy.

We were more than unhappy. We were furious, and we became ever more furious over the coming days. One particular aspect of the BHA's actions that bothered us was the very strong inference that our trade body, the Professional Jockeys' Association, was as one with the regulator. The BHA's initial press release included quotes of support from Tony McCoy and Frankie Dettori. Both had been informed about what the BHA was planning only the night before the announcement. They were caught on the hop and made to think that by not backing the new whip rules they would be shooting their own sport in the foot. The BHA gave the PJA similarly short notice about its intention to go public, which not only showed jockeys a lack of respect but also displayed an inner lack of confidence in their own policy.

Nobody came in for more criticism from jockeys than Jamie Stier. He gave the impression that jockeys had been widely consulted about whip policy over the previous months. That was not, in my opinion, the case. Stier also told us in the Newmarket meeting about ideas for either painting lines across racecourses or putting up large markers to signify the exact point of the final-furlong pole. Something like that was needed but none of Stier's ideas were activated. If you are riding down the centre of the Rowley Mile, a vast expanse of land, you do not see the furlong poles unless you are close to the rail. Very often, we could not be certain when we were reaching the point at which only five smacks were allowed. We needed help from Stier and his colleagues but did not receive it. Rather, we felt as though we had been bullied and belittled.

On the day that the rules came in, the Monday before the Saturday of British Champions Day, I rode at Salisbury. I became the second jockey to be banned under the new rules. My mount, Swift Blade, leant right throughout the closing stages. I used my whip six times in the final furlong – one more than the permitted number – but one of those smacks was down the neck and used only as a corrective measure. In an attempt to keep my horse straight and myself out of an inquiry into careless riding, I had broken the whip rules and was banned for five days.

I now knew that I had to be twice as careful as a second offence triggered double the penalty. Another five-day ban would become a ten-day ban. Three days later at Kempton, I received a ten-day ban. I don't think I have ever been as dejected on a racecourse as that night at Kempton. My crime was committed on More Than Words, one of Richard's two-year-old fillies, in a six-furlong maiden. Although she was racing for the first time, she was ready for a proper run. Had she won, she would have been the 100th winner for our biggest owner, Julie Wood. I wanted to be the one who rode that landmark winner and I was confident that More Than Words would be the horse on which I did it.

I had been secretly disgusted with myself for getting banned at Salisbury. I thought I should have been able to avoid what happened, but at Kempton I realised that I was not wholly in control of my actions. Once again I used the whip six times inside the final furlong. I had not realised. Nobody had been more adamant than me that jockeys would easily be able to count the number of strokes they had used. I was wrong. It would have been hard enough over jumps, but it was even harder amid the faster pace of Flat races. That was not the only thing wrong with the final-furlong rule. Flat jockeys now knew they were not allowed more than seven smacks in a race and only five in the final furlong so, in a bid to make sure they did not waste their quota, were regularly hitting horses twice before the furlong pole. This would not otherwise have happened. In effect, rules designed to make jockeys use the whip less were, at times, encouraging them to use the whip more. Jockeys were also using the whip harder. In the past, jockeys would often start by just flicking their whip, me in particular. I always like to flick a horse first to make sure that it does not resent the whip. Under the seven-smack rule, you could not afford to use up any of your permitted number with flicks. It was a case of hard hits only.

As I walked into the Kempton weighing room, I could see Steve Drowne shaking his head. I knew something was wrong. Then I saw more of the lads looking at me with pained expressions. A sense of impending doom came over me.

I was called into the stewards' room and, a few minutes later, told that I was being given a five-day ban. As it was my second offence, it was doubled to a ten-day ban. In all, that meant I had been handed 15 days of suspension that week. None of it seemed real or fair. Just a few days earlier, neither of the rides would have caused even the most critical eyebrow to be raised. Neither horse had been abused and nobody was claiming any different. I felt as though I was being punished for the sake of being punished.

I concluded there and then that I could no longer ride under the rules. The Breeders' Cup, at which I was supposed to be riding one of my season's top horses, Strong Suit, fell within the 15 days. I knew that I was going to miss that. I decided I should miss everything else as well. I did not want to ride under the stupid five-smacks-inside-the-final-furlong rule. I waved the white flag. I told Dave Mustow, my long-serving valet, that I would not be taking the rest of my rides that night. I added that I would not be taking any rides in the future. I was, metaphorically, handing in my licence. I vowed to myself that I would not ride again until the final-furlong rule was scrapped.

To the bewilderment of the other lads, I began to get dressed. Some of them thought I had lost my marbles and reminded me that I was booked for the remaining races. 'Not any more I'm not,' I said. And I meant it.

Then it kicked off. There were loud shouts of support. Plenty of the boys said they were going to follow my lead. I told them not to. I had not wanted to start a rebellion or a mass walkout. I was taking my own personal and principled stand. It would cost me the chance to ride at Ascot on Champions Day but I did not care. I could not carry on.

When word filtered out to the stewards' room, one of the stipendiary stewards asked me if I needed a doctor, thus offering me a potential way of leaving the racecourse without attracting too much controversy. I told him I did not, and as a result was also given a fine for crying off rides without good reason.

Without consciously trying to, I had instigated mass media interest. I received calls from the all the major newspapers, BBC Radio, Sky News and Racing UK. I gave interviews to them all. I also made sure that I rang Dad and told him what I had done. It was Dad who had drummed into me that the whip should only ever be used as the last resort and that the jockey who picked up his stick last usually went by the winning post first. Dad had still been left appalled by the BHA's new whip rules, however, and he backed what I was doing 100 per cent.

In the hours that followed my phone was red hot with jockeys telling me that we had to go on strike. There was talk of action being taken at Ascot, but that talk died down when the BHA promised to meet the PJA the following Monday. Racing was all over the newspapers, television screens and airwaves – and for all the wrong reasons. Qipco British Champions Day, a £3 million meeting that should have been a huge fillip to the sport, seemed set to be completely overshadowed. How the BHA could not have foreseen that happening remains nigh on unfathomable.

Various people impressed on me that I had to rise above the anger. I was told that for the good of the sport I must take on the role of a statesman. Accepting that to be true, I used my *Racing Post* column to offer the BHA an olive branch:

> Things might look bad now but I firmly believe that a solution is within touching distance. The whip debate has got massively out of hand – and I apologise to those who think that my actions have made matters worse – but I am absolutely sure that there is a simple way forward that is in the best interests of both jockeys and racing as a whole.
>
> Can I firstly stress that I am deeply embarrassed at having played a part in removing the spotlight from Qipco British Champions Day. That was never my intention. I apologise to Qipco, to Ascot and to everyone involved with the fixture. It is extremely bad luck that this issue has come to the fore this week when everyone should be concentrating solely on a wonderful day's horseracing and the mouthwatering prospect of the world's best racehorse playing a starring role at the world's best racecourse.
>
> When the new rules came out everybody in racing was supportive of them, including the jockeys and certainly including me. However, it is sometimes only when you start trying to put a rule into practice that you realise if it works or not. In the two weeks between the rules being unveiled and the first day of their implementation, it became obvious to us that we would find it difficult to comply with the stipulation that states we can only use the stick five times inside the final furlong. The BHA could not have foreseen that and we do not blame them for having framed that particular rule in the first place. I know people will say we should be able to count but when you get into the heat of a battle, which for us is in the closing stages of a race, it isn't that easy. Multi-tasking becomes difficult.
>
> Knowing that we were finding that aspect of the rules difficult – and knowing that jockeys being banned would create damaging

publicity for the sport – we went to Jamie Stier and asked him if he would revisit that part of the rules. He insisted that he would not, which led us to where we are now. People who support that aspect of the rule will point to the jockeys who have not been suspended this week, but those very same jockeys will tell you that they have not fully been able to do justice to their horses.

It is crucial to make clear that we have no problem with being restricted to seven smacks in a Flat race and I'm sure the jumps lads feel the same about not being allowed more than eight smacks. We all agreed on that from the start and ask only for some discretion if the whip is being used for corrective or safety purposes. No horse should need to be hit again and again, but just as importantly, we all recognise that the wider public does not believe that horses should be beaten up in the name of sport. Jockeys, who first and foremost are horse lovers, feel the same. We have been prepared to change the way we ride and have done so in a very short space of time.

It is now common knowledge that, as a measure of our frustration, jockeys have been talking about taking some form of action. There was a suggestion that this could happen at Ascot. It will not, principally because we all know how big a day this is for racing. We know full well that strike action would not be popular with racing professionals, punters or the general public, and it is not a course of action that anyone wants to take. The only reason it has been contemplated is because of frustration and the feeling that if we don't do something quickly the BHA will not take us seriously. If the BHA can give us an assurance that the five-smack rule is going to be dropped at a fixed point in the future I'm sure the lads would not contemplate taking action. I accept that a review has already been announced but I don't know if the rule is going to be changed in a week, a month or not at all, and under those circumstances it is not right that I ride.

I am happy to publicly give my support to the BHA. They reviewed the sport's whip rules for good reasons and with the best of intentions. What they announced seemed to make good sense at the time, and the

vast majority of it still does. I am firmly of the opinion that the BHA would have been applauded if they had originally made no mention of a final-furlong rule and instead just announced the limit of seven smacks on the Flat, eight over jumps and the massive penalties for those who blatantly flout the rules. We don't feel that removing this one troublesome aspect takes away anything from the BHA's overall message that as racing's regulator it is beefing up our whip rules and, in doing so, setting an example for the rest of the world.

At Ascot on Champions Day, the world saw British racing at its best and worst. Frankel was magnificent in the Queen Elizabeth II Stakes, and Cirrus Des Aigles got up close home at the end of a thrilling finish to the richest race ever run in Britain, the £1.3 million Qipco Champion Stakes. All that, however, was overshadowed by the unbelievably disproportionate penalty imposed on Cirrus Des Aigles's jockey, Christophe Soumillon. Having used his whip six times inside the final furlong, he was not only suspended but denied his share of the prize money. That amounted to a staggering £50,868.87. Unsurprisingly, Christophe was incandescent with rage. In a particularly memorable TV interview, he said, 'I'm very, very, very embarrassed for British racing. The people and the fans have been let down.' To highlight just how serious the situation was, he claimed he would now not be able to pay his dentist.

Regardless of the state of his teeth, Christophe helped to save us. He threatened to sue the BHA. The BHA must have realised that, regardless of their legal position, the publicity caused by a lawsuit would have been desperate for racing. Six days after British Champions Day, the BHA announced that they were scrapping the final-furlong rule and that all those who had broken it were having their punishments quashed. Christophe would get his money back and I would be free to ride at the Breeders' Cup. I had been in no way bluffing when I said that I would never again ride in Britain if that aspect of the rules remained. Once it was abandoned I returned the very same day at Newbury and won on my first ride back.

That, though, was certainly not that. I have never known jockeys to feel such venom towards those who run the sport as they did during the whip saga. The day after my race at Newbury, Ruby Walsh was slapped with a five-day whip ban at Aintree. It fired up talk of protest action. Further minor revisions were made to the rules and the penalties linked to them but they remained wrong to the core. It was only following the arrival of the BHA's new chief executive, Paul Bittar, that we finally saw introduced the sort of overhaul that had been so badly needed. Bittar described the changes introduced the previous October as 'fundamentally flawed'. Under his direction, the BHA kept the permitted number of smacks per race at seven on the Flat and eight over jumps, but now that number was only the trigger point for an inquiry as opposed to the trigger point for an automatic suspension. Stewards were given back the discretion they had lost. Another positive move was that riders who committed minor breaches of the rules were given bans that mirrored the severity of their crime. Both the rules and the punishments given to those who broke them were completely revisited.

And that has left us where we are today. In an attempt to clean up racing's image, the sport's leaders somehow managed to bring us not positive but negative headlines. The effort was to appease public opinion but I genuinely do not believe that the whip is something that concerns the man and woman on the street. They are bothered about mortgages, rents, bills, schools and hospitals. They are not fretting over whether Tony McCoy uses his whip eight, nine or ten times in a three-mile handicap chase at Towcester. Under the rules that were introduced in October 2011, I was allowed to use my whip seven times in a race and be adjudged to have done nothing wrong; if I used my whip nine times, I was deemed guilty of an offence that could cost me several thousands of pounds. The two responses, placed alongside each other, do not sit right. We should have had more confidence in ourselves and our sport.

I still do not think the whip rules we have now are the best possible whip rules we could have, but they are far better than the ones we had thrust on us in October 2011. Jockeys can now work with the rules without feeling that they excessively impinge on the way we do our job. Racing should not be about winning at all costs. Those jockeys who abuse the rules, and at the same time abuse horses, deserve to have the book thrown at them. They should not be excused. Cases of abuse will be obvious to anyone who sees them. We will not need to refer to a rule book to tell us what is right and what is wrong.

The whip is an essential tool of our job, both for safety purposes and as a means of encouraging horses to perform to the best of their ability. It is for that reason that racehorses are bred and looked after so well. Giving a horse a few smacks with a whip is not cruel. Indeed, I would even question the directive that says jockeys should always give a horse time to respond between strokes. There are occasions, such as on a sprinter who possesses only a short burst, when a few quick flicks can be the best way of producing maximum revs.

Following months of conflict, everyone has been left a little raw. It has not only been a case of us against them. Even within the sides there has been anger. I believe that the jockeys as a group were, at times, gutless. We did not act collectively in the way that we should have done. We have learnt lessons. There is, however, no point in any of us holding on to lasting bitterness towards anyone else. We must all move on. The jockeys certainly have done.

Paul Struthers began the whip war as the public face of the BHA. He is now the chief executive of the PJA. Paul has changed his position, but even when his views did not tally with ours, he meant us no ill will. The BHA at no stage had anything other than the very best intentions. We should all be able to accept that. We might not agree with how the BHA went about its business, but it meant well. Just as importantly, under its new leadership, it has been big enough to accept its own mistakes. Everyone should be sufficiently mature to do the same.

It is my great wish that the whip debate can now be put to bed. Should anyone want to bring it up again, I remain willing to bend over, bare my backside and be flogged.

EPILOGUE

I used to think I would quit the saddle when I was 40. I told everyone I would. I don't tell them that now because I can't envisage stopping for a good while yet. I know what I want to do when I finally do stop being a jockey, but that's all for the future. Right now, I'm enjoying the present way too much to even contemplate retiring.

My whole life has revolved around horses. They are at the centre of my very first memories and they have been at the heart of almost everything I have done since. I cannot recall a time when I did not want to ride racehorses. With the support of a lot of people, some family, some friends and some colleagues who have become friends, I have fulfilled my dream and then a bit more.

As I write these words, I have never been champion jockey and I have yet to win any of the British Classics, let alone the Derby – still, as it always was, the race I yearn to win most. However, in my head the list of what I have not done is far outweighed by the list of what I have done. I have been fortunate to sit on some wonderful horses that have been owned and trained by some extraordinary people. I am lucky now to ride as stable jockey to an excellent trainer who is also my father-in-law. Before that I was retained by one of the world's leading owners. We had seven successful years together and parted in the most amicable way. Not many jockeys can say they have done that. I have experienced the thrill of riding in some of the world's biggest races, both on the Flat and over jumps, and I have won more than my fair share. I have taken my saddle across Europe, to America, Australia, Hong Kong, Japan, South Africa and the never less than unbelievable India.

I appreciate that to many punters I am the Marmite jockey – you love me or you hate me. Even when I was wearing the Monksfield colours to ride little Chestnut Lady in those Sunday pony races, I was perfecting the style that people now associate with the guy they call Hughesie. I can ride in different ways depending on the horse, the track or the race, and you won't see me doing much other than dictating from the front at Windsor, but I do get the biggest buzz of all from coming late and fast to burgle a race. It is, I believe, what I do best. When it goes right I look a genius; when it goes wrong I look a fool. I know that. I genuinely do not ride the way I do to show off or showboat. I only ever ride a horse in the way I think gives it the best possible chance of winning.

Perhaps the biggest controversy of my riding career followed the 2008 1,000 Guineas, in which I finished fifth on the Mick Channon-trained Nahoodh. There is no doubt in my mind, nor probably in anyone else's, that Nahoodh should have won, but I remain convinced that I rode the right race. The filly had shown decent form as a juvenile but she ran appallingly on her three-year-old comeback in the Fred Darling Stakes. The bookmakers pushed her out to 33-1, understandably so, but Mick assured me that he had her back and told me to bury her and ride her for luck. We had no luck whatsoever. The stalls had been placed in the centre of the racecourse, but as soon as the gates opened everyone steered to the stands' rail. The entire field was concertinaed against the fence. The superb Christophe Lemaire got the 11-4 favourite Natagora into the lead and immediately slowed down the pace. It was exactly the right thing to do. Half the field was snookered, and in that situation the jockeys at the front of the race are invariably wise to keep a steady pace, so that when they eventually do kick for home, those in behind, who have had nowhere to go for so long, have precious little time in which to advance through the field. That is exactly what happened to me. Nine times out of ten I would have been saved as horses almost always drift off Newmarket's stands' rail. This time they did not. For the few strides in which Nahoodh saw daylight she flew, but she did not see enough of those strides. We were the unluckiest of losers.

If I had pulled back and steered around all the horses in front of me, I might just have nicked a place. I would not have won. By sitting and suffering, I gave my filly, her connections and the punters who backed me a shot at winning. The gamble did not come off, but it was a gamble worth taking. Mick was absolutely fine with the tactics I used. Very few trainers have ever been anything other than supportive. When they book me they know what they are going to get. As Richard Hannon said after one of our big wins together, 'There's nothing you can do about his style. You just say "Jesus" and hope everything goes right. He's different gear.'

Richard and Mick have been two of the greatest influences on my career, along, of course, with Dad. They have also been the very best of friends, loyal, supportive and forgiving. Throughout my career I have been able to count on some tremendous people, not least my long-term agent, Tony Hind, and my valet, Dave Mustow, both of whom work impossibly long hours and do an incredibly good job. Neither needs to be told that I could not do what I do without them.

As I write these words, I am getting used to the feeling of being 39. As I said, the intention for some time was to retire from the weighing room at 40, but I now think differently. For the last three or four years I believe I have been riding to the very best of my ability. I continue to love being a jockey every bit as much as I always did. And whereas some riders will openly tell you that they only get the special adrenalin rush from taking part in the biggest races, I am different. I love riding in any race, however good or bad. It bugs the hell out of me if trainers or owners think it's not worth engaging me to ride in a seller. Some of them think I would not give 100 per cent commitment in a race like that. I would, and I do. I once punched the air after winning a very ordinary contest at Salisbury. The other jockeys could not understand what I was thinking, but the horse was owned by the former captain of my local golf club. I knew how much winning a little race at Salisbury would mean to him so it meant a lot to me as well.

(And while we're on the subject of golf, I love it, and everyone knows I love it. It is the greatest of all releases for me. I love playing on Monday afternoons before heading off to Windsor, and some of my best holidays have been spent playing golf with the likes of Tony McCoy and Mick Fitzgerald. I could have written a whole chapter, maybe even a whole book, about golf, but Lizzie would have killed me.)

At this stage I reckon I have another four or five years' riding left in me. It does not help that Richard Hannon buys so many exciting yearlings every autumn. One of them could be something very special. One of them recently was Canford Cliffs. It would be too much to hope that another one might one day be as good, but if you don't hope, you don't get.

When I was drinking, I did not get the satisfaction from riding that I do now. The thrill of winning races is now as great, if not greater, than it ever has been. There are also no signs of me losing my bottle. At the height of my drinking days I did sometimes get a little nervous when a horse played up in the stalls. Not so anymore. I remain at my most comfortable when on the back of a horse. The job I do can be frightening, but I am not frightened. I sometimes think that the bravest jockeys are the ones who are scared. Should I ever start to get scared, I will not be brave, I will retire. For the moment, though, my job is way too easy to think about giving up. I am utterly content. My great mate Johnny Murtagh left Ballydoyle because he was not comfortable in his work situation. I could not be more comfortable in mine.

There is also a milestone I feel I must get through before I stop riding. At some point in the not too distant future, Richard Hannon will hand over to his son, Richard Hannon junior. When he does, I expect the transition to be seamless, and I intend to make it even more seamless by continuing as Junior's stable jockey. There is some truth in the statement that jockeys are ten a penny, but I am a cog in the wheel and would feel I was leaving him in the lurch if I moved on in my life before he had grown accustomed to a new stage in his. I owe the Hannon family that much.

And who knows? Before I do stop riding, maybe I will win the Derby. Maybe I will know how it feels to be champion jockey. I might even get to experience riding in a race over fences. When the time does come, I will be able to say that I gave it everything. I might not have achieved all that I wanted to achieve, but, apart from Tony McCoy, who has? I will be able to leave the weighing room with my head held high. I will know that at one time I was as good as anyone. I will be able to walk away saying that I no longer have anything to prove. And then I will spend less time in hot baths, eat a bit more, and become a trainer.

I want to be a trainer every bit as much as I once wanted to be a jockey. It is the one thing I want to do after I stop riding. I dearly want to be successful at it as well. There would be no point embarking on a training career unless you thought you could do it. As a job, it is demanding, stressful, time-consuming and potentially very expensive. You would be mad to take out a licence unless you were confident of making it work. Very few top jockeys go on to become top trainers. I hope I can buck the trend.

I have been thinking about it for a long time. My plan is to train on the Flat. Put simply, it is easier than training over jumps. In Flat racing, you get a large intake of new horses coming in every year. You can be stuck with the same jumpers for four, five, six, seven years or more, and in that time it is highly unlikely that injuries will not crop up along the way. I would not mind having a handful of jumpers as part of my string, but the Flat is where my primary focus will be.

In terms of numbers, there is no point thinking small. I want to start with a minimum of 60 horses, ideally 80 to 100. Even if you have 60 in your stable, it's likely that only 40 will be fit and available to run at any one time. I need horses who are able to run because I want to be competitive from day one. You need both quality and quantity to do that. In that first year as a trainer it will be essential that I do not disappear into the wilderness. I have to maintain my profile.

My aim will be to get the most I can possibly get out of my horses. I think one of the secrets behind training racehorses is to know how good a horse can be when it first comes to you. If you think you have a Group horse, let him get there via the handicap route by all means, but go that path knowing where you think the horse will end up. I also realise that as a new trainer my best opportunities will come with juveniles. You have a better chance of winning good races with two-year-olds than with any other sort of horse. As horses get older, they are more vulnerable to their better-bred contemporaries. With time, the horses with the classier pedigrees will nearly always come to the fore. When horses are in their first season racing, that is not necessarily the case.

Getting owners will, of course, be essential. I already have a lot of friends who have told me they'd be willing to support me. What I do not know is whether any of the sport's major owners would want to come on board. I hope some will. Acquiring the patronage of a top owner gives a trainer such a head start. For one thing, you know you are going to get paid. I also believe that the presence of big owners in a yard attracts other big owners. I would explain to those owners that, although on paper a new trainer, I am not new to training. I am the son of a trainer. I was brought up in a racing yard. Even as a jockey I have always been keen to watch and learn. When at East Everleigh or Herridge I like speaking with the head lads and the vets, I enjoy helping with the entries, and I like offering suggestions as to where horses might be aimed. When in India, I have always made a point of spending plenty of time in the yards that I ride for, not just in the mornings but also in the evenings. I get satisfaction from taking an interest and being involved. All the time I am soaking up information.

My one concern would be whether I could ever make owning a horse as much fun as it is with Richard Hannon. Hopefully, that is not essential. I cannot imagine, for example, that having a horse with Stoutey is always a barrel of laughs. It will not always be a barrel of laughs for me, either. When you get beat on a hot favourite, you can get off, pick up your saddle and walk away. As the trainer, you have owners to console. I must learn how to do that.

Richard already knows about my plans. When I told him, his reaction was, 'Are you effing mad?' I might be, but I don't think so.

I also don't think that I want to train anywhere far from where we live now. I love the counties of Wiltshire and Berkshire. They are great parts of England and I am certain that it is in England that I want to stay for the rest of my life. It hurts me to say this, but I have not the least desire to go home. I love English racing. Ireland is too small for me. You meet the same people every day, and I don't like the idea of that. I find that in Britain you are rewarded for working hard. I do not think that is necessarily the case in Ireland. Over there, you can work your balls off and still not climb a single rung of the ladder. Irish racing is too much of a closed shop. I would much rather train horses in a place where I felt I stood a chance. That means training horses in Britain, not Ireland. I'm afraid to say that I will never return home. My home now is in England. Dad knows that, and I did feel bad telling him. Everything he has done has been done so that a legacy can be passed on to Sandra and myself. It seems ungrateful to say that I do not want it. I hope he and Mam understand.

Lizzie has lived her life as a trainer's daughter and she seems happy at the prospect of being a trainer's wife. She knows that we will have to make sacrifices because financially it will be a stretch. At the moment, we cannot afford to buy a yard. We have created a beautiful family home, but when I find the right place to train, the home will have to be sold. We both know it will be worth it, undoubtedly for the two of us but even more so for the children. I am blessed to have Harvey and Phoebe in my life and I am sure that being brought up in a racing yard will be good for them. I want to bring my kids up around horses. I want them to help the stable lads, I want them to be sweeping the yard, mucking out the boxes and feeding the horses. They are good children and I want them to stay that way. Lizzie knows that the job always comes first but she also knows that nothing is more important to me than my family. Should Harvey and Phoebe grow up wanting to be jockeys, that will be fine by the both of us, so long as we know they could be successful. We wouldn't mind in the least if either wanted to be a nurse, plumber or road sweeper. As long as we know they are happy, we will be fine.

I do sense, though, that Harvey is thinking about being a jockey as he already enjoys watching me ride. If I get beat, he tells me that I should have kicked harder. Any jockey who beats me is immediately branded a naughty jockey. He is also a little boy with the most beautiful heart. Phoebe's character is still developing. She can be a tyrant when not happy, and aggressive towards Harvey, but he will never lay a finger on her. All Harvey ever wants to do is please.

We have been lucky enough to stay at the Sandy Lane resort in Barbados for family holidays. When I told Harvey at the end of one week that it was time to go home he was devastated. I explained to him that we could not afford to stay any longer. 'I'm sorry, Harvey,' I said, 'but Daddy's broke.' He then went round the apartment and collected four dollars in loose change. 'There you are, Daddy,' he said. 'We're not broke any more.'

That has been my life so far. If I have mentioned you, I hope you feel that I have represented you fairly and accurately. I have certainly tried to, just as I have tried to paint an accurate picture of myself. You already knew that I am the son of Dessie Hughes, stable jockey to Richard Hannon, and the man who rode Canford Cliffs. If I have been successful in the writing of this book you should also now feel that you know a bit more about not just Richard Hughes the jockey but Richard Hughes the person, warts and all.

I feel lucky. I am lucky to have been born the child of two amazing parents, lucky to have grown up with such a loving sister, lucky to have found the love of my life, lucky to have married into her wonderful family and lucky to have started a family of my own. I am lucky to have enjoyed such a long and fruitful career as a jockey. More than anything, though, I feel lucky to be alive. I feel lucky not to have killed myself or someone else during the days when I drank and drove. I regret that I did that, but I do not regret much else. I became an alcoholic but I enjoyed some incredible craic along the way. I wish that I could have stopped drinking sooner than I did, and there is no point pretending that those final years on the bottle were anything other than awful, but that was a part of my life that I had to go through and get through. And I did. Because of that time, I have gained knowledge and experience that I can now pass on to other people through Alcoholics Anonymous. Whatever I win on the racecourse, the times when I help those people will always be my greatest achievements.

My life now is so much better than it used to be. During the years when a young man is supposed to grow up, I never did. When they reach adulthood, most people are equipped with the tools that allow them to cope with life. I was not. I had to go through alcoholism before I became the person I am today, the person I was always destined to be, the person that the people who love me most always knew I could be. It took a long time to get there, but I have made it. I have learnt how to live.

APPENDIX 1

Group 1 Winners

RACE NAME	DATE	HORSE	TRAINER	PRIZE MONEY
Queen Anne Stakes	14 Jun 2011	Canford Cliffs	Richard Hannon	£141,925
JLT Lockinge Stakes	14 May 2011	Canford Cliffs	Richard Hannon	£99,348
Sussex Stakes	28 Jul 2010	Canford Cliffs	Richard Hannon	£179,677
Etihad Airways Falmouth Stakes	07 Jul 2010	Music Show	Mick Channon	£105,025
Prix Jean Prat	4 Jul 2010	Dick Turpin	Richard Hannon	£202,265
St James's Palace Stakes	15 Jun 2010	Canford Cliffs	Richard Hannon	£141,925
Abu Dhabi Irish 2,000 Guineas	22 May 2010	Canford Cliffs	Richard Hannon	£166,814
totesport.com Lockinge Stakes	15 May 2010	Paco Boy	Richard Hannon	£113,540
Queen Anne Stakes	16 Jun 2009	Paco Boy	Richard Hannon	£167,472
Grand Prix de Saint-Cloud	29 Jun 2008	Youmzain	Mick Channon	£168,059
Coronation Stakes	22 Jun 2007	Indian Ink	Richard Hannon	£141,950
Criterium de Saint-Cloud	12 Nov 2006	Passage Of Time	Sir Henry Cecil	£98,517
Sky Bet Cheveley Park Stakes	29 Sep2006	Indian Ink	Richard Hannon	£96,526
Stanleybet Sprint Cup	4 Sep 2004	Tante Rose	Roger Charlton	£130,500
Gainsborough Poule d'Essai des Poulains	16 May 2004	American Post	Criquette Head-Maarek	£140,838
Prix Jean Luc Lagardere	05 Oct 2003	American Post	Criquette Head-Maarek	£129,864
Netjets Prix du Moulin de Longchamp	07 Sep 2003	Nebraska Tornado	Andre Fabre	£111,312
Victor Chandler Nunthorpe Stakes	21 Aug 2003	Oasis Dream	John Gosden	£116,000
Darley July Cup	10 Jul 2003	Oasis Dream	John Gosden	£145,000
Prix de Diane Hermes	8 Jun 2003	Nebraska Tornado	Andre Fabre	£185,519
Gainsborough Poule d'Essai des Pouliches	12 May 2002	Zenda	John Gosden	£122,693
Prix d'Ispahan	20 May 2001	Observatory	John Gosden	£48,497
Prix du Cadran	3 Oct 1998	Invermark	James Fanshawe	£50,505
Premio Vittorio Di Capua	6 Oct 1996	Mistle Cat	Sean Woods	£54,084
Derby Italiano	26 May 1996	Bahamian Knight	David Loder	£209,536
Gran Premio d'Italia	16 Sep 1995	Posidonas	Paul Cole	£88,751

APPENDIX 2

Winners on the Flat in the UK

	WINS	RUNS	%	2NDS	3RDS	4THS	WIN PRIZE	TOTAL PRIZE
2011	130	722	18%	98	86	76	£1,771,219	£2,655,668
2010	192	1098	17%	171	123	113	£2,087,294	£3,169,420
2009	144	768	19%	98	92	70	£1,375,507	£2,246,022
2008	127	851	15%	124	90	82	£1,182,884	£2,121,258
2007	139	869	16%	115	108	76	£1,015,700	£1,882,973
2006	113	804	14%	95	107	76	£1,156,435	£1,854,639
2005	124	850	15%	108	92	76	£1,179,923	£1,795,004
2004	73	662	11%	76	70	67	£642,678	£1,070,722
2003	121	751	16%	88	80	89	£1,346,115	£2,066,141
2002	126	806	16%	137	92	89	£1,035,177	£1,981,399
2001	91	584	16%	59	70	55	£782,954	£1,361,013
2000	102	787	13%	98	81	97	£826,470	£1,443,025
1999	95	704	13%	90	75	61	£691,198	£1,128,039
1998	55	537	10%	52	67	44	£265,035	£542,216
1997	33	269	12%	33	37	28	£143,209	£235,028
1996	62	557	11%	68	64	47	£305,924	£647,935
1995	68	525	13%	75	54	46	£534,300	£802,384
1994	19	165	12%	15	21	14	£85,650	£135,813
1992	0	1	—	0	0	0	£0	£0

* Figures show results for calendar year, not championship season

APPENDIX 3

Winners in Ireland on the Flat

	WINS	RUNS	%	2NDS	3RDS	4THS	WIN PRIZE	TOTAL PRIZE
2011	2	9	22%	1	1	2	£82,888	£153,211
2010	2	10	20%	1	3	0	£204,204	£252,257
2009	2	5	40%	0	1	0	£1,099,029	£1,143,204
2008	1	10	10%	2	0	3	£724,265	£955,456
2007	0	8	—	0	1	2	£0	£39,865
2006	0	12	—	0	1	0	£0	£1,255
2005	0	14	—	2	2	1	£0	£19,168
2004	1	5	20%	0	1	0	£36,620	£53,099
2003	5	25	20%	3	2	4	£160,390	£227,414
2002	2	12	17%	0	1	1	£86,933	£130,525
2001	3	25	12%	3	3	4	£118,548	£182,117
2000	0	5	—	0	0	0	£0	£0
1999	2	18	11%	3	2	1	£18,458	£45,078
1998	7	41	17%	3	3	7	£78,561	£108,627
1997	0	14	—	2	1	1	£0	£30,916
1996	5	12	42%	3	0	1	£34,937	£80,530
1995	0	15	—	3	2	3	£0	£344,042
1994	9	124	7%	12	15	17	£38,110	£70,605
1993	38	299	13%	20	36	25	£173,055	£267,094
1992	35	349	10%	36	40	41	£143,368	£228,700
1991	30	331	9%	26	20	34	£117,819	£170,532
1990	19	339	6%	23	26	34	£46,184	£101,545
1989	16	229	7%	20	17	20	£56,630	£74,116
1988	6	120	5%	8	6	9	£7,441	£12,489

APPENDIX 4

Jumps Winners in the UK

	WINS	RUNS	%	2NDS	3RDS	4THS	WIN PRIZE	TOTAL PRIZE
2008-09	0	2	—	0	0	0	£0	£0
2007-08	1	5	20%	0	1	1	£6,494	£7,362
2006-07	0	1	—	0	0	0	£0	£0
2004-05	0	1	—	0	0	0	£0	£0
2003-04	0	1	—	0	0	0	£0	£0
2002-03	0	1	—	0	0	0	£0	£0
1998-99	0	5	—	1	1	0	£0	£10,669
1997-98	1	11	9%	3	0	1	£2,408	£22,510
1996-97	10	40	25%	1	8	2	£24,803	£47,343
1995-96	0	5	—	0	1	0	£0	£4,821
1994-95	0	1	—	0	0	0	£0	£0

APPENDIX 5

Jumps Winners in Ireland

	WINS	RUNS	%	2NDS	3RDS	4THS	WIN PRIZE	TOTAL PRIZE
2008-09	0	8	—	0	1	2	£0	£4,863
2007-08	0	3	—	1	1	0	£0	£2,303
1998-99	0	1	—	0	0	0	£0	£0
1997-98	2	26	8%	2	3	4	£11,962	£24,867
1996-97	9	59	15%	13	3	6	£68,511	£94,135
1995-96	0	6	—	1	1	0	£0	£1,021
1994-95	2	14	14%	2	1	0	£7,829	£9,596
1993-94	2	31	—	1	3	4	£5,967	£8,843
1992-93	0	6	—	1	0	0	0	£688

INDEX